W9-AXA-783

MIDLOTHIAN
PUBLIC LIBRARY

BAKER & TAYLOR

RADICAL
DISCIPLE

Father Pfleger, St. Sabina Church,
and the Fight for Social Justice

Robert McClory

Lawrence Hill Books

Library of Congress Cataloging-in-Publication Data

McClory, Robert, 1932-

Radical disciple : Father Pfleger, St. Sabina Church, and the fight for social justice / Robert McClory.

p. cm.

Includes bibliographical references and index.

ISBN 978-1-56976-528-9 (hardcover)

1. Pfleger, Michael. 2. Church and social problems—Catholic Church. 3. Social justice—Religious aspects—Catholic Church. 4. St. Sabina's (Church : Chicago, Ill.) 5. Chicago (Ill.)—Church history. I. Title.

BX4705.P44M33 2010

261.8092—dc22

[B]

2010018028

Interior design: Jonathan Hahn

Published by Lawrence Hill Books,

an imprint of Chicago Review Press, Incorporated

814 North Franklin Street

Chicago, Illinois 60610

ISBN 978-1-56976-528-9

Printed in the United States of America

5 4 3 2 1

To the Faith Communities of St. Sabina Church
Present, Past, and Future

CONTENTS

If there is no struggle, there is no progress. Those who profess to favor freedom, and yet deprecate agitation, are men who want crops without plowing up the ground. They want rain without thunder and lightning. They want the ocean without the awful roar of its many waters. This struggle may be a moral one; or it may be a physical one; or it may be both moral and physical; but it must be a struggle. Power concedes nothing without a demand. It never did and it never will.

—FREDERICK DOUGLASS

ACKNOWLEDGMENTS

I MET MICHAEL PFLEGER in 1976 when he was a newly ordained priest, and I was immediately impressed with his energy and creativity. I was inclined to attribute much of his enthusiasm to youth and inexperience, and I expected it to diminish with time. But when I visited with him a few years later, the zeal was still there, undiminished. And even after five years as pastor, he was as on fire as ever. Surely, I thought, no one, priest or layperson, could stay as engaged as he much longer, especially in view of the problems of the community. Yet ten years later he was still going, as strong as before, stronger in fact. Pastor Pfleger, it seemed to me, had become a veritable sacerdotal Energizer Bunny.

Several years ago an old friend, Fred Brandstrader, suggested I write a book about Pfleger and his parish, St. Sabina. It was an intriguing idea, and it marinated in the back of my brain for a long time. One day in 2007, I asked Pfleger if he or anyone else was chronicling the story. No one, he said, nor did he seem wildly excited when I offered to take on the task. Nevertheless, he agreed to cooperate and opened up his archives to me, such as they were. We met many, many times for interviews, and I always found him open, candid, and almost guileless in his responses, though his memory of dates and years left something to be desired. After his encounter with the press in the aftermath of his filmed imitation of Hillary Clinton in May 2008, our discussions and my research became more intense. I felt a kind of urgency to tell the story of this person and this church.

So I am first of all grateful to Father Mike Pfleger for opening his door and his life to me. I came to look forward to our meetings. They were not only enlightening, they were thoroughly enjoyable, sometimes hilarious. I found I could disagree with him and challenge his ideas at times without breaking our dialogue. I am grateful second of all to Vince Clark, the pastor's veteran aide who consistently went well beyond the call of duty in returning phone calls, providing ready access to other key persons in the parish, and responding to my sometimes outlandish requests with a laugh and a booming, "No problem!" Also at the staff level, I thank Randall Blakey, Kim Lymore, Leonard Langston, and Ann Gaskin—and of course Cory Williams, who makes St. Sabina that rarest of twenty-first-century institutions where phone calls are answered by a human voice and the flow of communication proceeds efficiently and without inhibition.

It was an honor for me to become acquainted with and learn so much from many pillars of the parish whose dedication to St. Sabina goals are of the highest order. The powerful women make things happen, like Jacqui Collins, Helen Dumas, April Dumas, Sharon Tillmon, Julie Welborn, and Lisa Ramsey, to name a few. Capable men take on heavy responsibility and are in for the long haul: Deacon Len Richardson, Rickey Harris, Gerald Stewart, Isadore Glover, Bob McCoy, and Bill Hynes.

To the many other members of the community who invariably greeted me like a long lost son at the Sunday service, I am grateful. I wish to thank also former Sabina members, like Chris Mallette and Virgil Jones, who spoke candidly of their experiences, as well as former members from a much earlier era, including Erv Schultz and Dee Foertsch, who provided helpful context information.

Thanks too to those who provided ideas and suggestions in the early research regarding this book project: Jason Bitner, Tom Artz, Dan Woods, Mike Leach, Bob Hercules, and Rick Kogan. Very helpful throughout the whole process was my regular Saturday board of advisers, including Bob Heineman, Lawrence McCarthy, Neil Gambow, Ray Bayless, Richard Adams, Jeff Shepard, Thom Clark, and Dan Maloney.

I appreciate the kindness, cooperation, and valued suggestions my editors Cynthia Sherry and Michelle Schoob of Chicago Review Press provided during the development of the book, as well as the input from other editors, readers, and Chicago Review Press staff members who gave of their time and talent.

At the summit of my appreciation list is my wife of thirty-nine years, Margaret, who has been editor, inspiration, critic, encourager, companion, and counselor of everything I've done in journalism and just about everything else. Alongside her as essential readers, editors, commentators, and personal supporters for the project are my daughter Jennifer, her partner Sarah Klein, and our beloved friend Judy Schoenherr.

PROLOGUE

===

W HEN REVEREND MICHAEL PFLEGER mocked Hillary Clinton at a
church service during the 2008 presidential primary, his remarks
were filmed and made their way onto YouTube and all the major television outlets in the United States. The result was a national broadside of
invective against the priest. He was labeled "ignorant, arrogant, caustic,
antagonistic, and racist." And that was just one person's reaction. He was
also called "a white nigger," and many hoped he would be yanked out of
his parish and eventually "burn in hell." The nature of his remarks notwithstanding, the public reaction seemed to me an exercise in overkill.
I've known Michael Pfleger since he came to his parish and had some
experience myself with St. Sabina Church long before he arrived, so it
was time, I thought, to look at the bigger, fuller picture.

My second appointment as a priest of the Catholic Archdiocese of
Chicago was to St. Sabina Church on the South Side, and I was excited
at the opportunity. The year was 1964, and it was well known that Sabina,
one of the largest and busiest churches in the whole city, was facing a
challenging crisis. I had been there less than a day when a parishioner
introduced himself and said, "Father, we're glad you're here, but you need
to know *they* are coming," and he gestured toward the northeast. I knew
what "they" meant: African Americans. I had been informed even before

I got to the parish that some of "them" were already living within the parish boundaries. But I had also been informed that St. Sabina was different from the dozens of other Catholic parishes east and north of us. Many had experienced a complete racial turnover from white to black in a period described by some as "overnight." The blacks had come, and the whites had fled as from an unstoppable army. But Sabina, I learned, was determined to become a successful interracial community. It was to stand as a model for large urban cities everywhere—blacks and whites living in harmony, proof that rational planning and common sense could overcome what seemed inevitable.

I met our leader, Monsignor John McMahon, the Sabina pastor who was overseeing this ambitious effort. He was a tall, thin man who, I thought, resembled Don Quixote—both in appearance, and, as I would soon learn, in temperament and personality too. He really did believe in the gospel and the equality of all human beings. He was putting the considerable savings of the parish into the creation and operation of a grand community organization that would hopefully make racial integration a reality. He was much influenced in his enthusiasms by another monsignor, Jack Egan, head of the archdiocese's office of urban affairs. Egan also believed fervently in the gospel of equality but was more worldly wise in making plans and nurturing friendships.

Egan's interest was not just St. Sabina but the larger Auburn Gresham area in which the parish resided, a ten-square-block sector centered roughly at the corner of 79th Street and Racine Avenue. He hoped the two largest parishes in that area, St. Sabina and St. Leo, would become the twin anchors of an integration plan. But he had little luck with St. Leo's pastor, Monsignor P. J. Molloy, a colorful, irascible wheeler-dealer who had long-standing relationships with insiders at city hall, business leaders, and even, in his earlier days, with the Chicago mob. Molloy gave only token encouragement to the plan at the start and never did become seriously involved. His advice to parishioners was "If you don't move out, they can't move in." When black families began moving in anyway, Molloy started rearranging St. Leo's boundaries, chopping off whole blocks to neighboring parishes and directing black newcomers to those churches.

So Egan turned his full attention to St. Sabina. He persuaded McMahon to hire the legendary community organizer Saul Alinsky to direct the project.

Under Alinsky's direction and amid many stops and starts, the Organization for the Southwest Communities, better known as the OSC, was launched in the early 1960s. Its goal was to mobilize businesses, banks, churches, corporations, and local citizen groups for "neighborhood stabilization." The term was deliberately ambiguous to insure a wide participation from the community. But it proved to be too broad—it came to attract both dedicated integrationists and hidebound segregationists determined to keep "them" out at any cost. The OSC was thus destined to become an arena of unending conflict during much of its history.

While all this maneuvering was going on, I was more than absorbed in the daily functions of a parish that had almost three thousand families. They were served by eleven masses on Sunday, starting at 6 A.M.—some in the upper church and some in the lower church and some going on in both places at the same time, many crowded to near capacity. There were five weekday masses and as many as an additional four funeral masses and perhaps two or three wedding masses each week. I was one of seven priests living in the rectory, two of whom were elderly, infirm, and unpredictable. The staff also included twenty Dominican sisters who handled the grammar school, which had an enrollment of almost eight hundred children. Besides the church, which could accommodate more than a thousand worshippers, the parish complex included a massive commmunity center constantly alive with sports events and featuring a legendary Sunday night dance that drew teens from all over the South Side, the school, the sisters' convent, the priests' rectory, and a building for meetings and celebrations across the street from the community center.

As I got accustomed to the often frantic ebb and flow of parish life, I couldn't dismiss the growing looks of apprehension and worry on the faces of longtime parishioners who feared a total racial turnover was inevitable. They dearly loved this community and this old church, regarding it as a kind of Camelot—a proud, white, largely Irish, self-sustaining village within the vast Chicago metropolis—but day by day the people were losing confidence. The OSC staff, we the priests, and the many activist parishioners, like Erv Schultz and Gene Tarpey, who shared Monsignor McMahon's dream were doing our best to bolster confidence and to thwart the major enemy, the so-called blockbuster real estate agents. These unscrupulous agents rang doorbells day and night offering homeowners money for their property and mentioning, by the way, that the price offered was for one week only, and, "Oh, did you know the house on the end of the block was sold yesterday to 'them'?" The OSC struggled to require that real estate companies monitor their agents and abide by ethical principles, but still they came. If not at the front door, then they were on the phone with a new offer or a rumor or a threat. There was blood in the water, and the sharks were swarming.

As I met people in the church and rectory and walked through the parish, I got to know some of the black families who had just arrived and who were delighted to be in this comfortable neighborhood. They were friendly, hopeful the integration plan would work, and eager to help. Yet every day we would hear of a few more veteran parish members who had sold their homes. Some would call or stop in to say good-bye. Others would just disappear without a word, some leaving in the middle of the night. And the mood of this white community was shifting from fear to anger—anger mainly at Monsignor McMahon for selling out to these strangers, for welcoming them into "our" parish. He did his best to rally the faithful, to assure them that if they would hold out a little longer, the tide would surely turn; the pressure on whites to sell would subside, and a balance of black and white residents would prevail. But McMahon was no Barack Obama. He tended to lecture rather than listen; he was not good at negotiation; and when push came to shove, he relied instinctively on his priestly authority.

Then came the evening of August 15, 1965, referred to by former Sabina families for years after as "the day the music died." I had just come back to my room in the rectory when I heard shouts and cries in the courtyard outside. I ran out along with Father Tom White, the associate priest in charge of the community center. There on the sidewalk in front of the center, Frank Kelly, a seventeen-year-old parishioner, lay motionless. He was surrounded by twenty or more white teens, who, like him, had just come out of the center. They said three young black people had appeared suddenly on the other side of the street, and two of them drew pistols and fired into the crowd. One shot struck a girl in the leg, and another, it appeared, hit Frank Kelly in the chest. He was not breathing and had no pulse. White gave him the last rites of the church. After the ambulances came and went, I stayed for a long time in front of the center trying (with minimal success) to calm the angry teens who were walking into the street and yelling racist remarks at any black motorists driving by on Racine Avenue. If their numbers had been larger, I thought, we might have had the start of a race riot. Later that night word circulated that the girl's injury was not serious but that Kelly was dead—a single bullet to the heart. He was a member of an active Sabina family, an alumnus of the parish school, and a student at a local Catholic high school.

For three or four days all parish activity seemed to halt. The only calls to the rectory were inquiries about funeral arrangements and some anonymous insults and threats aimed at Monsignor McMahon. Given the mood in the community, it was decided he would not preside at the funeral. Father White said the solemn high funeral mass, and I was the subdeacon at the service. As I looked out at the grim faces in the church, I saw that every pew was full, and people were standing in the back and in the aisles. It turned out to be the last time for many years that this large church would be full for any occasion. There would be no reversal of the tide. The dream of a stable, interracial community was dead.

In 1964, the year I came to Sabina, records reported just under three thousand families as registered parishioners. By the end of 1965, the year of young Kelly's death, the figure was 1,908. In 1966 the total was down to nine hundred. And in 1967 the parish claimed only 530 families.[1]

By 1971, the year I left to pursue a career in journalism, St. Sabina was a black parish—only a smattering of whites were still present. The school enrollment was black too. Longtime parishioner Dee Foertsch, who was still there with her family, said, "We had only twelve white children in the school that year, and four of them were mine." But there was a coterie of black Catholic newcomers like Elbert and Dolores Johnson, Herb and

Elsie Poleate, Otis and Vera Lyttle, and Charley and Mary Marble, who pledged to keep the parish alive. I bade farewell to them and other friends sadly. Despite all the good will in the world, how could such a small black congregation, less than 10 percent of the original Catholic population, maintain a complex of buildings the size of St. Sabina? Some predicted the church and the other buildings would eventually be sold or torn down. At best, it might eke out a modest existence for a while with subsidies from the archdiocese, as some other Catholic parishes that experienced a great racial turnover have done.

No one, absolutely no one, anticipated what actually lay ahead.

I

SUNDAY MORNING

===

> When you understand the kingdom, you feel compelled
> to become kingdom builders, to be agents of change, to
> transform society.
>
> —Reverend Michael Pfleger

IT'S TWENTY MINUTES before the start of the 11:15 A.M. mass on a beautiful, fall Sunday morning at St. Sabina, and the parking lot across the street is filling rapidly. The church is a large, gray stone structure with a flight of concrete steps rising to an expansive entranceway. Other lesser entrances line the sides of the building. It was built in the early 1930s in the midst of the Great Depression. Though the times were hard, the congregation obviously spared no expense in erecting a place of worship that has a solid, down-to-earth look. The single bell tower, flat on the top, rises up about eight stories. Today white-gloved greeters are at every door handing out orange sheets so worshippers can take notes on the sermon. Parishioner Terrence Marshall Haley, an energetic man in his mid-fifties, moves around to check the entrances, ensuring that every door is covered by a smiling greeter. This is one of his many volunteer jobs, though he is better known as the man who has taken part in virtually every march or public action the church has ever sponsored.

Early arrivals tend to fill the pews up front, in contradiction to the practice at many Catholic churches where the back half of the church fills first. Almost everyone seems to be in high spirits, greeting and God-blessing neighbors and friends with hugs, handshakes, and good-natured banter. Mattie George, a short, rotund woman with a head of blond curls, is in her usual seat in the front pew. She has her Bible and her small tambourine in hand, ready for the praise and worship segment of the service. In the vestibule, Debra Campbell is at the visitors' booth ready to answer questions and provide a free CD of information about the church, a sampling of the choirs singing, and words of welcome from Pastor Michael Pfleger. Campbell, a widow, is one of the many all-purpose volunteers at Sabina, assisting where she's needed. She frequently helps serve the breakfast (eggs, sausage, toast, sometimes pancakes) in the lower-level McMahon Hall for those who stay after the 8:30 service or come early for the 11:15.

Many who are moving steadily into the church carry well-worn Bibles; some also have notebooks for comments or inspirational thoughts that occur to them at the service. It is certain that at some point Pastor Pfleger will call on the congregation to open their Bibles to a certain passage and read it aloud along with him.

Little in the décor of this church is gaudy or ostentatious. The cushioned dark oak pews and carved oak wainscoting have weathered the years well. The stained glass windows, each with a dozen or more intricately designed miniature scenes from the Bible and church history, show few signs of age or wear. When Pfleger wanted to adapt the interior to African American culture, he sought an artist who could blend old and new. After a considerable search, he found such a one in Jerzy Kenar, an exile from Communist Poland who works in black walnut, a wood that easily blends with oak. Kenar came to St. Sabina to meet with the people and church leaders before undertaking his task. He produced the stately altar shaped like a massive African drum, the baptismal font in the middle of the church, the pulpit, podium, carved African scene sculptures behind the presider's chair, and the visitors' booth. Kenar also created the large sculpture of the Holy Family in the sanctuary that depicts an African Joseph with his arm raised high in the air in thanksgiving, holding the tiny, newborn Jesus in the palm of his hand. Beside him is the figure of an African Mary, not bending low in humility but dancing for sheer joy.

The most striking feature in the body of the church is a beautifully lit, twenty-foot-high mural on the front wall. It portrays a young black Jesus in a long robe standing in the immense, open hands of God the Father. One of Jesus's hands has an open palm, as if to say, "Here I am for you"; the other is beckoning the viewer to come forward. First-time visitors often find the painting riveting, almost hypnotic. The one art piece that has not been universally well received is a neon sign hanging over the sanctuary and spelling out in stark, red letters, "Jesus." It was a Christmas decoration years ago, and some have suggested it looks cheap and kitschy. But it stays because, according to Pfleger, it is a reminder that when St. Sabina was created in 1916, it was in a storefront church on Ashland Avenue—and many Sabina members today began their own spiritual journeys in such humble places.

Randall Blakey, the church's director of ministry, found the mural so powerful the first time he entered the church that it led to a renewal of his faith and brought about a sharp turn in the direction of his life. On this morning Blakey, an intense, purposeful man, is wearing a green dashiki and white pants as he prepares for the start of the service, during which he serves as an unofficial minister of ceremonies and sometime trouble-shooter. He is the founder of the St. Sabina armor bearers, so named for the Israelite men who carried the armor and weapons of King David when he marched into battle. At this mass, the armor bearers, some twenty Sabina men in dark suits and bow ties (not to be confused with the ushers, in dark suits and conventional ties), are stationed around the church in designated spots to assist ailing or disabled worshippers and to insure that nothing unexpected occurs. The armor bearers constitute a body of volunteer body-guards. One or more armor bearers often accompany the pastor when he travels to give a talk or attend a meeting. During several lengthy periods in Pfleger's pastorate, armed Chicago police have been in the pews at the 11:15 due to threats and the possibility of violence, but not this morning.

This, the faith community of St. Sabina, defies economic and social categorization. There are men in three-piece suits and women in high-fashion hats and dresses along with middle-class folks in jackets and jeans and some bedraggled-looking souls perhaps just a few steps from homelessness. The majority of the congregation is female, though not overwhelmingly so. Those who think all young black men are gangbanging thugs would be surprised at the respectable showing of well-dressed teens and twenty-somethings who seem as intent and interested as anyone else.

Sitting halfway back in the center aisle is Lonnie Washington, a senior citizen and the first person to move from a homeless shelter into St. Sabina's Samaritan House, an apartment rented by the church to provide full financial support, health coverage, and rehabilitation for a person or family for one year. The program, started in 2000, has proven successful for its participants. Washington, who admits his one-time addiction to "drugs, alcohol, and wild women," said it saved his life; he never misses the 11:15 mass these days.

Neither does Bill Hynes, a hopeless addict until he started coming to Sabina. He now heads Jesus the Next Step, the parish's version of All Addicts Anonymous. He also organizes large regular revivals for recovering addicts. Hynes is white, as is about 10 percent of the St. Sabina membership. Augustine Colon, a cheerful man who makes his way around the church before the service chatting with friends, was born in Puerto Rico. He was an activist for many years in his heavily Latino North Side neighborhood. He admits he became a "backslider" until he encountered St. Sabina and experienced activism on a scale he never knew before. That's when he decided "here's where I belong." He brings his wife, daughter, and granddaughter every Sunday.

Slipping quietly into a pew toward the middle of the church is Jacqui Collins, who worked for CBS radio and television before volunteering as communications director for St. Sabina. One day in 1992, Pfleger phoned her out of the blue and invited her to run for the Illinois senate. She agreed, won the election, has been reelected, and has become a powerhouse in the state for the kind of socially progressive legislation St. Sabina stands for.

In the cavernous rooms behind the sanctuary, the St. Sabina Levites choir, about twenty-five members on this day, are tuning up under the leadership of musical director Michael Drayton while artistic director Rickey Harris is assembling eighteen members of the Spirit of David liturgical dancers. The dancers are mostly young women, and they have to be in good physical condition for what lies ahead. Harris, who has been an intensely active church member since high school, rehearses with the dancers for three hours every Saturday.

Up in the balcony at the rear of the church, Vince Clark is readying the recording equipment as he does every Sunday. With him are his wife, Cheryl, and his young son, Chazz, who accompanies the musicians during the service (quietly) using sturdy cardboard drumsticks supplied by his father. Clark, Pfleger's closest aide, records the sermon every Sunday, and CDs of it are available for purchase after the service, which is also streamed every Sunday via the Internet to a national and international audience.

The musicians, known informally as the minstrels, are assembled to the right of the altar with their instruments—two keyboards, two drum sets (one bongo, one conventional), a saxophone, trumpet, flute, and violin. They are a mixed group of players, including a Jew and an immigrant from Bulgaria, whose weekly dedication to this long service seems boundless.

By 11:18, the church is beginning to look full. But easy to spot is one deacon, Len Richardson, a tall man with a prominent patch of white hair. Richardson and his family go all the way back to the mid-1960s at St. Sabina when black families were just beginning to move into Auburn Gresham. Another longtimer, Dolores Johnson, is also a regular at the service. She and her husband Elbert, since deceased, were among the contingent of early black leaders who longed to see St. Sabina become a proud, African American Catholic parish. She has lived to see it and is active among the lectors who proclaim the Scripture readings at the 11:15.

†

NOW THE COMMENTATOR for today's mass takes the microphone, calms the crowd, reads off a lengthy list of announcements, and the service begins. Suddenly, the old church rocks with the full power of the minstrels' instruments. The choir seems to appear out of thin air and is swaying, clapping, and singing, "Halleluiah, power and glory, honor and power unto the Lord our God. He is able! He is able, and he is our God!" They sing the words over and over and many in the pews join in with the singers' words or their own variations, "Thank you, Lord, for everything!" The dancers, all attired in red tops with flowing sleeves, are out in front of the pews in fast, perpetual motion, raising their arms to heaven, bowing low, and rising up again and again, as leader Rickey Harris, moving with the agility and grace of an NFL wide receiver, sets the pace. Most of the congregation are on their feet too, lifting arms in the air, clapping, rocking back and forth rhythmically, calling out, singing, "Yes, Lord, you are able!" "Thank you Jesus!"

This intense, nonstop celebration of sound and motion continues under full power for almost ten minutes, and just when it seems to be slowing a bit, the pace picks up with renewed vigor. Coming up the main aisle is a procession of lectors, altar servers, and Eucharist ministers. And standing tall and proud in their midst is their leader, "the Reverend Doctor Michael L. Pfleger," as he is identified at the beginning of every service. He is wearing a bright green, flowing chasuble, which contrasts with the dancers' red outfits. He is holding a microphone, and raising his arm he shouts, "If we had a thousand tongues we would praise the Lord! Use your tongue, use your tongue, praise the Lord!" The music grows louder, the motions of choir and dancers stronger still. They are singing one of Drayton's own compositions. It goes on for perhaps another fifteen minutes: "Clap your hands, all ye people, and give God praise. From the outer courts to the inner courts, into the holy place. Sing your song, all ye people, and give God praise . . . Do your dance . . . Leap for joy, all ye people, and give God praise."

To newcomers and visitors, there is an undeniable initial incongruity here. In this classic, African American liturgical ritual, the revered leader is white! Not just ordinary white, says Cathleen Falsani, a journalist who has followed Pfleger's career for twenty years. "No one is whiter than Pfleger; no one is whiter than this blond, blue-eyed, movie-star-handsome Catholic priest raised on the white South Side of Chicago." Yet here he stands in his twenty-eighth year of pastoring St. Sabina, building it up, baptizing, marrying, and burying these black parishioners. And it matters not to them what his race is. How is it possible that this white man has been so embraced by these church members?

One part of the answer is right here now before everyone's eyes and ears. It's this long, energized outpouring of praise and thanksgiving. In traditional Christian churches, there is a prayer called the Gloria. ("Glory to God in the highest. We praise you, we bless you, we worship you, we give you thanks for your glory," etc.) When recited, it takes probably thirty seconds; when sung, it might require three minutes. At St. Sabina, praise and thanks are not only said, they are performed, and not just by the choir and dancers. It is meant to be, and is for many, a lengthy, nourishing, spiritual experience that involves the mind and the whole body.

And it's not over yet. The music becomes softer now, the movements of choir and dancers slower. The mood shifts, and Pfleger calls on the congregation to worship God, not for what he's done for us but simply for who God is. "Come on, raise your hands. You are supreme, you are the Holy One, you are the Lord."

"Holy, holy, holy, Lord God, almighty," sings the choir. "Heaven and earth are full of your glory . . . Hosanna in the highest." Exhortations from the pastor are fewer as time passes, the music slower still, more meditative. By the time the choir and dancers finally depart and only a single instrument, the violin, is left playing, one full hour has passed. Even the most active, exuberant worshippers in the congregation look a bit fatigued as they sit down. The first meaning of the Greek word for liturgy is "work," the holy work of the people, and that is precisely what it has become at St. Sabina.

When Pfleger first introduced this concentration on praise and worship, some—especially those raised in traditional Catholic parishes—objected that it was too unsophisticated for their taste and way too long for anyone's taste. Others, Pfleger in particular, found it life-giving and wanted more. It has become a staple of the Sunday service, attracting people from well beyond the neighborhood for the effect it has on their lives. Lisa Ramsey, director of the St. Sabina Employment Resource Center, calls praise and worship the most important part of the Sunday service for her. "Isn't that what it's all about?" asks Ramsey, who attends the 11:15 every Sunday. She insists she needs it to cope with the three hundred or more unemployed persons her agency seeks to help every month.

Standing on the left side of the sanctuary and closely observing everything is Kimberly Lymore, who has been involved in liturgy planning since she first came to St. Sabina in 1983. She has since earned several degrees in theology including a doctorate and left her lucrative position as a systems analyst for several large firms to become an associate minister at the church. She is thus next to Pfleger in terms of ecclesial authority, although titles are not rigidly adhered to at St. Sabina. Lymore's special interest is the relationship between praise and worship on the one hand and social activism on the other.

†

THE SCRIPTURE READINGS for the day concern prophecies about the end of the world, and when Pfleger goes to the podium to preach, he passes over them rather quickly. His topic is not about the future but the present. His subject is from Matthew's Gospel, chapter six, verse nine: "Thy kingdom come," and he asks the congregation to open their Bibles to that location and read the whole verse with him. It is Jesus' famous prayer, the "Our Father."

Pfleger's sermon will be shorter than usual today, only fifty-five minutes, but he will make up in energy and volume for what may be lacking in length. As always in his sermons, he speaks in an informal style, with a Southern dialect indistinguishable from that of black Protestant preachers. He begins by presenting "the perspective" of the king: "People sit in church all their life," he says, "and never even know the king. In this day of prosperity teaching, God becomes their bellhop, their Santa Claus." They fail to understand, he explains, that in the kingdom God has established, "everything is in submission to the king." The king makes the rules, "and it's got nothin' to do with what you like or whether you agree or what you want. There's no cafeteria menu here. . . . You don't go through this book [the Bible] and decide what you like or don't like. . . . When you come under the kingdom, you come under authority."

He intersperses the talk with practical applications: "You can't be a thief or an adulterer. You can't be a Holy Roller on Sunday and a hell-raiser on Monday." And as he illustrates the hypocrisy of churchgoers, he humorously wonders if this tough talk is offending some in the crowd: "Uh-oh, I think I just lost another hundred people on that one."

"God is holy, omnipotent, and omnipresent," he says. "He's not just the God of the sanctuary, not just the God of the temple. He is a God without walls, a God who's everywhere. And where God is, there is power. In his name, walls fall down, doors open, waters part." As always, Pfleger's words are salted with an upbeat, running commentary from the congregation: "Tell it, pastor, tell it!" "Mercy!" "Praise Jesus!"

Next he talks about the importance of being prepared for the kingdom. "Don't pray for what you can't handle," he says. "Jesus' greatest conflict was that the people were not prepared. They saw a great light, but the people could not embrace it." When they saw him talking to prostitutes, touching lepers, healing on the Sabbath, says Pfleger, they said, "What's wrong with you?" "The people weren't ready, and they still aren't ready. That's why Jesus turned the tables upside down. . . . It's time for religion to think outside the box. . . . God wants to do something that's bigger than the church, and it makes people mad because he messes up people's individual kingdoms."

These first two sections of his presentation, which consume about thirty-five minutes, are, in fact, a prelude to the core message Pfleger really wants to deliver today. It concerns that other part of the answer that explains his longevity at St. Sabina and the magnetic attraction he holds for these believers. It is his insistent, urgent demand to live Christianity in a radical, totally involved way. He pauses, wipes his sweat-covered brow with his handkerchief for the second or third time, and warns the congregation that now he's "going for the jugular."

"When you understand the kingdom," he says slowly and deliberately, "you feel compelled to become kingdom builders, to be agents of change, to transform society." Quickly, he becomes aggressive: "Is Jesus king now?" He repeats the question three times in a row, louder each time until he hears enough vocal agreement from the pews. "If Jesus is king now, there's stuff we need to be changin' now. We ought not to become apathetic about an educational system that is not educating our children. We shouldn't be tolerant that people are sleeping under viaducts and people are standing in line to get crumbs thrown out of somebody's kitchen. . . . I want to impregnate you with a now mentality . . . with a conviction and restlessness that says I ain't waiting any longer! I'm not gonna put up with this. It's got to change! Militarism has to die, classism has to die, sexism has to die, racism has to die."

Another pause and he comes on from another angle. "Watch this," he says, as if he's a magician about to perform an amazing card trick. "We've been taught wrong for too long that heaven is a place to go up to when we die, and so we become passive while we live. We become tolerant about living and simply wait for the day," and he sings in a high-pitched, mocking voice, "I'm goin' up yonder to be with my Lord." He is getting still louder, and the musicians are beginning to play in the background, taking their cue from his words. "This is the same theology that kept the slaves in bondage. The slave master taught the slaves, 'Don't worry about how you're treated 'cuz one day you'll get it all.' That slave mentality has been passed on from generation to generation to generation. But look what Paul says." He cites a passage from the First Epistle to the Thessalonians: "Brothers, sisters, we do not want you to be ignorant concerning those who are asleep. For the trumpet will sound [there's a quick blast from the band's trumpeter] and the angel's voice will command . . . and the Lord shall come *down* . . . and we will meet him in the air. He is coming *down*. You're looking to sit on some cloud, and he is coming *down*!"

Pfleger raises another passage, this from the book of Revelation: "I saw a new city, a holy city coming down from heaven—coming down!" He shouts, "Hear me, St. Sabina. Heaven is not where I'm going up to. Heaven is coming *down* to the earth to invade the earth, to impact the earth, and the government shall be on his shoulders. . . . If the kingdom is getting ready to come down, we are called to begin to establish the kingdom right now, right here on this earth. Look at the person next to you and say, 'Neighbor, you are supposed to establish the kingdom now.'" Many in the congregation may be tiring, but most comply, especially since Pfleger repeats the order, asking that this order be spoken again, to the person on "your other side" and to the "person in the pew in front of you."

He mops his face, bracing for a final charge, quoting from the Gospel of Matthew: "You are Peter and upon this rock I will build my church." But he gives the text an interesting, Pflegerian spin. "Read further," he says, "and see that Jesus gives the keys of the kingdom of heaven, the keys that bind and loosen [to challenge others and to deliver them from their hang-ups]. You are ready and you are empowered. Say to somebody, 'You have power, you have power, you have *power!*'" Then he says to the whole gathering, "I command you in the name of Jesus, the king of kings and the lord of lords. I deputize you when you leave this place, start binding and loosing in your house, start binding and loosing on your block, start binding and loosing in the city, start binding and loosing in the country!

"Do you have power?" he shouts, or rather tries to shout, his voice becoming raspy and weak. "Go kick the devil. Thy kingdom come!"

This was not a classic Pfleger presentation. He did not jump up and down to emphasize a point or invite the congregation to dance in the aisles. He didn't even have an altar call after the sermon as he often does, inviting people to come forward to pledge their loyalty to the king or confess their weakness. Yet, he got across this key idea: passive religion is not acceptable; all are summoned to action. What is amazing is that he finds so many different ways to impregnate his people with the urgency of the mission.

†

THE IMAGE HE used this day—building the kingdom—is not a fanciful conceit at St. Sabina. The city blocks around the church, as well as blocks half a mile or more away, have been transformed by the presence of this pastor and this community. Across the street on 78th Place, within the shadow of the church, is Samaritan House, where Lonnie Washington and others have recovered their lives. Across the street on Racine is the office of the Beloved Community, an independent development corporation founded by Sabina; it supports new housing ventures and business opportunities in Auburn Gresham and provides technical assistance to small businesses that are already in the area. The director, April Dumas, is a regular at the 11:15. Just steps away is the Ark, St. Sabina's mammoth community center, whose activities touch more than two hundred young people every day. Director Leonard Langston, in his dark suit and bow tie, is at his post in the church this morning as a member of the armor bearers. Adjacent to the church on Throop Street is the St. Sabina Academy, a K–8 school that has consistently earned high ratings. Principal Helen Dumas regarded the school so highly she took a forty-thousand-dollar cut in pay to take the job, and she's still there seventeen years later.

Half a block from the church on the northwest corner of 79th and Racine is BJ's Market and Bakery, a sit-down restaurant that opened in 2005 after Pfleger persuaded the owner of another South Side eatery to expand because the community was on the way back. On the southwest corner is the Agape Clothing Store, which specializes in women's and children's wear, picture frames, candles, and other home-related items. Pfleger urged the two female owners to open here, since the presence of such small businesses sends a loud message to the community. Mattie George, the front-pew lady with the tambourine, is an employee at the store. Next door to Agape is Jacqui Collins's senatorial office, and next to that a child-care center. On the southeast corner is a new Walgreen's drug store, which came only because Pfleger and other Sabina boosters, after much tugging and pulling, convinced skeptical Walgreen's executives that Auburn Gresham was in resurrection mode. Pressure also brought about the new CVS store four blocks east of Sabina on Halsted Street. Ten years ago there were no drug stores within a mile of the church, and no banks either. Today there are three banks, one four blocks east of Sabina and one six blocks west. Two blocks north on Racine is a large bowling and skating center, built thanks to a cooperative arrangement between Sabina and the Chicago Park District. Also several blocks east are the two Sabina-sponsored safe homes for foster children. Not visible in the immediate neighborhood but just as important in the Sabina community is the AIDS clinic they founded in Ghana.

The 1200 block of 79th, once the province of drug dealers and prostitutes, is now dominated by the six-story, eighty-apartment St. Sabina Elders Village, which was erected with the cooperation of Catholic Charities and the federal Department of Housing and Urban Development. Pfleger begged and pushed for its construction when he discovered there were more than ten thousand seniors living in Auburn Gresham, many alone and in unsuitable housing. Some Sabina regulars live there now. Others live at the very similar six-story Senior Suites building two blocks east on 79th. Next door to that is a Women, Infants, and Children center maintained by the Illinois Department of Health. Sabina facilitated the coming of both these additions to the community.

Farther up the block is the St. Sabina–Catholic Charities Social Service Center, which distributes yearly 1.2 million pounds of food to the needy and serves over 2,500 clients a month. Its director, Sharon Tillmon, says her regular attendance at the Sunday mass and the Tuesday Bible study helps her handle the overload. On Racine south of 79th, near the site of a motel once occupied largely by prostitutes (now torn down), stands the Sabina Employment Resource Center, which is an especially popular destination due to the high unemployment rate. Director Lisa Ramsey relishes the praise and worship portion of the Sunday liturgy, which she says helps her maintain a sense of calm as she looks at the packed waiting room outside her office every morning.

Truth be told, Pfleger did not achieve all this by himself. When Terry Peterson was the alderman of the 17th Ward in the late 1990s and early 2000s, he and Pfleger formed a team. Together they were able to cut through enough bureaucratic red tape and put enough sustained pressure on church, state, city, and federal agencies to lay the groundwork for this renovation.

South of the church on 79th Street is the Perfect Peace Café and Bakery, a top-end business started by two St. Sabina regulars, Julie Welborn and Denise Nicholes. With Pfleger's encouragement, they "stepped out on a dream," concentrating on custom-made sandwiches and quality pies and cakes. Their products have been well received in the community. Welborn, a former youth director at the church, also manages the Thea Bowman retreat house in the buildings of a closed parish west of St. Sabina. She is in the church every Sunday for the 11:15, except on those occasions when the congregation is invited to her restaurant for brunch after mass.

Right across the street from Perfect Peace (where there once was a car wash infested with drug traffic) is the topping for this neighborhood reconstitution: a beautiful, one-acre garden of trees, flowers, and benches called Renaissance Park, honoring the children who have lost their lives to violence. It is a "passive park," which means no basketball playing, skateboarding, or carousing, and it is maintained by the Chicago Park District. At the entrance is a fountain and sculpture by Jerzy Kenar, the artist who designed much of the Afrocentric furniture in the church. With a cluster of black granite balls, it celebrates great African American achievers: Martin Luther King Jr., Maya Angelou, Muhammad Ali, Gwendolyn Brooks, Harold Washington, Mahalia Jackson, and others.

Obviously, the Faith Community of St. Sabina is not the kingdom of God—not yet. But when people walk through that garden on a fall day and see the tower of St. Sabina rising up less than a block away, they may get a fleeting sense of what Michael Pfleger is driving at and where all the sweat and passion comes from.

†

BACK IN CHURCH, following the sermon and the prayers of the faithful, the collection is taken up. At Sabina this is no small detail. Everyone who can walk, limp, or be pushed in a wheelchair moves slowly up the center aisle, envelope in hand. Before the altar, ushers are in position holding two large wicker baskets to receive this week's offerings, one by one. The procession, directed by ushers and greeters, begins with the first pew and proceeds in an orderly fashion to the back pews until everyone has come forward. The movement has a certain reverent quality that is rarely seen at collection time in most churches, and it moves so slowly partly because some individuals and couples stop at the basket and seem to be in prayer before dropping in their contribution. St. Sabina has been a tithing parish since 1982, which means parishioners are urged, encouraged, and expected to give 10 percent of their income to the works of the parish.

In the midst of the procession is Sabina Academy principal Helen Dumas, who, with her late husband Martin, has been a longtime advocate of tithing. She recommends the practice wherever she goes. If you give

10 percent, even when it hurts or seems foolish, she contends, God will find a way for you. She often tells the story of her own providential benefits from tithing. Tithing has proved providential for St. Sabina as well. The Sunday total had averaged around thirty-five thousand dollars a week through most of the 2000s, making it one of the largest weekly collections in the archdiocese, the middle- and low-middle-class nature of the Sabina neighborhood notwithstanding. Thanks to tithing, in 1990 the parish was able to pay off the considerable debt it owed the archdiocese, and it has been a solvent operation since. With the recession in 2008 the amount dipped, but the total for the previous week, according to the announcements before mass, was $32,240.

Pfleger interrupts the service momentarily to introduce to the congregation his daughter-in-law Dia and her five young children, who are living temporarily in the Chicago area. He asks them to come to the front of the church, and the crowd applauds warmly, though some people seem puzzled by this first view of Pastor Pfleger's grandchildren. Perhaps, as newer church members, they were not aware that Pfleger adopted a nine-year-old son in 1983. Now in his late thirties, Lamar and his family live in Seattle. Dia, and the children are here while Lamar is on an extensive job search.

From this point on, the service is more clearly recognizable as a Roman Catholic mass. Parishioners process up the aisle and present containers with communion bread to presider Pfleger, the servers, and other attendants. Standing at the altar, he says the offering prayers while the choir sings quietly in the background. Then in succession, Pfleger recites the traditional preface and the solemn eucharistic prayer, including the words of consecration, "This my body" and "This is my blood" over the bread and wine. This part of the mass ends with the so called Great Amen, which is proclaimed loudly by all the people. After the congregation recites the Lord's Prayer together, everyone is invited to offer peace to those around them. At many parishes this amounts to little more than a quick handshake and the words, "Peace be with you," to those nearby. At Sabina, this is done on a grander scale, some people moving out of their pews and up the aisles to hug and kiss friends and strangers alike. The activity takes about five minutes.

Then comes the communion procession, which imitates almost exactly the procedure of the collection procession, except that a gospel hymn is sung by the choir. Eucharistic ministers stationed near the altar place a portion of the consecrated bread in the hands of each worshipper, who immediately consumes it and returns to the pew. A kind of meditative hush comes over the crowd as they sit awaiting the final blessing from Pfleger. And with that blessing, the worshippers are sent off "to love and serve the Lord." Closure this day comes precisely at 2:25 in the afternoon, just over three hours from the start. One weary visitor marvels at the "sheer stamina of these folks," most of whom seem buoyed and energized by their participation.

On the way out, the cheerful mood persists. Ushers hand out the Sunday bulletin packed with news about the upcoming Thanksgiving eve dinner for young people fifteen to twenty-one, the Christmas feast for the homeless and elderly, the family ministry night, the armor bearers dance, the youth ministry debate team presentation, the new believers teaching series, the addict recovery revival, and a dozen other events and appeals for volunteers in various Sabina ministries. Downstairs in McMahon Hall, a scattering of people, mostly teens, are lining up for nachos at the cafeteria counter while other folks are checking out the booths where clothing, banners, stationery, and Christmas cards are for sale. The parking lot clears quickly, but a few people head over to 79th Street on this unseasonably warm day and take a leisurely walk through the greenery in the Renaissance Park.

2

DEEP ROOTS

═══════════

WELCOME TO AMERICA, MIKE! IF YOU WANT TO FIGHT INJUSTICE,
YOU DON'T HAVE TO GO TO OKLAHOMA. WE HAVE PLENTY IN
CHICAGO.

—MARION NOBLE PFLEGER

WHEREVER HE GOES to give a speech or receive an award, people ask
Michael Pfleger how he became the Reverend Doctor Michael
Louis Pfleger. They are genuinely curious about the deep roots of this
blue-eyed, sandy-haired, youthful-looking white man who became the
unquestioned leader of a highly self-conscious black community and the
revered hero to black civil rights leaders and activists all over the country.

Pfleger is quizzed about his background so often that his standard
answer seems almost scripted. There is the time he witnessed segregation firsthand at an Indian reservation in Oklahoma, and there's the
fleeting glimpse he had of Dr. Martin Luther King Jr. when he was marching in Chicago. That usually satisfies the audience, but his story is more
complicated than that, full of odd quirks, strange turns, and unexpected
coincidences, just like everyone else's. Yet in Michael Pfleger's case, one
observes a kind of single-mindedness, a consistency of vision that runs

17

through all the contingencies and makes his story different. He has been called stubborn, self-absorbed, even crazy. He's also been called amazingly open, compassionate, and self-giving well beyond the call of duty. There is something of the Biblical prophet here, his friend Giles Conwell, a black priest from Nashville, once observed. "He's in the tradition of Jeremiah and John the Baptist, someone in whose head God's word dances, plays, and sizzles, and who's got to speak even though he knows speaking out can get you in a lot of trouble."[1]

Michael Pfleger was born in 1949 and bred in Chicago's South Side Ashburn community, about two miles west of St. Sabina parish. It was an all-white, mostly Catholic, middle-class neighborhood of single-family dwellings. It was "a little like growing up in a bubble," says Pfleger, "everybody pretty much alike, almost everyone's father working for the police department or the fire department." Michael was the second child of Louis Pfleger and Marion Noble Pfleger, a couple whose story has its own unique twist. Marion had become pregnant by Louis out of wedlock in the late 1930s—a development viewed at the time as a terrible disgrace and scandal. A hasty church wedding was arranged, and Marion gave birth to a daughter, Joan. Unfortunately, no one apparently thought it was important that Louis and Marion actually be in love. They weren't, and their attempt to live together lasted less than a year. They talked of getting a divorce but abandoned the idea when their pastor assured them they would certainly go to hell. Louis and Marion each went their own way for ten years, and the separation seemed destined to become permanent. But it happened that they went on a double date arranged by their friends one night and suddenly discovered in each other something they hadn't seen before. They came together as committed spouses at last, and Marion in due time gave birth to their second child, Michael, in 1949.

Pfleger credits his close relationship with his sister, eleven years older than himself, with giving him an early awareness of life's unfairness. Joan had been mentally challenged since her early years, never going beyond the fifth grade and living her entire life at home. "I could see the pain and hurt she suffered when people called her retarded and when she was denied job opportunities," says Pfleger. She worked for a time in the kitchen of a Chicago Park District facility and later held a job working with mentally disabled adults, but she was unable to rise very far in life. "Her disappointment created a kind of tension in me. I think it was the beginning of my hunger for justice in this world," Pfleger says. Joan died in 1995 after a long illness.

During Pfleger's boyhood his father worked for a mattress company, then became office manager for the local 18th Ward headquarters. Marion worked as a secretary at St. Thomas More Church before taking a similar job with the Chicago Board of Education. Pfleger believes his first awareness of racial inequality occurred when he was in fourth and fifth grades at St. Thomas More School. Since his mother was working in the rectory, he would occasionally drop in during lunch hour and eat his sandwich in the kitchen with the rectory cook, Mary Betts. She was the first black person he had ever met, let alone talked to, and he recalls sitting on a stool listening to her tell of her experiences. "She wasn't angry or confrontational," he says, "but it was clear she had faced a lot of prejudice and struggle as a black woman. She was going to do whatever it took to raise her kids. At that point it meant traveling a long way to be a cook in this all-white community. I didn't know it at the time, but here she was teaching me black history." Pfleger kept in touch with Mary Betts until her death, and he calls her "my John Hope Franklin," comparing her to the eminent black historian.

In his early grammar school years, Pfleger was only vaguely aware of racial fear and anxiety in the community. Everyone knew black families were moving their way from the east and north, but they were still considered a long way off in the 1950s since the racial boundaries were thought to be shifting slowly. Young Michael discovered they were shifting faster than everyone thought when he and a few school friends attended a movie at the popular Capitol Theatre several miles east of his home and realized they were the only white kids in the house. They never went back.

Although the word "nigger" was often used in the school and community, it was strictly banned in the Pfleger household. Marion and Louis did not often lecture on racism; instead, they made sure their children understood that everybody stood equal before God. That was a lesson Michael learned the hard way, since he was getting consistently high grades at school. Instead of receiving praise for his brilliance, his mother would invariably use the occasion to remind him that neither high grades nor one's race nor any other accident of brain or birth justified looking down on others. "To tell the truth, that sometimes pissed me off," he recalled.

He was also offended when his eighth grade teacher, a nun, recommended that he not enroll at Quigley South High School, a preparatory seminary for future priests, because she considered him "too wild" and was afraid he might embarrass the parish. "That really motivated me," says Pfleger. "I've never liked to be told no." So he did enroll at Quigley, along with about a dozen of his classmates. The notion of becoming a priest had attracted him at an early age, and family photos show a very young Michael attired in a homemade "vestment," celebrating "mass" on an altar made of orange crates in the basement of his home. But priesthood was not on his mind by his teenage years. Quigley was close to home and had a reputation for quality education.

After his first year in high school, Pfleger and five other students volunteered to work during the summer at a Native American reservation in Wilburton, Oklahoma, some eight hundred miles from Chicago. Pfleger was impressed with the history and tradition that was being passed on to the younger generation as he worked with the teens in the community. But here for the first time he came face to face with racial bigotry. One day as he and several Native American teenagers walked into a reservation store to purchase candy bars, the man behind the counter stopped them cold. "Only whites allowed in here," he said. "You kids get out!" Fair-skinned Pfleger of course was allowed to stay, so he bought the candy while the others waited outside. "It was mind-boggling," he says. "They couldn't go into a store in their own territory." That night he called his mother and told her he intended to transfer to a school in Oklahoma "because they have real problems here."

"Welcome to America, Mike!" his mother responded prophetically. "If you want to fight injustice, you don't have to go to Oklahoma. We have plenty in Chicago."

He went back to the reservation the next summer, older and wiser, and gave no further thought to moving. Yet that quick, unexpected sting, which he has shared in countless talks over the years, remains fixed in his mind.

More deeply fixed in mind and spirit is his one and only sighting of Dr. King. It occurred on a summer day in 1966 after his third year in high school. He and two friends had bicycled several miles to Marquette Park, a middle-class neighborhood as white and bubble-like as his own. They came to see the much-anticipated march of King and his entourage through the streets in support of open housing. Pfleger was not prepared for what he saw.

"There was a terrific crowd," he recalls. "They were screaming and cursing and throwing stuff. I never saw such hate in my life. Some of the people I recognized as neighbors or people from our own church. I was really scared. I guess I had never connected all the dots before." And there walked Martin Luther King, "calm and erect, saying, 'We love you, we love you.'" Pfleger didn't know it then, but King had been struck in the head by part of a brick earlier in the march.

As Pfleger has stated many times since, he was so moved by that moment that he said to himself, "Either he [King] is crazy or he has a strength I want to know about." King became a kind of obsession with him. He read King's books, put up posters of King in his bedroom, tracked King's ongoing civil rights moves in the country. "I saw Martin Luther King using faith as a transitional agent for building community," he says. "I decided then I wanted to be a priest because the church can be an element for change."

†

FOLLOWING HIS GRADUATION from Quigley, Pfleger continued his studies for the priesthood at Niles College, affiliated with Loyola University. While there he got the opportunity for real-life ministry, the chance to put into action what was simmering in his soul. He was assigned by Niles superiors to work in ministry at Precious Blood parish near Western Avenue and the Eisenhower Expressway, an impoverished black and Hispanic community on the West Side with a church building overlooking the expressway. Jerry Maloney, the pastor at the time, said it was a struggle to realize as much as one hundred dollars in the average Sunday collection. Michael Pfleger instantly fell in love with the problem-ridden place and the poverty-stricken people. He visited homes, put new life in the teen club, and formed a youth choir. He got to know the Black Panthers, the militant, much-feared organization promoting black power and identity, whom Maloney had welcomed into the church basement for their regular meetings.

He was especially impressed with the Panthers' community outreach, which included free breakfasts for children living in the nearby Henry Horner public housing project and free after-school tutoring for children. In many ways they were advocates of the people. He became friends with Fred Hampton, the charismatic Panther leader who would be shot to death in 1969 during a raid on his apartment led by Chicago police under the direction of Cook County State's Attorney Edward Hanrahan. The killing, which many still consider a deliberate assassination, did a lot to shake Pfleger's meager faith in the justice system. "I saw at Precious Blood what people could do when they worked together. I was also seeing how damned unresponsive the city and the people in power can be." The Panthers, he says, "taught me everything I know about effective community organizing. They were doing more to serve the people than the church, the police, or the city were."

Pfleger got to know the local storefront ministers in the area and began to sit in on their church services, carefully observing their lively teaching and worship styles. "I saw how they helped people bring their whole selves into the service, not just their minds but their bodies," Pfleger notes. "I found things there I never found in the white church." It was especially at one of these small churches, Hopewell Baptist, Pfleger says, that he developed "a personal relation with Jesus." And it was out of those praying and learning experiences, he adds, that he personally came to "confess Jesus as my Lord and Savior." In later years at St. Sabina, Pfleger would sometimes recall in a sermon, "I learned about sin and guilt in the Catholic Church. But at Hopewell Baptist I learned about Jesus." Eager for more of the black experience, he attended some of the larger Protestant churches in Chicago, sitting in the back pews and taking in the preaching of T. L.

Barrett of the Life Center Church of God in Christ and Clay Evans at Fellowship Baptist Church.

Meanwhile, Pfleger was far from impressed by the curriculum at Niles College. American history, he felt, misrepresented and dismissed Native Americans. Social studies fixated on one culture and one race. "It was all European and all white. I realized the Catholic Church wasn't relating to the black community in any serious way. And the seminary wasn't preparing us to make much difference." But he stayed, he says, because "I love the Catholic Church, its history, its tradition, its flexibility, because it's the church I grew up in, because Dr. King taught transformation can come through faith." He stayed too because he saw in Jerry Maloney a man of conviction who quietly made small but important differences in the Precious Blood neighborhood. Maloney had opened doors to the Black Panthers when virtually every institution of society considered them dangerous. Maloney had openly opposed the Vietnam War, placing a large sign outside the church (in view of motorists on the Eisenhower Expressway), that said, "Stop the God Damned Bombing." Perhaps most importantly, Maloney validated young Pfleger in his myriad ministries and explorations. The things he was doing were worthwhile, Maloney told him, assuring Pfleger that in the long run, he and the Catholic Church would make a difference.

Today, Maloney takes pride in his encouragement and mentoring. "Mike was just so dedicated, so great with people. He was always in the present, giving it his full and undivided attention. Of course he could go overboard, go out on a limb now and then and make mistakes. That's how he was then, and I think that's how he is now. There are few priests in the Church who have earned genuine credibility in the black community. Mike is one."

The murder of Dr. King in 1968 all by itself might have pushed Pfleger over the edge and out of ministry. King had been his guide since that transformative day in Marquette Park. "I was devastated," he says. "He was the hero who would lead us into the promised land. In a single moment we lost him and his prophetic voice." Then came what he calls one of those "aha moments." A few days after the shooting he was standing on Madison Street a few blocks from the church, viewing the burned-out buildings and cars, the shattered windows, and the heaps of rubble left over from the riots and looting. A woman emerged from a house nearby, holding a broom, and spoke to a small cluster of people standing in the street as if in shock. "Time to clean up," she said. "Time to start going forward."

"I took it as a message meant for me," says Pfleger. "I remember that woman to this day."

†

WHEN PFLEGER ENTERED the major seminary at Mundelein, Illinois, in 1971 for his final four years of formation in philosophy, theology, and spirituality before ordination to the priesthood, his interests remained at Precious Blood. And for the most part, so did he. Archdiocesan leaders were attempting something new that year. For fifty years the seminary had been more like a monastery set on a beautiful lake than a training ground for activists. Prayer, study, discipline, and silence comprised the order of the day. Those restless types who could not conform were gradually sifted out of the student body, leaving presumably a residue of talented, obedient, and celibate men—but men with neither experience nor understanding of the real world. Now it would be different. The prayerful, disciplined life would be balanced with time for "clinical pastoral education"—ministry assignments in the churches or other institutions throughout the Chicago archdiocese. Many of the seminarians received the news like manna from heaven—none more so than Michael Pfleger.

His parents bought him a new Chevrolet Vega, and he began commuting the forty miles between Mundelein and his ongoing assignment, Precious Blood Church. He would attend classes, but often his work in the parish prevented him from taking part in other seminary activity. In fact, Pfleger had basically moved into the Precious Blood rectory, and his ministry there constituted his major work while the seminary became a part-time job. At least, that's the way some of his superiors viewed the situation.

In the middle of his second year at the seminary he was called in by the rector, Monsignor John Gorman, who complained that Pfleger did not have a "significant presence" on the campus and was therefore not receiving the kind of formation required. He insisted Pfleger move back to campus and lead a more balanced life. Pfleger was stunned. He took Gorman's words as an ultimatum: conform or be expelled. "That broke me," says Pfleger. "I was hooked on ministry, on faith, on the church as a way to better people's lives. I didn't know what to do." He called Maloney, who, with some other priests from the West Side, came out to Mundelein and interceded with Gorman on Pfleger's behalf.

Gorman has since said there was never any question of throwing Pfleger out. "The whole program was new," he says, "and it wasn't easy to get a balance. Sure, some people pushed hard on the envelope [overdoing their outside ministry] and Mike was one of them. But he wasn't the only one." Pfleger remained in a kind of limbo for months, awaiting word of his dismissal. But he did little to mollify the authorities. He was still commuting, still making Precious Blood his home and center of activity, though he says he "tried to be a little bit more visible" at seminary meetings and other activities. Then the following summer, Gorman resigned as rector, and the pressure was off—for a while.

Reverend Bill Stenzel, a classmate of Pfleger's at Mundelein, says he considers Pfleger his hero because "he made me hungry for people to serve. He was never distant or remote, but we always knew he had a bigger agenda, a passion for ministry." At the same time, notes Stenzel, "Mike was not a regular collaborator with others on projects; he was more of an independent operator." And this is a characteristic, he believes, Pfleger has carried into his work as a priest.

With a new rector, Reverend Thomas Murphy, installed, most of Pfleger's classmates were on their best behavior during their third year at Mundelein. At the end of that school year, decisions would be made by a screening committee as to who should be ordained to the deaconate and who should not. Those who became deacons took upon themselves the obligation of lifelong celibacy and were virtually assured of ordination to the priesthood the following year. But Michael Pfleger was no more cautious than he had been in the past. He continued to make Precious Blood his priority and let everyone at the Mundelein campus know in a variety of ways that he considered the seminary training there superficial and inadequate. On one occasion the twenty-four-year-old seminarian wrote a letter and put a copy under the door of each student and faculty member. The immediate occasion was a proposed vote on whether the seminary's new set of ciboria (the cups that hold communion wafers) should be plated with gold or ceramic, but that set Pfleger off on a host of issues in his craw. "If I didn't do something, I would have busted," he says.

The letter drew on contrasts between the hardships of the inner-city poor and the overweening comforts at the seminary on the lake. He wrote about "the newly carpeted chapel and freshly painted walls . . . the newly furnished faculty rooms, new offices, and new faculty lounge. . . . I drive past many empty buildings that exist here, heated, cleaned, and maintained for what? I drive around the grounds and find its many workers plowing the snow, raking the leaves, or cutting its massive lawns. . . . I experience the delivery of new sofa beds for many of the students. I look at the practically nonexistent Apostolate Fund [donations for the inner city] and observe the rooms of some students turned into hotel suites . . . while programs to attract minority students and courses to sensitize students to life in the real world remain in oblivion. . . . We have watched many disturbed people pacified. We have watched questions drift into silence. My fear is that if we don't stop now, words like poverty and injustice will escape our vocabulary . . . and perhaps we will even lose our touch with reality itself."

Back at Precious Blood, matters had taken a turn for the worse. Maloney left the parish, and the new pastor, Tom Millea, was less than impressed with the high-powered young man living in his house. "It wasn't just me," said Pfleger. "He was a dictator, and he wasn't treating the people with respect." Some offended church members went so far as to hold their own prayer service in front of the church while the new pastor was saying mass. "I stood with them," says Pfleger. After several heated discussions, Pfleger says, Millea ordered him to get out, but he refused to go. So one morning as Pfleger was finishing shaving, the police arrived and removed him from the rectory. Angry, embarrassed, aghast, and hardly believing what had just happened, he called the archdiocesan vicar general, who informed him that pastors are in charge of their churches and there was nothing he could do.

"Well, that did it!" says Pfleger. "I had it at that point. I quit the church, the seminary, the diocese, the whole thing! I drove home to my parents' house." An hour passed and the seminary rector, Murphy, drove up to the Pfleger's South Side home. "I saw him coming, and I didn't want to talk to him," says Pfleger, "so I went into the kitchen." Pfleger's mother let Murphy in and then went to the kitchen and told her son, "Get your ass into the living room and talk to the man!" He did.

Pfleger has only a sketchy memory of their conversation, and Murphy, who later became the archbishop of Seattle, Washington, is deceased. "He said he understood my reaction, but he urged me not to throw everything away that I had worked for just because I was hurt and angry," says Pfleger. By the time Murphy left the house, Pfleger had cooled off and knew he still had a place in the seminary, though the exciting, formative days at Precious Blood were history.

Asked about the abrupt removal of the young seminarian from the premises, Millea, now retired, acknowledges that he regarded Pfleger as a renegade and troublemaker. However, he attributes Pfleger's account of his ouster from the rectory to the young man's "creative imagination." He says police were called about that time due to a break-in at the rectory, and they questioned a number of people, but he professes no knowledge of why Pfleger departed so abruptly.

Back at the Mundelein seminary, Pfleger still faced serious obstacles. The decision about the deaconate was just around the corner, and he had hardly endeared himself to the seminary professors, department heads, and administrators who would vote on his worthiness. His lack of "significant presence" on campus throughout his three years irritated many of them and some fellow students as well. Accepting strong-willed, rebellious Michael Pfleger, it was argued, might set a dangerous precedent for the future. The day soon came when Michael Pfleger was ushered into a room crowded with a dozen or more priests waiting to discuss his qualifications and vote as they saw fit. His spirits fell as the conversation proceeded. Yes, he was a highly intelligent young man; yes, he was extraordinarily zealous and committed to the poor; yes, he had an outgoing, pleasing personality—most of time; yes, he seemed to have a solid spiritual life. However, would he be an obedient priest? Was his commitment to Catholic doctrine sufficiently solid? Above all, had he had "a significant presence" at the seminary over the years?

Time came for the vote, and Rector Murphy asked everyone who approved this candidate for the deaconate to raise his hand. A long pause followed, and it seemed to Pfleger that he was doomed. Then slowly, deliberately, Murphy raised his own hand. Another pause, another hand, two more, three more rose, until the silent vote was nearly unanimous. They all congratulated Pfleger. Afterward, Murphy quietly told him, "Such, you see, is the power of the rector." Many times since, Pfleger has told friends and parishioners, "I am a priest today only because of Tom Murphy."

Of course, the absolutely final decision in such matters rested with the Chicago archbishop, Cardinal John Cody. And Pfleger was on shaky ground here too. It was well known that he had picketed the cardinal's residence on several occasions over Cody's decision to close inner-city schools. Pfleger's constant and sharp criticism of the seminary, including his letter to the students, his clash with a pastor, and the recent incident with the Chicago police—any one of these departures from protocol could persuade Cody to veto the screening committee decision and scuttle Pfleger's chances of becoming a deacon and thereby a priest.

When Pfleger met one-on-one with Cody for the mandatory pre-ordination interview, the cardinal let him know immediately who was in charge. "Take off that ring," said Cody, pointing to a ring Pfleger had been wearing for several years. "I alone wear the ring in this archdiocese." Cody presented his concerns with Pfleger's "extremism" and speculated that he might have been unduly influenced by Jerry Maloney. But he did not badger the candidate on any of the issues Pfleger most feared and in the end gave him his blessing and seal of approval.

After his ordination as deacon in 1974, Pfleger was assigned for further ministerial training. It was not to an all-black parish as he had hoped, but to Our Lady of Perpetual Help, a large, all-white, affluent parish in suburban Glenview. At first he viewed the one-year assignment as punishment for his impudence, but he later made peace with it, seeing here an opportunity to experience the other face of Chicagoland. At the parish he met two Franciscan nuns, Sisters Marie Kripner and Paul Anne Held, with whom he formed lasting friendships. Their support and prayers for him have transcended the years, and Sister Marie has designed several sets of vestments for use in the liturgy at Sabina. In Glenview Pfleger shared with the parish teens his love for the poor and neglected, taking the young people on field trips to the inner city, to the Audy Home for juvenile offenders, and to the county courts.

He had passed the major hurdles, though with little room to spare. He was ready for the priesthood and the future. Did he ever think about what he had given up by his decision—the opportunity for marriage and a family? "It was a hard choice in the early days in the seminary," he says. "Then as I grew and matured I saw that my life's work was ministry, totally ministry. If I ever married a woman, I knew the first thing she'd do was leave me."

3

A SERIES OF COINCIDENCES

Young, old, rich and poor, everybody was unanimous. It had to be Mike.

—Reverend Michael Nallen

JUST TWO MONTHS before his ordination to the priesthood in 1975, Michael Pfleger's mother died. She had been suffering from cancer and had undergone a mastectomy the previous year. While she was in the hospital for what was considered a routine blood transfusion, Pfleger phoned to find out how she was doing. "Could you come now?" she asked. "I'm slipping." He rushed to the hospital and found her failing rapidly and unable to speak. "I held her hand," he says, "and she knew me." Soon Marion Pfleger was gone. The loss was profound for Michael, his father, and his sister. "I always knew she loved me," Pfleger says. "Even if no one else in the world loved me, she did."

Grief put a damper on his ordination preparations but did not prevent him from rewarding old friends. Seminary regulations allotted only a handful of guest tickets for the ordination mass in the large colonial-style chapel at Mundelein, so Pfleger had thirty counterfeit tickets printed, allowing him to invite supporters from Precious Blood and the parish he served as a deacon in Glenview. As a result, he received more applause and cheers than any of the others when the newly ordained were introduced.

His first assignment was to St. Sabina, just a mile from his home parish of St. Thomas More. He had already met the pastor, Reverend Henry Pehler, who later attended the ordination itself and received the customary first blessing from his new associate pastor. In the seminary parking lot afterward, Pehler suffered a severe heart attack and was rushed to the hospital, where he underwent open-heart surgery. His recuperation would keep him away from the parish for more than six months.

Meanwhile, the single associate pastor who had been serving at St. Sabina was leaving. So the newly minted Father Pfleger was largely on his own right at the start of his priestly career. His only companion in the rectory was Monsignor John McMahon, the aged, ailing, retired pastor who had struggled unsuccessfully throughout the 1960s to create an integrated community in Auburn Gresham.

"It was a pretty dark scene," recalls Pfleger: the rambling, multilevel rectory could easily accommodate seven or eight priests, with bedrooms and anterooms and offices and long halls all built around a concrete-paved courtyard. The whole rectory had been painted a pale green, making the place seem cold, sterile, and empty. Emptier still was the cavernous church, built to hold more than a thousand worshippers but now usually drawing no more than sixty persons (almost evenly split between white and black) for each of the three Sunday masses. The downstairs church, which once accommodated the overflow of parishioners, was closed and deteriorating. St. Sabina was deep in a debt that was growing by the month and would have soon put the whole enterprise out of business if it were not for subsidies from the archdiocese—and bingo.

Pfleger despises bingo. "It's the most depressing thing a church can do; it demands loads of work from volunteer and staff so old ladies can come and spend their money. And it doesn't bring in that much anyway." Yet bingo was a major activity of St. Sabina, drawing two to three hundred players to the community center every Thursday evening.

The whole operation of the church, including worship, was more traditional and staid than what Pfleger had experienced at his home parish even in the 1950s and 1960s. "At least we had decent sermons there and a welcoming, family feeling. Here, the remaining white folks were the backbone of the parish, and we had no formation of black leadership at all. But what facilities we had! What great potential! We had this great institution sort of divorced from the people who lived here." Awaiting the return of Father Pehler, Pfleger busied himself making contacts and learning about what was going on in the community.

Monsignor McMahon was at first wary of this hyperactive young man, but when he saw how much energy he had, how he was greeting everyone at church, visiting parishioners in their homes, how he kept talking about the future of the parish while the dwindling whites talked mostly about the past, McMahon's attitude changed. "He kind of opened up to me one night," says Pfleger. "He talked about bringing in Saul Alinsky to create integration, about how he went out into the neighborhood to welcome the newcomers, while on the other side of Ashland [Avenue], an Augustinian priest was playing on fear and rallying the people to keep the blacks out." McMahon went to his room and brought down a stack of letters and notes he had never shown anyone. It was the hate mail he had received from parishioners moving out of the parish, many of them families he had ministered to for more than twenty years and considered his friends. "They turned on him," says Pfleger, "considered him a traitor for letting the blacks push them out. He was deeply hurt."

Pastor Pehler's return following his recuperation opened an era of quiet tension between pastor and associate pastor. Pfleger remembered the stunned look on Pehler's face as he walked through the rectory, looked out a window, and saw for the first time the old school bus that had been donated to the parish by Pfleger's friends in Glenview. It had been painted, under Pfleger's direction, red, black, and green, the traditional colors of African American pride. It was not so much that Pehler railed against the young man's ideas and enthusiasms, just that the two were never on the same page.

"Henry was very German, very unemotional, very structured and traditional," notes Pfleger. "He saw his role as pastor as one of maintenance: keeping the lights on and the doors open until the archdiocese decided to close the place." To Pehler, who knew well the history of black movement on the South Side and its effect on Catholic churches, St. Sabina was just too big and unwieldy an institution to survive much longer.

On the other hand, Pfleger was aflame with its possibilities. He got banners celebrating black history and hung them in the church. He launched a post-service coffee shop in the church vestibule. In his homilies at mass, he tried to be very personal and very positive about his vision for St. Sabina. His preaching manner had not yet evolved into the high-voltage style that would characterize his later ministry, he admits, but he has always denied ever consciously speaking with a Southern or black inflection, though he admits, "I've lived with black people most of my life. They're my people, they're my staff, they're my social friends. I guess that's all had some effect."

Elbert and Dolores Johnson and their eight children (with another on the way) were among the first black Catholic families to move into Sabina in the mid-1960s. Elbert, a husky, outgoing, friendly man, used his considerable conversational skills to become a successful sausage salesman for a large meatpacking company. When he arrived, he was forthright about his hopes that his new parish might be an active, involved, black community, not the sort of pray-pay-and-obey community he and Dolores had experienced in some other Catholic parishes. There were similar high hopes, along with leadership potential and a willingness to give time and talent, among other Sabina newcomers like Charles and Mary Marble, Leslie and Beverly Allen, and Herb and Elsie Poleate. But with St. Sabina in a state of instability at the time—ongoing white retreat and black arrival—they quickly learned community-building was difficult, often frustrating work. To these relative newcomers, the coming of Michael Pfleger was a godsend. One night, Elbert Johnson gripped Pfleger on the shoulder and said, "We've been watching you, and we're convinced you're genuine. What you're trying to do here is what I've been hungering for all my life."

Meanwhile, Pfleger introduced gospel music at some of the masses, occasionally playing the piano himself. He is a capable pianist though he's never had a lesson. (As a youngster he learned to play the accordion and claims it was a relatively easy jump from one instrument to the other.) Pfleger arranged in 1976 for a well-known black Catholic priest, James

Goode, to preach a revival at the church, advertising the event with flyers and signs in the neighborhood. For Easter, he took down the prominent crucifix at the front of the church and erected a painting by a black artist. It depicted the resurrected Jesus as a black man in slave attire, with wild hair and broken manacles on his hands and feet. Some white parishioners thought the painting in bad taste and complained to Father Pehler. But black parishioners countered, telling the pastor how moved and delighted they were at seeing Afrocentric culture expressed in a Catholic church.

Pfleger persuaded Pehler to let him oversee a renovation of the unused lower church. The pews were removed and sold, providing enough money to renovate the space into a large hall for meetings and after-worship fellowship; it was named McMahon Hall to honor the veteran pastor. In addition, he also managed to bring in the first of what would become an unending procession of prominent, black guest speakers: Rosa Parks, the woman who would not sit in the back of the bus.

†

DESPITE THESE CONSIDERABLE achievements, the youthful associate pastor was unable to move Pehler out of his gloomy maintenance mode during his first five years in the parish. His own innate conservatism made Pehler increasingly hesitant and doubtful about further adaptations to the African American experience. "It was like pulling teeth, like we were butting heads all the time," says Pfleger. "For me, the worst night of the week was Thursday—and bingo. I kept saying to myself, is this what we're supposed to be doing?"

He looked around the archdiocese at other parishes serving black communities and found little that was hopeful or life-giving there. He resented the fact that the archdiocese had not embraced black culture and was not about to now. He was haunted by an image he had heard the charismatic black nun Sister Thea Bowman use in her talks. The Church, she said, was proud of every ethnic group that had arrived in the United States, be it German, Polish, or Irish, and presented each as an entree dish on the menu of Catholicism. But blacks, she said, were never considered more than an appetizer! Pfleger came to believe that the Church of the

late 1970s was nationally shifting from the activist and prophetic stance
of earlier days, symbolized by the Berrigan brothers and Monsignor Jack
Egan, to one of passivity and safety.

By 1980 Pfleger felt burned out. He could, of course, go to another
parish as an associate pastor, yet he felt certain it would be more teeth
pulling and head butting there. Of course, there was no chance that he at
age thirty-one could be named pastor somewhere in the Chicago archdiocese and develop his own ideas for authentic black ministry; he was
too young, too inexperienced. After conferring with a few close associates, he decided to take a leave of absence from ministry altogether. With
some recommendations from friends in Glenview and without informing
Pehler, he signed a lease in early November for a studio apartment in
downtown Chicago, on McClurg Court, for six hundred dollars a month.
He planned to move in right after Christmas and had no idea how long
he would stay or what he would do.

On November 19, Pfleger was saying mass in the church when someone came in and told him that Father Pehler had just suffered another
heart attack. Parishioner Dorothy Banks rushed to the rectory and found
him slumped over at the breakfast table, unconscious and not breathing.
She performed CPR until an ambulance arrived. Pfleger gave him the last
rites, and medics worked on Pehler for forty-five minutes, trying in vain
to resuscitate him. He was declared dead on arrival at the hospital. Later
in the day, Cardinal Cody called Pfleger and appointed him temporary
administrator, since he was the only priest at Sabina. "He told me to make
absolutely no changes and no plans for change of any kind. I wasn't to do
anything but pay the bills."

Nevertheless, the new administrator managed to rile Cody within
minutes of ending the conversation. He scheduled the funeral mass for
Pehler in the evening because that had become the practice at the parish.
When priest friends of Pehler heard of the arrangement, they complained
that evening services were inconvenient for the clergy and urged that the
mass be scheduled in the morning, as was the long-standing custom in
most Chicago churches. Pfleger refused, arguing that most black parishioners had daytime jobs and could not easily attend morning services.

"Who's the funeral for," he responded to inquiries, "a bunch of priests or the people of the community?" This precipitated an angry call from the cardinal, demanding a morning service. So Pfleger scheduled two funeral masses, one in the evening, which was celebrated by a black bishop from Cleveland and attended by a substantial representation of Sabina members, and one the next morning, attended by Cardinal Cody, a coterie of priests, and virtually no one from the parish community.

Aware of the arrangement, Cody came to the rectory afterward and rebuked Pfleger for this act of wanton insubordination. "The whole incident ended up kind of funny," recalls Pfleger. "Cody asked to use the bathroom, and somehow he got locked inside. I had to pry him out. I took it as a sign from the Lord—I wasn't sure of what."

Pfleger was forced to delay his moving plans indefinitely, or at least until a new pastor was named. However, the wheels of church bureaucracy, as usual, moved exceedingly slowly, and he continued as temporary administrator for several months. The archdiocesan process regarding pastoral succession called for an open town hall meeting between parishioners and members of the priest personnel board. The purpose was to inform board members of the people's hopes for the parish and the sort of characteristics they would like to see in a new pastor. The final selection would be made, of course, by the archbishop, Cardinal Cody. Not for a minute did Pfleger think he had a chance in view of his turbulent history with Cody.

During the interim period, Pfleger became aware that parish members were meeting in the school hall to prepare for the arrival of the personnel board. He was not invited to these meetings, nor did he think it strange that his advice was not sought. After all, he was a lame duck, and his days at St. Sabina were numbered. "I did think it strange though," he says, "that there were so many people coming to these meetings, and some, I knew, weren't even members of the church. It was like a big deal in the community."

Indeed, it was. When the personnel board members finally arrived, they faced a standing-room-only phalanx of determined people in McMahon Hall. They didn't want to talk about the "characteristics" of their new leader; they wanted Pfleger. "I have never seen such an outpouring of genuine support for one man," said Father Michael Nallen, a personnel board member at the meeting. "Young, old, rich, and poor, everybody was unanimous. It had to be Mike."

Pfleger was touched by the single-minded unanimity at the meeting, which had been planned and orchestrated by Elbert Johnson, Charley Marble, and a few others in the small, emerging cadre of parish leaders. Still, the cardinal, never one to be easily swayed by public opinion or the recommendations of his own committees, could choose whomever he wanted. Cody was known to tell priests or laypersons who became too insistent on presenting their demands, "In this jurisdiction, there is only one successor of the apostles!" Namely, himself.

But as it happened at the time, Cody's options were limited. He had recently alienated a large segment of the black South Side by unilaterally closing down several Catholic parish schools, and he did not want to risk further confrontation. So he called Pfleger and told him he was appointing him "permanent administrator" of St. Sabina parish. "What does that mean?" asked Pfleger. "I've never heard of such a title in canon law."

"There is no such title," the cardinal replied brusquely. "I created it. You are in charge until things calm down, and I'll replace you as soon as I can."

Pfleger hardly knew what to make of it. He was in charge, really in charge. But how long could it last? He would have, at best, a very brief window of opportunity. He called Father Howard Tuite, the pastor of St. Leo parish and highly respected dean of a cluster of parishes in the area, and asked for advice. Tuite recommended he never identify himself publicly as administrator. "Tell the people you are the pastor," he said, "because in fact you are. And act like a pastor."

That Sunday at mass when he informed the congregation, the people went wild, shouting praise to God, applauding, and dancing in the aisles. Few were aware of Pfleger's dismal relationship with the cardinal; they viewed the appointment as entirely appropriate and looked forward to years of his leadership. Weeks later a formal installation ceremony of the new pastor was held in the church, with Tuite, the local dean, presiding.

Pfleger decided then to abandon his fears, forget about his leave and his Chicago apartment, and hurl himself into the work he loved. He hadn't conspired or connived to be in this position; it was just that circumstances and coincidences had put him here. He decided to take it all as another sign from the Lord.

†

HIS FIRST OFFICIAL act as pastor was to end bingo forever. "And there will be no spaghetti dinners and no Vegas nights either," he told the congregation. "From here on, I believe we can get what we need another way—by tithing." That is, by parish members freely giving 10 percent of their income to the church. He knew tithing was a gamble, especially in a parish like St. Sabina where families with disposable income were exceedingly rare. But he had been impressed with the success of tithing programs in many of the Protestant churches he visited. He knew too that Sabina parishioners were on his side and eager for the new pastor to succeed. For several Sundays he preached and taught about tithing: how in the Old Testament God commanded the Israelites to give a tenth of their income and possessions to the temple every year, how the requirement is repeated more than thirty-five times in the Scriptures, how tithing was considered a fitting return to God for all that God had given to his people. The practice had lapsed in the Christian era, though a constant refrain in the epistles of Paul is an appeal to give more than the minimum for the ministries of the church, since "God loves a cheerful giver."

"I wasn't sure how this would work here," says Pfleger, "so I presented tithing as a kind of challenge, a dare, a dream to the people, like, let's do it God's way for a while and see what happens." He and the staff were delighted with the results. The Sunday mass collections rose immediately and kept rising, doubling and tripling over the next few years, with Pfleger feeling it necessary to tout the advantages of the system only two or three times a year. By 1990 the parish would pay back more than one hundred thousand dollars to the archdiocese; it would be debt-free and financially independent. Sunday attendance began to grow too, not dramatically but steadily. The new churchgoers came from the Auburn Gresham neighborhood, from surrounding communities, from the far South Side and the North Side; some were starting to arrive from as far away as Indiana. Emboldened by this growing congregation, Pfleger adopted the more exuberant, high-spirited preaching style he found so attractive in black Protestant churches. And the hearty reception of the congregation moved him to become even freer in his delivery.

After Reverend Willie Barrow, then president of Operation PUSH, attended a service to see this phenomenon in action, she said, "I had to look twice to make sure what was happening. Most white preachers, you know, don't have a lot of spirit and emotionalism. But this boy, he can whoop!"

Pfleger was determined to give the church an African American look. A bronze bust of Martin Luther King Jr. was placed in a prominent place. Traditional West African kente cloth was used in the sanctuary. Plans were soon underway for a new altar, carved wooden sanctuary furniture and statues, and a large baptistery—all reflecting the African heritage of most worshippers. He was also determined in those early days that the people take primary ownership of the parish. Despite his own full-speed-ahead, type A management tendencies, he sought widespread input from the congregation on major decisions. A decision-making parish council was formed, emphasizing social service in the community, and great attention was given to the formation of a quality gospel choir and active youth group.

The Richardsons and their seven daughters, early arrivals during the 1960s racial transition, became involved in every aspect of St. Sabina life. But Len, a tall, trim, easygoing administrator with the Water Reclamation District, and his wife, Beverly, had become disenchanted with the low level of activity and absence of vision at the church in the 1970s. During a dispute over a tuition raise in the school in 1975 (when young Pfleger was just arriving), the family "took a leave" from St. Sabina and put their energies and contributions into another parish. By the early 1980s, Len said, "People we knew were talking about all the action going on at Sabina and this young pastor who's gonna knock your socks off! My daughters were even getting involved with the youth group. We went back to see what it was all about. There was a new vibrance we had never experienced. We had to wonder where Mike Pfleger was coming from. Was his energy and zest just a façade? In time we came to see everything was real: the black-style preaching that lifts you up, the emphasis on our relationship with Jesus, the mass as a celebration—not the quickie, genuflect, move in, move out, twenty-minute service at some other places." The Richardsons were back for good. Len remarried after Beverly died in the 1990s, and he became one of St. Sabina's three ordained, permanent deacons.

No addition to the church has had a greater impact than the twenty-foot-high mural mounted at the front of the church where the spires of the altar once reached up toward the ceiling. The painting, titled *For God So Loved the World* (a quote from the third chapter of St. John's gospel), depicts a young, black Jesus, standing confidently in the immense black hands of God the Father and beckoning for viewers to come. It is the work of a Mexican-born Jesuit priest, Fernando Arizti, who served for some years in Nigeria and had a special interest in African American culture. He began attending St. Sabina in the early 1980s and became acquainted with Pfleger and other church members. After learning of his experience as a painter of religious murals, the parish commissioned him to produce something reflecting the spirit of the place. Arizti worked on the project for a year, laboring in the former handball pit in the basement of the Sabina community center. When the painting was unveiled in mid-1984, Arizti told a packed church, "I couldn't help but fall in love with St. Sabina, for we are family. . . . You, St. Sabina, are my inspiration because the Lord Jesus lives in you." The painting has since achieved a life of its own, with some nine thousand full-color reproductions published by Loyola Press and sold in the United States and abroad.

Its transformative impact on church members and visitors is legendary. Randall Blakey's first viewing of it was, he says, "an overwhelming, mind-blowing experience." He was a twenty-something, single cameraman and photojournalist for CBS television news in Chicago and came to St. Sabina one Sunday in the 1980s.

"I knew what Catholic churches were like," he says. "Always prominent and out in front is the crucifix with Jesus, this dead white man on it. And when I walked into St. Sabina, here was this black guy, this Jesus, and he's alive! It's like he's reaching out to embrace us and saying, 'Come, I'm not dead, I'm alive.' To see ourselves reflected in that image, man, that's monumental!" Blakey has been coming to St. Sabina ever since.

Pfleger was determined that St. Sabina would not be a typical Catholic parish. "Lots of churches are full of believers," he says. "They give themselves to Christ, establish a relationship with Christ, and they're promised a place in the kingdom. But it's the church's job to send them out into the world with the responsibility of bringing the kingdom of God to this earth. Everybody is to be a leader, not just a few. People need to know who you are and what your convictions are—the people in the community, the boss at work, your coworkers, your children, and your family. When you're there, the atmosphere of the workplace changes because you're there. You set a standard and hold others to it." He began to express these ideas in his Sunday sermons and was delighted with the positive response. Eventually, Pfleger expanded his teaching ministry through voluntary Tuesday evening Bible study sessions in McMahon Hall. The turnout steadily grew until as many as two to three hundred were coming faithfully to absorb the word. The working motto of St. Sabina, "See how they love one another," would gradually evolve into "Turning believers into disciples."

The arrival of guest speakers formed an important element in educating and inspiring the people. In the years ahead, every member of Dr. King's family would speak at the church. After her visit, Coretta King became a personal friend and confidante of Pfleger; they spoke regularly in person and on the phone until her death. Others who have drawn overflow crowds to the church include Harry Belafonte, Archbishop Desmond Tutu, Maya Angelou, Michael Eric Dyson, Cornel West, Reverend Al Sharpton, and Minister Louis Farrakhan. Needless to say, some of the guests Pfleger invited have ignited controversy and inspired questions about Pfleger's own judgment.

†

IF ST. SABINA was becoming a nontypical Catholic parish, Pfleger decided he would become an even more nontypical Catholic priest than he already was. He began the process of adopting a son. Pfleger had become friends with Father George Clements, the square-jawed pastor of Holy Angels parish in Chicago, one of only three black priests in the archdiocese, and a man considered something of a maverick himself. In the late 1970s, Clements had approached Cardinal Cody about approval to adopt, and the cardinal, Clements said, "blew a gasket." He absolutely forbade Clements to go forward with any plans, since adoption by a cleric was "out of the question," and besides, it had never been done before. However, a story about Clements's hopes appeared in *L'osservatore Romano*, the official publication of the Vatican. Pope John Paul II saw it and commented in a subsequent issue of the paper that he thought such an adoption would be a good idea. Cody reluctantly withdrew his objection, and Clements adopted a son, Joey, in 1981.

Pfleger was attracted to adoption because, he says, "I'd seen so many kids put in institutions. It's hard enough to make it anywhere, let alone with no parents. I thought now is the time." Unlike Clements, he did not ask permission. He approached the Catholic Charities adoption agency and was turned down flat. He then turned to the Illinois Department of Children and Family Services (DCFS), where he was welcomed. After filling out endless forms and undergoing a rigorous investigation, he was tentatively matched with an eight-year-old biracial boy, Lamar, who had been living in a series of foster homes in the Rockford, Illinois, area. There was a six-month getting-acquainted period, with multiple visits in Chicago and Rockford, then six months of Lamar living at St. Sabina before the adoption was finalized in 1982. In the midst of the process, Cardinal Cody heard of Pfleger's intentions and ordered him to cancel the adoption immediately. Pfleger refused, saying it would be criminal to dash the hopes of a young child. The cardinal took no disciplinary action.

"We got along pretty well," says Pfleger. "Lamar has the biggest heart in the world. He would just give away his possessions to people and never think twice about it." Pfleger made a commitment to cook breakfast for his son every day—oatmeal, waffles, French toast—"but he was mainly a meat man, and his favorite place was McDonald's." A video made at that time shows Pfleger reading to his son, putting him to bed, the two of them bicycling, picnicking on a beach, and paddleboating. A lot of adjustment in his own life became necessary, admits Pfleger. "I discovered for the first time I couldn't just make my own plans."

Lamar attended St. Sabina school, where he was treated like a celebrity at first. But after about a year, he was getting razzed as "the pastor's kid," and he got into some fights. With Pfleger too, he became restless and argumentative. "It was as if he didn't want our arrangement to work," says Pfleger. "I didn't know what to do." He consulted a psychologist, who met with both of them and got to the heart of the problem. She told Pfleger that Lamar had been in quite a few foster homes, and every time he had been moved out, rejected by his new family. He thought it would happen this time too, the psychologist explained, only this time he wanted to be able to think he set up the rejection himself. She advised Pfleger to spend more time with Lamar, do more things he liked to do, like lying on the bed watching Saturday morning Superman cartoons, and never, ever suggest that their relationship was not working. Pfleger followed these directions, and the difficult period passed. "I learned how important a job raising children is," says Pfleger. "The most important job in the world, and I saw how difficult it is. I think I'm a better person and a better priest for it."

Lamar, now in his mid-thirties and living in Seattle, says coming to Sabina was a rags-to-riches experience. He remembers the feeling of being something of a celebrity. "People would say, 'Wow! You the pastor's son?'" He remembers too his fear that this would be just another temporary foster-home situation. "I wasn't sure this was permanent," he says. "I never really called him 'Dad' until I was seventeen." After high school, he tried college for a time, then enlisted in the army. He settled in Washington state after his release and got married. Lamar has held a series of jobs, including work with the U.S. Postal Service. He and Dia have five children. When Pfleger turned sixty in 2009, personal greetings to "Grandpa Pfleger" arrived from the whole family. The oldest granddaughter, Samara, wrote, "I told my teacher Mrs. Burke that my grandfather is a saint . . . that you share God's love every day with everyone."

Pfleger's second venture in parenting would begin about ten years later under truly bizarre circumstances. He got a letter from a Maryknoll priest in Seoul, Korea, who said he had custody of a twelve-year-old son of an African American U.S. soldier and a young Korean woman who was no longer able to care for him. The priest had read about Lamar in an article in *Catholic Digest* magazine and wondered if Pfleger might be able to find a family to take the boy. Pfleger explained the situation to the congregation at Sunday mass and was still seeking a volunteer family when a second letter from the priest informed Pfleger that he and the boy would be arriving at O'Hare Airport within a few days, with the time and flight number indicated. When Pfleger went to the airport, he was met only by the boy, a tall, timid lad named Beronti Simms. Pfleger learned that the priest had suffered a heart attack and was in a hospital, so he had sent the youth alone. And with him Beronti had legal documents signed by the priest, naming "Michael Pfleger" as his new guardian! "What could I do?" says Pfleger. "I talked to the DCFS people, and they said Beronti was too old for adoption, so I just moved him into the rectory and became his official guardian."

Currently in his late twenties, Beronti lives in Florida and works in customer service for a phone company. In high school, the six-foot-seven Beronti won a basketball scholarship to Central Florida University, where he excelled at the game and was considering a professional career until he tore his ACL in his junior year and required surgery. He did not completely recover from the operation and dropped out of school before graduation. Beronti feels fortunate that Pfleger took him in. "I wouldn't have had a childhood without him," he says. "I remember going on marches where he took on the gangbangers. He wasn't scared of anyone, but sometimes I was scared for him."

Four years after taking in Beronti, Pfleger added to his family yet again, this time a sixteen-year-old boy named Jarvis from the Sabina neighborhood. He was in an intolerable family situation and had become involved in gangs and drugs. Under the direction of the DCFS, Pfleger moved him in and was given a letter of custody. His experience with Jarvis would reinforce his conviction that faith and determination can move mountains, but he would learn through Jarvis's premature death in 1998 that not everything is possible.

As a parent, Pfleger was greatly assisted by his own father, Louis, who became a close adoptive grandfather to the children. Until his death in 2008, he attended mass at Sabina every Sunday, where he joyfully adapted to the energized worship style of his fellow worshippers, a style radically different from what he had known most of his life. In his latter years, four St. Sabina men were assigned to help Grandpa Pfleger from his car to his official seat of honor in the church.

4

THE PARAPHERNALIA WARS

I THINK THAT'S WHEN I GOT SAVVY ON THE MEDIA, LEARNING
WHO WAS ON THE ASSIGNMENT DESK AND THE POWER THOSE
PEOPLE HAD. WE WERE DISCOVERING HOW TO USE THE MEDIA
INSTEAD OF THEM USING US.
                                        —MICHAEL PFLEGER

FROM HIS EARLIEST days at St. Sabina, Pfleger was aware of the stark contrast between block after block of well-maintained homes and lawns in Auburn Gresham and the seedy condition of 79th Street, Racine Avenue, and other business thoroughfares in the parish. Families, determined to find a better life, moved to Auburn Gresham to escape deteriorated conditions in the older neighborhoods. Yet 79th Street had come to represent everything they fled from: vacant lots, empty storefronts, broken windows, trash in the street, and just a handful of small businesses—a grocery and liquor store or two, mom and pop convenience stores, and an auto repair shop much in need of repair itself.

What appeared to be an economic and social wasteland in the daytime came alive at night with the flourishing business of illegal drugs. Everything was out in the open. Pfleger remembers, "You could drive along and see the sales being made right on the sidewalk or at the curb—marijuana, heroin, crack, you name it. Everyone in the parish knew someone who was in trouble with the stuff." He talked to everyone he knew about the problem and found no ready answers. Addiction was on the rise, and so was crime. It was as if the blight on 79th Street was seeping into the community like poison gas. To complicate matters, a kind of legitimacy had been granted to the flourishing drug culture by the ready availability of drug paraphernalia for sale in the businesses on the street.

"I went into these stores and looked around," says Pfleger. "They would have all these items, little pipes and scales to weigh the stuff and syringes. And some would have these hollow canes and fake cans and bottles to stash it in and packages for dealers to wrap it up. It was all there, often for sale beside the bread or the candy the kids bought." He began talking to the clerks, first suggesting, then demanding, that they get rid of it all. "Kids come in here every day," he would say, "and here's all this junk right out in the open. What kind of a message is that sending?"

In rare cases a manager would admit the impropriety of the display and agree to stop. More often the clerk on duty would insist the materials were only for tobacco users or refer Pfleger to the owner. Many told him to mind his own business. "One guy on Ashland said, 'Hell, no!'" says Pfleger. "He said he made five thousand dollars a month on sales of these things, and he wasn't about to torpedo his business for us." Pfleger talked to the police but was told there was nothing they could do since these drug accessories were legal. Besides, the police had their hands full just trying to cut down on actual drug sales.

One Sunday in 1988 Pfleger sponsored a Save Our Children Mass and introduced the idea of an all-out anti-drug-paraphernalia campaign. "If we don't take action," he said, "we're like absentee landlords who are not in control of our streets. We surrender them to these negative influences and finally to the loss of our own children." Sodom and Gomorrah perished, he said, citing a story from the book of Genesis, because "God could not find even ten righteous citizens in those cities. . . . We cannot let that happen here." Many responded, saying they were ready for direct action, though at the time neither they nor Pfleger knew where this was all going.

He started working closely with Reverend George Clements, who had acquired a national reputation by developing a thriving parish at Holy Angels in the Grand Boulevard neighborhood and the largest black Catholic elementary school in the country. He was also gravely concerned about the spreading drug epidemic and the supportive role played by drug paraphernalia. He had been "awakened," he said, after a gratifying visit one evening with a sixteen-year-old high school sophomore from his parish who seemed to be excelling, academically and otherwise. "Tom told me he wanted to be an obstetrician," Clements said, "and I was sure he was going to make it. Then I was shocked at two o'clock the next morning by a call from the hospital with the news that I should come right away because Tom was near death from a drug overdose. I can tell you I said the funeral mass in a daze. It was as if the Holy Spirit had grabbed me by the neck and said, 'Get off your bad ass and do something!'"

Clements and Pfleger became a kind of God squad, going together into stores on Chicago's South Side, sometimes just the two of them, sometimes with groups of parishioners. "We'd plan for three visits," says Pfleger. "First, go in and ask that they quit selling the drug stuff. Second, come back if they haven't complied and demand that they get rid of it. Third, come again, and if they still had the stuff out, we would sit in the store, sometimes for hours, until they complied or had us arrested." And they were arrested, many times. Their exploits generated a lot of newspaper and television interest, usually because Pfleger would call the downtown media ahead of time, telling them where and when they intended to strike. "I think that's when I got savvy on the media," says Pfleger, "learning who was on the assignment desk and the power those people had. We were discovering how to use the media instead of them using us."

That too is when Pfleger began to acquire the reputation of being a newshound. But he is always unapologetic about those criticisms. "If good happens and nobody knows about it, then for practical purposes it didn't happen," he contends. "You can't hide the light under a bushel."

For many months the two priests used every opportunity to raise the paraphernalia issue. In addition to aggressive visits and sit-ins at stores and shops, they worked with state legislators and finally got a bill introduced in the Illinois General Assembly to make sales of paraphernalia illegal throughout the state. They also traveled to Washington, D.C., to make their case directly to William Bennett, the U.S. drug czar. During this period in the late 1980s, Clements, seventeen years older than Pfleger, got the major share of press attention. He was Batman, and Pfleger was Robin, the boy wonder, usually a step behind but still in the picture. Pfleger has always denied he ever felt any jealousy toward his older and far better known companion at the time.

Perhaps their most publicized action occurred on June 20, 1989, after they learned that a major wholesale supplier of drug paraphernalia, the Good Deal One Stop Distributing Company, was less than a mile from St. Sabina Church. Their attempts to meet with company officials had been spurned. So, flanked by some fifty protesters from the two parishes and a contingent of newspersons, the priests rapped on the door of the company, located (appropriately) on 79th Street. The door was locked, and it soon became apparent no one inside was going to unlock it. Pfleger addressed the crowd: "We've come [alone] before, and we've come here together, and they've refused to speak to us. My insult level has reached its peak!" Clements meanwhile kept banging on the glass door, while the crowd took up the chant, "Open the door!"

"Mike was preaching a revival," says Clements, "and he got me so worked up I banged too hard and broke the glass." Clements reached inside and opened the door. He, Pfleger, a Baptist minister who had joined the group, and some of the other protestors walked in. "It was quite an experience," said Pfleger later. "You could see the employees running in all directions." The police arrived quickly and arrested Pfleger and the minister. But Clements was nowhere to be seen. He had sustained a cut on his arm from a piece of glass and was hustled off to a hospital by several in the crowd. He later appeared outside the hospital where he was liberally photographed by the press with a bandage running from his fingers to his elbow. "It was an accident," he explained. "I'm not involved in violence, but I'm not going to stand by and let my people die."

†

IN ADDITION TO the publicity it generated, the campaign against drug products spawned a horde of threatening phone calls and letters, all anonymous. Some samples received by Pfleger:

Watch your back. This is not a joke!
You got no business on our turf, white boy. Get out or face the
    consequences!
Your days are numbered, you piece of shit!

The calls at first came four or more a night, usually around 3:00 A.M. Both priests were provided police escorts. Eventually the calls trailed off to two or three a night, but the police were concerned enough to maintain the escorts indefinitely. The harassment was a positive sign, Pfleger told the congregation at a Sunday mass. It meant the drug dealers were hurting, and indeed, there were indications that drug sales were down on 79th Street. "I'm not really afraid," Pfleger said. "If you're in a leadership position, you've got to lead. And if you're concerned about my safety, then you better come out, stand by me, and march with me."

Among those who have stood closest by Pfleger is Vince Clark, who had first gotten involved at the church as a high school student in a summer youth employment and training program funded by the City of Chicago in the early 1980s. His strong voice, booming laugh, and personal loyalty to Pfleger have suited him well for countless projects in the parish. He was raised in the nearby Englewood community, the sixth of seven sons of Henry and Carolyn Clark (who also adopted three girls to even out the gender imbalance a bit). Young Vince was impressed with the activity and attitude of the Sabina church family—especially, he noted, "the authentic youth presence at Sunday mass." Pfleger gave him a number of jobs in the rectory while he attended Chicago State University, studying computer science, and then made him his administrative aide at eighteen and an assistant pastor at twenty-one. Since then, Clark has been Pfleger's representative at meetings, major researcher and fact finder, and strong right arm in every campaign, starting with the drug paraphernalia effort. He became especially skilled at posing as a laid-back druggie checking on the prices of the items in the showcase.

Pfleger's race was never an obstacle for Clark because, he says, "we were used to white priests as leaders in the Catholic Church." What he was not used to was the energy and dedication of this leader. "Father Pfleger is a man of God," says Clark, emphasizing the last three words. "You can see it in the way he carries himself, the way he witnesses to what he believes, the way he treats people, the way he's transformed this community. It comes to a point where skin is irrelevant. He's been transplanted since he came here. It's more about being a man of God than about color!" Now married and the father of a son, Clark puts in more than forty hours a week in parish-related activity. "This place is a second home to me," he says.

While generally supportive of the antidrug effort, some segments of the media became concerned when footage of Clements and Pfleger exchanging sharp words with store owners seemed to be dominating the nightly news. The *Southtown Economist* newspaper wondered editorially why so much attention was given to Clements and "his new sidekick," Michael Pfleger, regarding the paraphernalia issue, "a virtually insignificant part of the drug problem." What their efforts have in common, said the paper, "is that they are high on publicity and low on results." The paper recommended that the two priests change their tactics: "They should start programs to keep kids away from drugs, counsel those trying to get away from drugs or lobby politicians to provide more money to law enforcement professionals."[1]

But in terms of results, just over a month after the confrontation at the Good Deal One Stop Distributing Company, the Illinois legislature passed a bill outlawing the sale of drug paraphernalia throughout the state. The bill revised a 1983 law and made sales to anyone under eighteen a felony with a possible sentence of three years in prison and a ten-thousand-dollar fine. Sales to those over eighteen result in a fine of one thousand dollars for each item confiscated. Lest anyone miss the connection between the new legislation and the Clements-Pfleger collaboration, Governor James Thompson (with the two priests at his side) signed it into law on August 22, 1989, under a tent in front of Clements's Holy Angels Church, with some two hundred leaders and community members looking on. Clements called drugs "the worst plague to hit the world since the Black Death in the Middle Ages." He added, "We are here because we're in a mighty struggle to save the United States and the world."

Illinois State Representative Monique Davis, cosponsor of the new legislation, said previous efforts to outlaw drug-related items had failed because many of her colleagues feared offending businesses in their district that profited from paraphernalia sales. With all the publicity about the priests' activities, they had come to fear that continuing to block a ban on sales would cause outrage among their antidrug constituents. So, said Davis, "We had the votes we needed at last."

In October 1989, Cardinal Joseph Bernardin, archbishop of Chicago, announced at a press conference attended by 130 priests that the Catholic Church would participate in a citywide campaign against drugs. He praised Clements and Pfleger for their dedication to the cause but was not pleased when the two priests took the occasion and the microphone to call for more than generic "participation." The National Conference of Catholic Bishops should immediately produce an action agenda on the drug threat, they declared. The Chicago church should inaugurate drug education programs in all parishes, empty church properties should be transformed into drug treatment centers, and mandatory drug testing of students should begin in all Catholic schools!

Said Pfleger, "Mandatory testing may be a drastic solution, but I think we need this kind of solution right now.... We have a drastic problem." He said the parents of children in the St. Sabina school had already agreed to such testing. Bernardin, who had no warning of this declaration, shuffled nervously during the statement and remarked only that he would take it under consideration. Some priests regarded the Clements-Pfleger remarks as rude, disrespectful, and out of place—not to mention that mandatory testing would create a major burden for them if it became a requirement. It did not, though, except in St. Sabina school, where it has continued to be a requirement throughout Pfleger's pastorship. He has reiterated on many occasions what he said at the press conference: "If tomorrow every church in Chicago decided to get serious about drug sales in their own neighborhood, and if school authorities decided to crack down, they could stop the waste of human life overnight. I'm convinced tremendous things can be accomplished by nonviolent people who get serious."

†

BUOYED BY THEIR victory in the paraphernalia war, the two priests carried their message far and wide over several months. On the basis of tips and invitations from antidrug groups, they traveled to Indiana, Wisconsin, New York, Louisiana, and other states, targeting stores that sold drug-related products. Invariably, their tactics got them arrested, and just as invariably the charges were dropped. It was during this time that many state legislatures, noting the publicity, began clamping down on para-phernalia sales in their own territories. On some of their treks, Clements and Pfleger were accompanied by comedian-activist Dick Gregory, whose presence always guaranteed even wider news coverage.

During a protest in Milwaukee, the three, accompanied by thirty sup-porters, crowded into a shop called the Smoke Connection and refused to leave until the owner agreed to remove drug pipes, roach clips, and other items. Instead, he pressed a robbery alarm, which summoned several police cars to the scene. On arrival, the officers at first thought they were encountering the largest robbery gang in history, but they soon realized what was occurring in the crowded store. They arrested Gregory, Pfleger, Clements, and four others when they insisted on staying and dispersed the rest of the protesters. Within weeks, Wisconsin governor Tommy Thomp-son signed an anti-paraphernalia bill similar to the one in Illinois.

In Hammond, Indiana, Clements and Pfleger were arrested at the Good Stuff store, where sales of drug paraphernalia had been booming since the crackdown in Illinois. They found a counter packed with pipes decorated with the grim reaper, clips, spoons, bongs, and other items suited for heroin and cocaine use. These are products found in crack houses, said Pfleger, the very things that contribute to the deaths of drug users and the births of drug addicts. Not so, said the owner, insisting with a straight face that they were for tobacco users only. He then announced the store was closed and threatened to call the police. "That's what we're waiting for," said Clements. The two were taken before Hammond City

Judge Peter Katic, who showed little interest in the charges of trespassing and disturbing the peace and indicated they would probably be dismissed. "I believe in the cause," he said. "This incident is not an intent to trespass as much as it is an intent to dispose of drug paraphernalia in the community."

Back in Illinois, Clements and Pfleger descended on stores that were still selling drug-related products despite the new state law. At the Trend Setter Clothing and Video Movie Rentals store in the Chicago suburb of Harvey, they volleyed with the owner, Leonard Kucharzyk, urging him to get rid of the illegal products displayed in plain view to customers. He called the police. While waiting for their arrival, Clements left the store to make a phone call, and Kucharzyk followed him out and locked the door, leaving Pfleger and two fellow protesters alone inside the store for some forty minutes. When the police arrived and viewed the spoons, pipes, and syringes on display, it was Kucharzyk they arrested and the priests they commended in a rare turning of the tide.

The fruitful collaboration would continue on a lesser basis in 1990 but ended rather abruptly when Clements resigned as pastor of Holy Angels. He had been much occupied in the rebuilding of the church, which had burned in 1986. Then just two weeks after the dedication of the new, solar-powered structure in 1991, Clements announced his decision to turn to other matters, including counseling, meditation, and retreats. But his major interest lay in the development of a project he had founded to persuade parishes to adopt children. His experience as a father to his adopted son, Joey, became a central theme in a made-for-television movie (with Lou Gossett Jr., as Clements, Malcolm-Jamal Warner as Joey, and Carroll O'Connor as Cardinal John Cody). His One Church One Child movement was spreading throughout the country and continues today as a valuable resource for bringing religious congregations and needy children together. Clements, who moved for a time to Washington, D.C., to direct the operation, later founded the One Church One Addict and the One Church One Inmate movements.

His departure left Pfleger as the lone member of the God squad, and he was beginning to feel very much alone in his dedication to direct action.

He told the *Chicago Tribune* that Clements was a "truly prophetic voice who challenged the church to get out from behind the stained glass and dogma and deal with real issues. . . . George, more than any other person in the country, has given credibility to the Catholic Church for African Americans. In a church that seems sometimes comatose, George is an active, passionate voice of conscience."

Some eighteen years after leaving parish work in Chicago, Clements has only praise for what Pfleger has done. "He's made St. Sabina the most dynamic black parish in the United States," he says. Clements was less enthusiastic about the attention given by church leaders to black Catholics in the new millennium. "There's a lot of concern about ministry in the Latino population, but about blacks, I have the impression they could care less," says Clements. He calls Pfleger "our solitary boast," a tongue-in-cheek reference to a phrase sometimes applied to the Virgin Mary.

Meanwhile, Pfleger told the parish in 1990 that they were "now moving into phase two" of the war on drugs. At a press conference on the steps of St. Sabina Church, he called on the public "to turn in the names or addresses or license plate numbers of known drug dealers or pushers in the community. We will be exposing them, marching on them, and turning them over to the police. This is an important step in making our community drug free. It is also a dangerous step. But I am not afraid!"

The issue of safety has come up often during his long ministry at Sabina. Fear is likely what keeps many, even those who admire his courage, from following his lead. In the face of regular arrests, the strain of repeated, heated confrontations with individuals and groups, and the ongoing string of threats, prudence might seem the better part of valor. But not to him. "What motivates me," he acknowledged on one occasion, "is outrage! Outrage at the ruined lives of addicts, especially the young, at the greed of those who are in the drug trade for profit, at the irresponsibility of parents who just don't care, at the indifference of politicians, school boards and teachers, and law enforcement personnel who shrug their shoulders." Pfleger admits that he does have a sense of fear. "But fear can paralyze you, or it can motivate you, as it motivated Dr. King. For me it's outrage that overcomes fear," he explains.

Phase two, as it developed, put an emphasis on marches through the neighborhoods. They soon became a staple of St. Sabina life, just as bingo and carnivals previously had been through much of the twentieth century. The marches are held from April through October, often on Friday evenings—the police told Pfleger that was when street drug sales were at their highest. Singing, praying, and proclaiming antidrug slogans through a megaphone, the marchers spend hours on foot and cover up to four miles on a given night. Sometimes the marchers stop at residences that have been identified by tipsters as the homes of drug sellers or gang leaders. Pfleger rings the bell and tells what he's heard to whomever answers the door (usually a parent or other relative of the person in question). He declares that the people of this community, a representative assembly of which is now crowded on the porch and sidewalk, do not tolerate drug or gang activity but will gladly help those who want to straighten out their lives.

The number of marchers usually runs between thirty and fifty. On certain special occasions, there can be upward of three hundred who take part. For some, like Laura Matthew, who has two grown sons and is raising three foster children, marching has become a way of life. She has even been arrested. She originally lived on the North Side and saw Pfleger for the first time when he was being interviewed on television. She was struck with his "humble confidence." On her first trip to St. Sabina, she recalls, "Pastor Pfleger said in his sermon that morning, 'I'm looking for people so hungry for God they think they're gonna die.' That's exactly the way I felt. I had this long yearning for more of God or I thought I couldn't go on. When he said that, I felt like I was floating."

She moved to Auburn Gresham, took classes in the Catholic faith, and became a member of the church. "I'm part of a supportive family that's in this place," says Matthew, who is white. "I feel now God is with me and won't leave me. I have a different sense of self." An integral part of that is participating in the direct social action that Pfleger endlessly promotes. "He's changed the lives of thousands around here," she says, "and he doesn't want a dime for all he's done."

5

PAINTING THE TOWN RED

═══════════

THE EXPERIENCE WAS AN EYE-OPENER FOR ME—TO BE ABLE
TO IDENTIFY AN INJUSTICE AND NOT JUST COMPLAIN ABOUT IT
AND NOT JUST ACCEPT IT, BUT TO BE ABLE TO DO SOMETHING!
THAT WAS DIFFERENT.
                            —RICKEY HARRIS, PARISH ACTIVIST

DURING THE CAMPAIGN against drug paraphernalia, several veteran
church members told Pfleger, "If you're serious about keeping drugs
away from our kids, you need to start from the bottom up. You need to get
at the gateway drugs—alcohol and cigarettes—because that's where it all
begins." He heard the same thing when he talked about drugs to community organizations and at high schools and universities. "Over and over, I
was told, 'These are the substances that are whetting the appetites of our
children.'" He had no trouble finding evidence to back up the assertions.
Researchers had been complaining for years that cigarette and alcohol
advertising was deliberately designed to attract the young. One study, for
example, found that 30 percent of three-year-olds could correctly match
the "Smokin' Joe Camel" character with Camel cigarettes, and 60 percent
of six-year-olds could do so. Studies also linked early smoking and drink-

ing habits with later use of marijuana and other drugs. Pfleger learned how dependent the tobacco and alcohol industries had become on out-door advertising since the 1971 federal ban on advertising these products on television and radio. According to industry figures, tobacco advertisers had spent $385 million on outdoor ads in 1988; brewers and distillers had poured $112 million into such advertising.

Pfleger was well aware of the dominance of billboards featuring these products in Auburn Gresham. "They were everywhere," he said, "like twenty-four-hour [drug] pushers. A kid couldn't come out of his house to go to school without getting hit with the images." There were attractive and seductive images of young people on all of them: a cool-looking musi-cal combo "Jazzin' with the Brothers," said a Christian Brothers brandy billboard; an elegantly dressed black couple "Mist Behavin'" on a Cana-dian Mist whiskey ad; two beautiful black women with a man sporting a pack of Newport cigarettes, all three obviously "Alive with Pleasure" on still another.

Pfleger decided serious action was required. One day in 1988, he asked his administrative aide Vince Clark to research just how many billboards existed in the community and what they were selling. Clark spent the better part of three days driving around the ten square blocks surround-ing the St. Sabina complex, taking detailed notes. He reported finding 118 billboards of various sizes ranging from six-foot by twelve-foot signs to large, well-lit, dominant boards looming over busy streets, advertising "butts and booze"; they were the overwhelming majority of ads in the area. For comparison, Pfleger drove through the white neighborhood two miles west and found only three boards promoting alcohol and cigarettes in an area comparable to that researched by Clark.

He began to talk about "the gateway drugs" and "the twenty-four-hour pushers" to his staff, parish council, and other key church members, and he spoke loud and often in his Sunday sermons about the "unjust saturation" of tobacco and alcohol ads in the community. Any attempt to take on these industries, he believed, had to be done both boldly and thoughtfully. These were not the little neighborhood stores and shops they had targeted in their antidrug campaign; those could be often cowed by demonstrations and the threat of withdrawing business. These were multimillion-dollar institutions that would fight back.

He tried to get city zoning officials to limit the number of boards in a community; he urged local aldermen to introduce legislation banning booze-and-butts saturation; he invited city council members to come see what his community was up against; and he took a dozen of them on a billboard bus tour of the area. Over many months in 1989, Pfleger personally visited with officials of some of the major companies involved: Gateway Outdoor Advertising and United Advertising, which controlled most of the billboards on Chicago's South Side; Philip Morris and Lorillard tobacco companies; Miller, Anheuser-Busch, and other breweries; and Union Liquors, a major bottler and distributor of alcoholic beverages in the Midwest. He traveled to Washington, D.C., to meet with William Bennett again and testified on the saturation problem before a U.S. congressional committee. Officials of the companies he spoke with were polite at first, but discussions soon became contentious when he started asking the hard questions: Why are these ads concentrated in black neighborhoods? Why is the advertising so relentlessly targeted to young blacks? Why are white neighborhoods, on the other hand, presented with a variety of products? If he did not use the word *racism* in these early exchanges, everyone knew where he was headed.

The billboard people protested their innocence. It wasn't their job to select the products displayed or censor those that might offend self-righteous folks like the Reverend Pfleger. The tobacco and alcohol officials flatly denied they were targeting only one group. Naturally, they explained, they tried to match their messages to the ethnic or racial makeup of a given community, which is sound, accepted advertising strategy. It was certainly not their fault if producers of other products chose not to advertise in certain areas of the city. Besides, they insisted, at bottom this was an issue of free speech, and attempts by preachers or others to curtail it would be stiffly resisted in the name of the Constitution and Bill of Rights.

Pfleger was getting nowhere. He felt like David confronting Goliath without a slingshot. "There was no real negotiation with these people," he says. "I was patronized, dismissed, and I was angry." At the end of one unproductive meeting he asked a billboard official if he would ever consider saturating the Chicago Gold Coast or the affluent North Shore with the kind of concentrated advertising accorded the minority communities. "No," said the official, "they wouldn't allow us to do that."

"Then neither will we!" said Pfleger as he left the meeting.

Certainly at that moment no one in the room had any reason to consider those words as more than an empty bluff by a frustrated, impotent do-gooder. Yet it was precisely out of that kind of frustration that he would conceive the idea of a stealth campaign designed to do what had to be done.

†

ALREADY IN THE late 1980s there were press reports of activists whitewashing alcohol and cigarette billboards in the Harlem and Bronx areas of New York City, and in Dallas, Texas. Even on the West Side of Chicago, a one-man crusader who called himself Mandrake had damaged some billboards. But these were sporadic forays, lacking the dedication, duration, and deliberation Michael Pfleger had in mind.

The campaign began in mid-January 1990. Two cars left St. Sabina at about 10:00 P.M., one car to take care of the action, the other to provide a lookout. They traveled some three blocks south and pulled up in front of a large billboard featuring cigarettes at 80th Street and Racine Avenue. Three men got out of the first car and pulled a five-gallon can of red paint, a roller brush, and a retractable, sixteen-foot extension pole from the trunk. The brush was soaked in paint and hoisted up to the billboard by Father Pfleger. With a few swashes back and forth, he obliterated the image of the pack and the name of the brand. The deed took about four minutes. The culprits got back in the car and returned to the church.

"I got a kind of rush from the experience," admits Vince Clark, who was a crew member on that first sortie. He says he and the others were not fearful, since they had planned what they were about to do and had prayerfully discussed the five steps Dr. King proposed to anyone embarking on nonviolent civil rights action. They had just begun to take the most exciting and dangerous step—demonstration—and had to be prepared for whatever might happen. But on that night, nothing did. A few cars passed on the street while they were at work, but the drivers did not stop and appeared not even to notice. The only downside of the action was the residue of paint on the hands and arms of the crew as well as the thickness of the paint itself, which made it difficult to spread evenly.

Clark, who has a knack for technical matters, thought he could improve the process. He acquired a pair of pressurized cans equipped with short hoses, the kind exterminators use to rout vermin. He started experimenting with various combinations of paint and thinner, plus a little water, to create an easier-to-apply blend. On their second mission a few nights later, Clark showed off his invention, and it worked. The paint mixture could be aimed by the hose and shot accurately a considerable distance, the painters discovered. No need for rollers or extensions except for the highest billboards. Clark became the group's unquestioned mechanic and troubleshooter. Pfleger referred to him ever after as the parish "genius" and the "Einstein" of the project. A variety of St. Sabina members participated in the months ahead, but Pfleger was most often the shooter—not because he wanted the glory, he insisted, but so that he would be in a position to take full blame if anything went wrong.

And for a long time, with raids on billboards scheduled two or three nights a week, nothing did go wrong. Rickey Harris, an occasional nightrider and a sixteen-year-old student at Quigley South Seminary at the time, never hesitated about participating in this defacement of private property. "I trusted him [Pfleger]," he says. "He always explained to everybody what we were doing and why. The experience was an eye-opener for me—to be able to identify an injustice and not just complain about it and not just accept it, but to be able to do something! That was different."

There were a few occasions, however, when he nearly lost his composure. Harris was sitting in the lookout car one night while others were at work on a billboard. Suddenly the horn started beeping of its own accord and would not stop. The painters outside panicked, thinking Harris had spotted a police car. They were stumbling around, he said, gathering their gear and yelling at him to get off the horn. "It was one of those moments," Harris says. "But the horn finally stopped and it turned out OK."

Harris, who is now a teacher at Whitney Young High School in Chicago, first met Pfleger when he was preaching a black, African-style revival at Quigley. Harris's parents later broke up, and when Harris did not want to move away with his mother, Pfleger invited him to live at the Sabina rectory. He accepted the offer and stayed for seven years while finishing high school and attending Chicago State University. For a time he headed the church's youth ministry program and later taught at the St. Sabina Academy; he then worked five years as the academy's assistant principal. Although raised Catholic, Harris had shown little interest in Catholicism before he encountered Pfleger. But his experience of worship in the church was transforming. "I was just amazed and intrigued," he says. "It was so free and liberating. For the first time I felt like I really mattered to God and had a relationship with the Lord. There was a level of comfort there and nothing culturally stifling about the place."

To those who fault Pfleger for deviating from liturgical law, not to mention civil law, Harris says, "People get too caught up in regulations. They think anything different has to be wrong. As a teacher, I know kids have different ways of learning." Likewise the Church, he believes, must make room for different ways of worshipping.

As Harris, Clark, and others assisted, the billboard painting campaign expanded its boundaries beyond Auburn Gresham and into the greater South Side and in the southeast, and even into North Side areas. The painting crews became so adept, says Clark, that they could easily hit twenty or thirty boards in an evening. "It didn't take any time at all. If we had a station wagon, we could open the back window and spray without even getting out of the car." The effort had become so easy that many billboards were resprayed two or more times immediately after the advertising companies had repaired the damage.

Pfleger organized petition drives and demonstrations protesting the proliferation of cigarette and alcohol ads in minority neighborhoods, but he did not publicly acknowledge the role of St. Sabina in the damage. Nevertheless, he knew it was an ill-kept secret by the mounting number of angry and threatening messages he was receiving. The tires of the parish car were slashed, and a church window was broken. Pfleger tended to regard this as collateral damage since it indicated someone was getting the message.

Vince Clark, possessor of a smooth, clear speaking voice, was assigned the responsibility of calling the city's major newspapers and news radio and television stations every morning following an evening sortie and reporting anonymously the location of vandalized billboards. Soon photos and news stories began to appear, some reports assuming on the basis of the amount and widespread nature of billboard damage that mobs of vandals must be circulating around the city. By the spring of 1990 it was common knowledge in Chicago and the country that outdoor cigarette and alcohol advertising was under assault in Chicago. In all these efforts, the Sabina painters were aided by the counsel of Jacqueline Collins, who had become the church's communications director and who had firsthand knowledge of the Chicago media.

Sparked by this wave of vandalism, a national Gallup poll at the time indicated somewhat ambivalent opinions about all this in the general public. To the statement, "If the members of a community find an advertisement offensive, they should use any means they can to cause the advertiser to remove the advertisement," 40 percent of all respondents agreed or strongly agreed. But minority respondents (54 percent among blacks, 52 percent of Hispanics, 50 percent of Asians) agreed or agreed strongly. When a more specific proposition was proposed, minorities tended to back away. To the statement, "Defacement is against the law and shouldn't be allowed under any circumstances," 75 percent of respondents, regardless of race, agreed or agreed strongly.[1]

But that did not seem the predominant view on the Chicago South Side. Pfleger found outspoken support and virtually no opposition among St. Sabina members. Clark reported that an employee of the store where he was returning again and again to buy inordinate amounts of red paint asked him what he as doing with it. "I just told him we were the ones painting over billboards, and after that he gave me his employee discount when I came in." Even law enforcement officers seemed to back the campaign. On one occasion a police patrol apprehended the painters in the act of spraying a billboard. "They asked what we were doing," says Clark, "and when we explained, they just got back in their car and drove off. I felt bad because one of the cops shook hands with me and I'm sure I got a lot of red paint on his hand."

Having dodged the bullet, the Pfleger brigade was emboldened to extend the sorties still farther and wider. One night they traveled to downtown Chicago and sprayed two large boards on the side of a building that were in full view to drivers on the Ontario Street ramp leading to the Dan Ryan Expressway. It is one of the busiest traffic lanes in the city, accommodating thousands of cars every day, especially during rush hours. Pfleger suspected someone had spotted him at the time because of an increase in the number of calls to the rectory accusing him of wanton destruction. Still, he would not be accused publicly for many weeks, nor did he curtail the raids in any way.

†

BUT ON THE night of July 9, 1990, Michael Pfleger, Vince Clark, and four others were literally caught red-handed. They were putting the finishing touches to a billboard (advertising Smirnoff vodka) on the 8100 block of Racine Avenue when two men emerged from a car parked across the street with its lights off. One of them was Milton Steffen, general manager of Gateway Advertising, who knew Pfleger from their meetings at the Gateway office. He was mad and he was loud, demanding to know what the hell a Catholic priest was doing defacing property in the middle of the night. Pfleger, equally loud, wanted to know what the hell Steffen was doing saturating a neighborhood with ads for death-dealing substances. A profanity-laden argument ensued, after which Steffen, with a large splotch of red paint on his pants, got back in his car and followed the Pfleger group to another site some three blocks away. He watched while Pfleger brazenly sprayed yet another billboard (Miller Lite beer) before returning to St. Sabina.

Steffen drove to the Gresham police station and filed charges against Pfleger for criminal damage to two Gateway boards and for battery, claiming Pfleger threw paint on him during the confrontation. Meanwhile, sent his accomplices home and waited at the rectory for the police, who arrived after midnight. He was read his rights, told the charges, and taken to the station in handcuffs. Pfleger neither denied nor admitted to painting the billboards, but he did claim Steffen had threatened his associates with a flashlight. He also said Steffen's pants got soaked when Steffen kicked a five-gallon paint can in anger and some of it splashed on him. Hearing of the arrest, Clark came to the station, though at the time he thought he too might be charged. But Steffen had accused only the ringleader, Pfleger, who was released on his own recognizance after the charges were filed.

In the morning reporters were at the rectory door. Looking like he had not slept well, Pfleger told them, "I hate being arrested and I hate jail, but I believe you have to fight for what's right." He defended "whoever it was who painted over the ads" as a legitimate defense of a community under siege. "If money is the reason the ads are there, money is going to be the reason they're going to have to stop," he said, referring to the costs advertisers were incurring in repairing their billboards.

Pfleger got no sympathy from his superior, Cardinal Joseph Bernardin. In response to reporters' inquiries, a statement from the chancery office said, "While the archdiocese supports efforts to sensitize people to the need for greater responsibility with regard to alcohol and tobacco advertising, acts of vandalism are inappropriate and counterproductive. The cause would be better served by reasonable dialogue and other efforts to persuade than by unilateral actions which invade the property rights of others."[2]

The arrest of the priest was widely reported. "Priest charged in paint 'war' over smoke, drink billboards," said the *Chicago Sun-Times*. "Billboard war rages in Englewood," declared the *Chicago Tribune* (incorrectly identifying the community at the center of the controversy). "Priest pleads moral right to deface ads," said the *Los Angeles Times*. Various press estimates placed the number of defaced billboards at 500 to 750, though no one, including Pfleger, kept an accurate count.

In spite of his arrest, Pfleger did not cease the defacement project. The regular treks continued, although with a bit more care and caution to avoid unwanted observers if possible. Meanwhile, Pfleger discovered a

new tack to take in the campaign. He obtained from the city hall officials
a list of all the billboards for which city permits had been issued. With
the cooperation of Sabina church volunteers and other interested citizens,
a survey was conducted along a two-and-a-half-mile stretch of Racine
Avenue and a one-and-a-half-mile length of Damen Avenue, match-
ing the city's list against the existing billboards. In August, Pfleger held
a press conference at the corner of 79th Street and Loomis Boulevard to
announce that the citizen survey had identified eighty-five billboards that
lacked permits required by the city code, the majority advertising alcohol
or tobacco. "We want these ads that are saturated in black, Hispanic, and
poor communities stopped," he announced. "We have a real problem in
our society, and we don't want these messages in our community." He then
mounted a ladder, and while photographers' cameras flashed, he pasted a
large "ILLEGAL" sign on a billboard at the corner.

The publicity that followed reflected badly on the city's enforcement
record. And it only got worse when the *Chicago Reporter*, an investiga-
tive monthly, followed up with a far more thorough survey of its own,
covering fifteen community areas of Chicago. It reported finding six hundred boards lacking permits. In one black neighborhood 78 percent of
the billboards were unlicensed, in another 60 percent, said the *Reporter*.
The publication noted that Gateway Outdoor Advertising was among the
biggest violators, depriving the city of some $116,000 in permit fees in
1989 alone.[3]

Rumblings were heard at city hall. Officials pledged to create a new
enforcement bureau to rectify the permit violation problem. Aldermen
sponsored various ordinances, one of which would remove all tobacco and
alcohol billboard advertising in the city, another to ban cigarette vending
machines, still another to halt the construction of new billboards. But
the proposals were not considered likely to move out of committees in
the near future, if ever. One reason, suggested the *Chicago Reporter*, was
the contributions Chicago politicians were receiving regularly from billboard lobbyists. In one fourteen-month period, noted the *Reporter*, Mayor
Richard Daley alone had been the beneficiary of $47,500 (for his reelec-
tion efforts). "Apparently," commented Patrick Quinn, a member of the

Illinois General Assembly (and future governor of the state), "the owners of billboards have fallen through the cracks."

Seeking to repair its reputation, Gateway owners met with the Mothers Against Gangs organization, but the meeting turned sour when the company refused to decrease its saturation in minority communities. Instead, the owners offered to pay the mothers a 15 percent commission to sell billboard advertising to companies whose products they might find more acceptable. In other words, more billboards, not fewer. The Gateway offer was flatly rejected.

Despite the charges hanging over his head, Pfleger was growing more convinced than ever of the rightness of his cause. In a letter to a supporter, he wrote,

> For me the advertising of tobacco on billboards is particularly heinous in that it does not discriminate against anyone. It is there for all to see. Not only do adults receive these messages but children as well, children who have a wonderful capacity to take in information uncritically. Unlike magazine and newspaper ads, which involve a somewhat conscious decision to peruse the printed material, the tobacco billboard seduces us without conscious, critical thought ever entering the process. When directed at adults, this is merely wrong, when directed at children, this is most criminal and must be stopped. How can our government profess to be fighting a war on drugs when it is subsidizing and protecting an industry that produces and markets our most lethal drug? To my mind this is the height of hypocrisy.

†

WHETHER HE WON or lost his case in court, Pfleger had no intention of backing away and seeking less troublesome challenges. He had asked for a jury trial and was told he could face up to five years in jail and a stiff fine if found guilty. The trial could be over very quickly since his role in damaging property was beyond dispute. A friend suggested he speak to Michael Monico, an experienced criminal attorney who had represented some highly publicized political figures, including Chicago Alderman Edward "Fast Eddie" Vrdolyak, notorious for his questionable business dealings. Monico was interested in Pfleger's situation and quickly agreed to take on the case pro bono, though he said he could make no promises, given the evidence.

Together, Monico and Pfleger decided to attempt the so-called necessity defense. To be effective, this legal maneuver requires the defendant to admit that he committed an illegal act but did so because he believed it necessary in order to avert a greater evil. And he must establish he had beforehand done everything legally possible to avert the evil but was unsuccessful. The defense has been used by antiwar activists who commit civil disobedience—for example, trespassing on government property—in order to arouse the public to the evil of war. However, judges often disallow the necessity defense, finding it arbitrary and capricious. Monico and Pfleger regarded it as a long shot, since clearly the Sabina war had been waged so flagrantly over so many months and had caused thousands of dollars in damage to private business owners and their clients. As he was preparing his case, Monico was approached by James Serritella, a major attorney for the Archdiocese of Chicago. Serritella expressed concern about the "possible liability and financial exposure" of the archdiocese due to Pfleger's action, says Monico, and strongly recommended that Pfleger be persuaded to plead guilty and agree to cease any illegal activity.

Monico was irate at this approach, saying he found "dark irony" in the fact that Serritella (and the archdiocese) showed no interest whatsoever in Pfleger's well-being while at this time the archdiocese was "paying lawyers four hundred dollars an hour or more to defend several priests accused of sexually abusing children."

As the date of the trial drew closer in the spring of 1991, Pfleger was also sensing a dark irony in his relationship with the Church he worked for. He wrote a long letter to his archbishop.

"Dear Cardinal Bernardin: It is 3:00 A.M. and I have prayed and prayed for months, and now I cannot sleep. I must write to you. I would rather see you in person, but I would not waste my time." In deliberations over several major issues including "allegations regarding the billboard issue," he wrote, "not once was I ever asked to come sit and voice my thoughts or concerns to my Bishop. I have been called by Bishops and heads of other religions throughout the country, and asked questions about the billboard issue and given support—yet my own Bishop has never asked to even understand the issue." Pfleger went on to lament the closing of Catholic schools in the minority communities, the closing of Quigley South, a high school seminary that had attracted black teens, the shutdown of the black ministries office, the casual way the poorest parishes in the archdiocese were being pressured to give more and more to the cardinal's annual appeal for money, and the fact that Bernardin's chief advisors within diocesan offices "continue to be of one color." He finished, "I will continue to pray for this church that I love, but I will not be still and see injustice and hurt continue. Our number one problem in the Diocese is still a spiritual hunger and we must address it. Our whiteness is still a disgrace and we must end it."

Bernardin called him after receiving the letter, saying he felt Pfleger's hurt and anger and respected the passion Pfleger brought to ministry. It marked the first step in a reconciliation that would mature several years later.

The trial was held on a humid July 2, 1991, in the courtroom of Cook County Court Judge Stuart Nudelman. The room was packed, mostly with St. Sabina parishioners, and the tension in the air was palpable. Assistant state's attorney prosecutors held a strong upper hand at the beginning.

"He stepped over the line," they said. Whatever his motives, he went too far. "He decided on his own authority that the powers that be were not responding, and he took the law in his own hands." In their eyes he had become that most dangerous of all lawbreakers—a vigilante.

"Who will be the next person to draw the line?" they asked. "You cannot give one person that kind of power." Give a man like that a free pass, and you're on your way down the slippery slope.[4]

"He attacked the fundamental right of free speech." They accused him, a clergyman, of knowingly trampling on the Constitution.

But Nudelman allowed Monico to use the necessity defense, so the lawyer put Pfleger on the stand and let him tell the what and the why of his story, starting with the 118 alcohol and cigarette billboards grabbing the attention of children first thing on their way to school. "When you walk out the door and you're hit with thirty-five billboards within three blocks, you have to do something," he said. He presented the problems of chronic drug addiction in the community, the established link between the "gateway drugs" and the illegal ones, the terrible toll of addiction and sickness and despair.

And then he told of what he did about all this. Pfleger spoke of his endless travels seeking concessions, and he could have gone on and on all day about his deliberations with city officials, his meetings with tobacco and alcohol officials, his pleading with billboard moguls, his testimony in Congress, the petitions, the marches, the leaflets.

And what was the result of this sustained effort? Nothing.

So what did he do? He started painting.

There, Monico told the jury, is the classic necessity defense. Father Pfleger "reasonably believed that his conduct was necessary to avoid a greater injury than that which might reasonably have resulted from his conduct."

Perhaps sealing the defense argument was the testimony of Diana Hackbarth, a professor of community health nursing at Loyola University in Chicago. She released for the first time the results of a nine-month study of all the billboards in the entire city of Chicago. Sponsored by the American Lung Association of Metropolitan Chicago and completed just a month before the trial, the study corroborated and expanded on, in technical language, virtually everything Pfleger had been claiming. Hackbarth and her colleagues found that 86 percent of all billboards were in minority wards, that these wards had an average of more than five times as many alcohol billboards as white wards, and three times as many tobacco billboards. The data confirm that "minority neighborhoods are more likely to have billboards hawking dangerous products than white areas of the city," declared the study.

As the jury of eight white and four black people deliberated, people in the hallway, including Pfleger, formed a prayer circle. "Send your angels into the jury room," said a woman. "Let your truth be known so that it will make us free." After just ninety minutes the jurors returned with a unanimous verdict: not guilty. Someone in the courtroom yelled, "Thank you, Jesus!" Pfleger shouted back, "Thank you, jury!" Everyone seemed to be crying—even the court reporter, even St. Sabina member Beverly Allen, who was suffering with terminal cancer. "This is such a happy day," she said. "We thought we might lose him." Judge Nudelman warned Pfleger that he should not consider his exoneration a mandate to continue breaking the law, and the priest nodded dutifully.

The publicity that attended his arrest almost exactly a year before was nothing compared to the deluge accompanying the exoneration. Pfleger appeared on the Larry King show and a segment on his battle was done on the *20/20* program. Many newspapers saw a David-beats-Goliath undercurrent in the acquittal.

"Priest freed in billboard attack," said the *Chicago Sun-Times*. "Jury acquits rebel priest on 'necessity defense,'" wrote the *National Catholic Reporter*. "Pfleger declares victory in battle over signs," said the *Chicago Defender*.

Washington Post columnist Colman McCarthy wrote that St. Sabina's parishioners were blessed to have a pastor willing to express some holy wrath against the butts-and-booze peddlers. "For nearly two years, Pfleger worked the gears of good citizenship. The machinery didn't move. Painted into a corner, he painted his way out. . . . St. Sabina happened to have a priest with the pluck and imagination to take a stand. At St. Sabina's, never was painting the town red more apt."[5]

Not everyone was so elated. Some newspaper letter writers chided Pfleger for refusing to take responsibility for his criminal actions. Others attacked the verdict as an example of the legal system surrendering to relativism. Billboard operators were especially indignant. The verdict "opens the door for an awful lot of dangerous things," claimed the director of an outdoor advertising association in Missouri. And Craig Heard, the president of Gateway declared, "Here's a priest who should be setting an example for his congregation and has become a vigilante." He said Pfleger had caused the firm more than one hundred thousand dollars in damage and lost advertising.

Pfleger took a few days to enjoy the moment. "This is a real victory for the community," he told the Associated Press. "It was the alcohol and tobacco companies and the billboard companies that were on trial here, not me. And they lost."

Or did they? A month after the trial, all the "twenty-four-hour pushers" were still standing and visible, doing their job in the St. Sabina neighborhood and throughout the city. The battle to put them out of business, Pfleger would learn, was far from over.

6

VICTORY AND BEYOND

I'D RATHER SEE FATHER PFLEGER OUT THERE WITH HIS PAINTBRUSH, PRACTICING A LITTLE CIVIL DISOBEDIENCE, THAN DOING WHAT HE'S DOING RIGHT NOW. BECAUSE WHAT HE'S DOING NOW IS PERFECTLY LEGAL, BUT FAR MORE DAMAGING.
—R. BRUCE DOLD, *CHICAGO TRIBUNE* COLUMNIST

MICHAEL PFLEGER HAS a supply of favorite slogans that slip often into his talks, sermons, even everyday conversation. One of these, "If you're not in it for the long haul, you shouldn't get in it at all," had special relevance for him in the 1990s. After battling with billboards for almost five years and narrowly escaping a felony conviction, he had so little to show. It was true that publicity generated by his activities at St. Sabina had moved city councils in several large cities to take notice of the saturation of butts-and-booze billboards in their own minority areas and some were taking legal action. It was also significant that he had met with Mayor Richard M. Daley after his acquittal and gotten the mayor's endorsement of legislation to keep alcohol and cigarette ads at least five hundred feet from schools, playgrounds, and parks. And yes, the R.J. Reynolds Tobacco Company had announced its intent in 1991 to remove all its billboard ads from African American and Latino communities in Chicago after meeting with Pfleger and other minority leaders. (Reynolds representatives at company headquarters in North Carolina later downplayed community pressure as a motive for their withdrawal. The cutback was strictly "a marketing decision based on competitive factors," according to Reynolds spokesman John Singleton.)[1]

But Pfleger was still unable to get the Chicago City Council to budge on the issue of outlawing the offensive billboards, despite lip service from some minority aldermen. What he did not fully understand at the time was the deeply entrenched political and financial relationship between the council and the three industries he was fighting: big alcohol, big tobacco, and billboard advertising. High-ranking city, county, and state officials and former officials, along with top Chicago attorneys, were among the paid lobbyists for the three industries. And city council members were the grateful recipients of generous, ongoing campaign contributions from these industries.

Given the situation, Pfleger found other ways to keep the pressure on. He formed a parish organization called Standing Up, Taking Back, whose purpose was to find fresh, imaginative ways to keep the issue in the public eye. He invited parishioners to join in marches, protests, sit-ins, and demonstrations and recruited willing college students and summer interns to help organize these activities. One of the first projects was a recount of billboards in the community in 1992, this time covering an extensive swath of the South Side more than three times the size of the original survey. It was obvious, says Vince Clark, who headed the project, that the saturation of cigarette and alcohol ads had not decreased. When an advertiser like Reynolds backed off or when an outdoor advertising company left, another advertiser and another company were ready to move in. "We could see billboard advertising had to be a precious source of income for these people or they wouldn't have been so protective of it," says Clark. In an area covering some six hundred blocks, Clark and his crew identified 464 liquor or tobacco boards, more than half of which were owned by Gateway. Some 330 advertised liquor, 125 cigarettes. (A survey in a smaller area of a nearby predominantly white community found only eighteen tobacco or liquor ads, their message almost lost amid the proliferation of advertising for other products.) Of the 125 cigarette ads the majority, 66, promoted the Newport brand, with Virginia Slims a distant second.

As a result, Standing Up, Taking Back organized a two-day sit-in at the Midwest office of the Lorillard Tobacco Company, the manufacturer of Newports, in the upscale Chicago suburb of Naperville. More than one hundred protesters milled around the company grounds for the better part of the two days, demanding that Lorillard cease inundating the minority community with ads and stop distributing caps and T-shirts that linked Newports with good times. "Bouncing balls, skates, happy people—that's the image they give of cigarettes," said Pfleger. "They should be showing coffins instead."

Clark added, "When you're driving in Naperville, you're not bombarded by billboards pushing cigarettes and beer. All we're saying is be fair. We've been trying to set up meetings with this company for three years; not once have they responded." They did not respond this time either. None of the protestors was arrested, although Pfleger put some pressure on the security detail by insisting on sitting in the company offices all night.

Two weeks later, the buses full of demonstrators unloaded at the offices of Gateway, the largest Chicago billboard company at the time. Pfleger labeled it "the main perpetrator of this plague." He noted that, although there had been some minimal response from Gannett Outdoor and Salem cigarettes, Gateway remained insensitive. He took the occasion to chastise city hall for its reluctance to take legal action against billboards and its continued toleration of ads that lacked city permits. Because of "this contemptuous disregard and disrespect for our communities, we are determined to fight," he said. "We will not allow our children to become the victims of this insidious targeting by alcohol and tobacco billboard companies." This demonstration proceeded without incident but yielded enough press coverage that the Standing Up, Taking Back initiative continued in the months ahead, sometimes with the cooperation of Operation PUSH and other civil rights organizations.

Gateway, which remained a major target of its activities, responded at last—by filing a one-hundred-thousand-dollar civil lawsuit against Pfleger for wantonly destroying company property. The suit failed because a jury had found Pfleger not guilty of destroying Gateway property. Gateway itself soon failed, declaring bankruptcy in the early 1990s and eventually going out of business. It has never been made clear to what extent the damage of its property and the community protests were responsible for Gateway's collapse.

†

STANDING UP, TAKING Back also sponsored projects at the local level, one of which eventually created citywide reverberations. It was well known to Auburn Gresham parents that children as young as twelve were able to buy beer at local liquor and convenience stores—no identification required and no questions asked by clerks or owners. Pfleger decided it was time to determine how widespread the practice was, and he devised a carefully choreographed sting operation to provide answers. Three fourteen- and fifteen-year-old boys who had summer jobs at St. Sabina were recruited and trained. One or more would enter a store and attempt to buy a six-pack or a quart of beer. Several adults from a parish team would wait outside in a car. If the purchase was successful, the youths would get in the car and turn over the beer, the receipt, a description of the clerk, and any other relevant information, which was dutifully recorded. Over a two-month period the team visited thirty-four South Side stores along a three-mile stretch of 79th Street and a mile and a half of Halsted Street. The receipts and the alcohol the youths provided established that they had been successful in purchasing beer in twenty-two of the thirty-four stores.

Pfleger held a press conference in a vacant lot on 79th, providing all present with the names of the stores, copies of the receipts, and information about the whole operation. "A young person who looks fourteen or fifteen years old can walk in and ask for a quart of Old English or a quart of Colt 45," he said. "These people [store owners] do not give a damn about our kids. They care about one thing: how much money they can make before they close their doors and drive off to another community." He then turned all the evidence over to the district police commander.

That evening Pfleger got a personal call from Mayor Daley, who asked that Pfleger present himself in the mayor's office in city hall the next morning. Pfleger was immediately concerned about what this meant. Hiring underage youth to commit unlawful activity was clearly illegal. He could be arrested and prosecuted for his audacity. Besides, this sting operation showed up and embarrassed Daley's police force, which should have been cracking down on establishments so openly selling liquor to children.

When Pfleger walked into the mayor's office, his fears seemed justified. Sitting with Daley were Police Superintendent Philip Cline, the city corporation counsel, and the head of the city zoning board. Daley immediately asked Pfleger to explain what he had been doing regarding liquor sales to young people. Pfleger described at length the details of the sting, emphasizing his motives and his abiding concern about the easy access children have to liquor and cigarettes, "the gateway drugs" to narcotics. When he finished there was a moment of silence. Then, according to Pfleger, Daley turned toward the police superintendent and demanded, "Why haven't you been doing this? Why does it take the reverend here to expose this criminal activity?" Cline and the corporation counsel tried to explain that the law does not permit police to involve underage youth in deceptive practices. "I don't care," thundered Daley. "I want this stopped, and you find a way to do it!" Daley then politely thanked Pfleger for his work and wished him well.

Feeling relieved and vindicated, Pfleger decided to move the initiative several steps further. Over the course of six weeks, he and parish volunteers met with store owners who sold liquor in the Auburn Gresham area and developed a multipart agreement that the owners were asked to sign. In November, at what Pfleger called "an historic moment," some forty (of the sixty-five owners contacted) gathered at St. Sabina to sign a covenant. They agreed to require valid identification when there was any doubt about a liquor purchaser's age, to remove all liquor and tobacco banners from the outside of their stores, to stop selling loose cigarettes and cigarette wrapping papers, to cease selling grain alcohol, to support African

American community activities, and to post copies of the commitment in their stores. (The grain alcohol ban was entered into the agreement because it is primarily used to cook cocaine to make crack.) The owners—black, white, and Arab American—came forward one by one and put their signatures on the covenant, most without comment. "Some of the stores that refused to sign are presenting the biggest problem," said Pfleger, "and they may even have to be closed if they don't join this positive effort." But he denied any suggestion that the agreement amounted to extortion. "The best monitor is not city government, it's not law or law enforcement, it's the neighbors," he said. Parishioners were encouraged to patronize these stores over the others in an effort to reward this action.

Almost exactly one year after the sting operation orchestrated by St. Sabina, Mayor Daley announced at a press conference the results of a sting operation of his own. The police had quietly hired eighteen youthful-looking persons, eighteen to twenty years of age, and sent them to buy alcohol at stores in all twenty-five of the city police districts. Of the 240 stores visited, he reported, 130, or well over half, sold alcohol beverages without seeking identification. More than one hundred of these, said the mayor, had already been fined, and fourteen others were facing license revocation for repeated illegal sales. This new initiative, called Stop Alcohol to Minors Program (STAMP), would be continued indefinitely, said Daley. "We're serving notice to store owners: check IDs and stick to the law if you want to stay in business." The press conference, at Daley's request, was held at St. Sabina, where Daley praised Pfleger for taking the first steps. STAMP, he acknowledged, was essentially the Sabina sting writ large, made permanent, and (unexplainably) legal when practiced by the city.[2]

The sting was just one of those occasions when Daley and Pfleger found themselves in warm agreement, but their relationship has often been ambivalent. In some cases, Pfleger has loudly supported city hall decisions; in others, such as the city council's reluctance to take legal action against billboards, he's been loudly critical. It all depends on the issues. On one occasion, recalled Pfleger, he and a crowd of demonstrators were emerging from a bus in front of city hall just as Mayor Daley was entering the building. The mayor looked at the assembly and asked Pfleger good-naturedly, "Are you here today for me or against me?" Overall, said Pfleger, he respects the mayor. "He's a good man. He really cares about Chicago and its people."

In 1994 a potential breakthrough occurred when the city council of Baltimore, Maryland, passed an ordinance prohibiting all alcohol and tobacco ads in residential areas. Their reasoning, identical to the position of Pfleger, was that enticing children to use these products is harmful in itself and a step toward the use of illegal drugs. Pfleger immediately petitioned the Chicago City Council to follow Baltimore's lead, but the council refused, fearing a lawsuit. In Baltimore opponents of the ruling had already appealed the judgment in court, claiming it violated their fundamental right of free speech. It was clear they intended to appeal, fighting all the way to the U.S. Supreme Court if necessary.

During the next two years Pfleger tried a variety of new tacks. He organized a letter-writing campaign in which community organizations, churches, and residents in a four-square-mile area of the South Side del-uged the city council, demanding that alcohol ads be removed from the area because they were preparing to designate it an alcohol-free zone. The effort produced some media notice but no concrete action. The letters were ignored by city council members. Next he called a press conference, charging that scores of billboards still lacked city permits even three or more years after he had complained about their illegality. He saw irony in the fact that a huge outdoor sign featuring outrageous basketball star Dennis Rodman had been ordered removed by the city because it caused traffic congestion on a nearby expressway. "It seems to me if such an ad can be removed because it slows down traffic," said Pfleger, "ads ought to be removed if they are contributing to the death and destruction of human lives."

Then came the idea of fighting fire with fire. In cooperation with several minority health organizations, an association of Chicago black ministers, and the Black Contractors Union, he announced a plan to rent fifty billboards in black and Hispanic neighborhoods. The message printed in stark black-and-white was "WARNING Advertising alcohol and cigarettes to minors is hazardous to the health of our community."

At the bottom in smaller type were the words "Protect our kids from destructive messages." Since the sponsors were prepared to pay the going rate for billboard rental, the owners of the billboards, Universal Outdoor, Inc., consented to a six-month lease. Almost immediately the company changed its mind, saying the ad copy "attacks advertising as such" and not the real problem. "If you don't like the message, don't shoot the messenger," declared Paul G. Simon, Universal Outdoor spokesman. So Pfleger led a protest rally at the company headquarters in downtown Chicago, and Universal Outdoor reversed itself again. Said Simon, "While our company does not agree with the message, we firmly support the right of this group . . . to promote their views, and we will accept their advertising message on our standard terms."[3] The signs went up and stayed up for six months. No one in the community protested or attempted to vandalize them.

†

FOR SEVERAL YEARS Pfleger had been a friend of Terry Peterson, chief of staff to Allan Streeter, alderman of the 17th Ward, which included the Auburn Gresham community. In fact, the ward offices were directly across the street from the St. Sabina community center, the Ark. Peterson was greatly impressed with the long struggle by Pfleger and the Sabina community over the billboard issue and their determined effort to quell drugs and crime. Although not a member of the church, Peterson frequently participated in the Friday night marches organized by the church. In 1995 Alderman Streeter was forced out of office, charged with extortion and filing false income tax returns. Peterson was appointed his temporary replacement by Mayor Daley, and he won the 17th Ward seat on his own in the 1996 election. (During the campaign, Pfleger on one occasion substituted for Peterson in a debate when the alderman was unable to attend.)

After the election, the two went to work together in a big way. Pfleger realized that even if all the drugs and gangbangers and billboards and other ingredients of neighborhood deterioration were to disappear from Auburn Gresham, it would still be a lost cause. "You can't stabilize a community if it's not a working neighborhood, if there's no businesses and no commerce, no jobs. You have to put some life in the community." With Peterson at city hall, Mayor Daley generally supportive of Pfleger's local activism, and Barack Obama, whom Pfleger knew from the mid-1980s, in the state legislature, the way was open for constructive collaboration. Peterson and Pfleger made contacts, submitted proposals, and met with decision makers. Slowly, progress began to occur. One of the first signs was an Obama-backed $250,000 state grant for an employee resource center in Auburn Gresham. Then the city, the federal government, and Chicago's Catholic Charities agreed to cooperate on an eighty-apartment seniors' building half a block from St. Sabina. Catholic Charities and Sabina teamed up on plans for a new social service center. The team got in touch with businesses and banks, promoting their vision of a new, stable Auburn Gresham. With the crime rate still alarmingly high, this was no easy sale. But there was no denying that St. Sabina provided a kind of community anchor with strong, visible leadership and an activist membership. By 2000, the results began to appear. "If anyone says activism hasn't done any good around here," says Peterson, "they've never come to this church or this community. There's a long history of fighting for justice, and it's made a big difference."

Meanwhile, the team drafted an anti-billboard ordinance that they felt could pass in the city council. The wording was similar to that of the Baltimore ruling, which had resisted stiff efforts by the advertising industry to strike it down. It had survived assaults in the federal court of appeals, and the case had finally reached the U.S. Supreme Court. But in 1996 the high court decided not to hear the case. Thus, the Baltimore ban stood vindicated, and the barrier that had kept the timid Chicago City Council from taking action was removed. The new ordinance was introduced in the council cosponsored by Peterson, representing the black community, and by Alderman Danny Solis of the 25th Ward, representing the Latino community. The cosponsors, along with Pfleger, met with Mayor Daley, who put his stamp of approval on the proposed legislation. Pfleger sensed victory at long last, but he didn't underestimate the opposition. As written, the ordinance was not perfect in his view. Tobacco and alcohol billboards would still be permitted along expressways, at sports stadiums, in industrial areas, and on mass transit vehicles. But lawyers who scrutinized the ordinance agreed these exceptions would prevent a flood of lawsuits from the opposition. At least the blackout of objectionable billboards in residential neighborhoods would be citywide.

During a series of packed public hearings at city hall in the summer of 1997, the proposed ordinance was denounced as an attack on the First Amendment of the Constitution. Speaking for the Chicago Advertising Federation, David Feldman said, "There's no such thing as a little censorship." Restricting outdoor advertising would not only "tear at the fabric of basic citizen rights," it would also have a domino effect, "setting the stage for restrictions on the advertising of milk and eggs, because these products are high in cholesterol and potentially may pose health problems for certain individuals." Chris Stone, an official with the Wholesale Liquor Dealers Association, cited a Pennsylvania study that claimed restrictions on billboard ads have no effect on drinking patterns and "trample on the rights of billboard owners." David Jaffe of the Association of National Advertisers, Inc., warned that the ordinance was "bad public policy" since it could lead to "substantial legal and court costs for the city without furthering the goals of the legislation."[4]

Pfleger arrived at the hearings fully armed. In a prepared statement he compared the 185 billboards in the overwhelmingly black 17th Ward with the 50 in the largely white, North Side 50th Ward. Citing a study from the U.S. Department of Alcohol and Substance Abuse, he said 80 percent of children who drink or smoke are likely to try illicit drugs. He cited recent admissions by major tobacco companies that they had aimed ads at young people, and he charged that the alcohol industry had done the same. "We know also from the obscene amount of billboards of tobacco and alcohol in African American and Hispanic communities that these two industries have not only targeted children but chosen to saturate particular communities. When you target and saturate children and minorities with the top two killers in America, that's genocide!"

Less bombastic but perhaps more persuasive was Diana Hackbarth, a Loyola University professor and board member of the Chicago branch of the American Lung Association. Six years earlier at Pfleger's trial her testimony had proved crucial. She told the city council, "Every day three thousand to five thousand young people become addicted to tobacco in the U.S." Currently, she said, "almost 14 percent of students in grades nine through twelve are regular smokers, and more than 30 percent have used cigarettes in the previous thirty days."[5] Still, it was not clear the measure would pass in the council. Some council members worried that the ordinance would lead to lawsuits costing the city money it did not have; the City of Baltimore had paid a heavy price in legal costs defending its anti-advertising legislation. Others argued that children could still see ads on trains and buses and at sporting events, so what was the point? Some, everyone knew, were reluctant to take a stand because of their friendly and lucrative relationships with lobbyists from the three industries.

The major news media provided no encouragement to the Pfleger forces. A *Chicago Sun-Times* editorial stated, "Communities have a right to control signs to reduce visual pollution. But to pick out a few products— legal products—and remove them from a particular advertising forum is an improper infringement on free speech." In a *Chicago Tribune* op-ed essay titled "Even the 'wrong' billboard deserves protection," R. Bruce Dold, deputy editorial director of that newspaper, said the same thing but in greatly extended form. "Father Pfleger is a man who speaks his mind to full advantage and sometimes steps beyond the law, and that's great. The harm was modest—the companies had to repair their billboards. . . . I'd rather see Father Pfleger out there with his paintbrush, practicing a little civil disobedience, than doing what he's doing right now. Because what he's doing now is perfectly legal, but far more damaging." Those signs may be a public nuisance, preying on poor kids in poor neighborhoods, wrote Dold, but they also inform adults of something they might like to know about, that cigarettes and alcohol are legal for adults. Dold concluded with a dire warning: Though Pfleger and his forces may have the ability to silence these major industries, he hoped they would reconsider the implication of their actions. "What if the alcohol and tobacco industries had the votes in the City Council to silence them?"[6]

†

THE HEARINGS WERE followed by weeks and weeks of delay. It was as if city council members knew what they had to do but didn't want to budge, especially when the lobbyists were pressuring them daily to choose free speech over the demands of the community. But on September 9, 1997, the vote was called, and the opposition crumbled. The ordinance banning alcohol and tobacco billboards in all residential areas of Chicago was approved forty-four to one, and suddenly city hall seemed to be in a self-congratulatory frame of mind. Mayor Daley said, "The block clubs, the churches, and everybody said, 'We don't want them here. We're tired of having them in our community.' How many times can we say it? If they would have listened to the community and taken them out where they wanted them out, this would not be an ordinance today, but they didn't."[7] But if city hall had been listening to the community itself, the anti-billboard legislation would have passed six years earlier.

Alderman Edward Burke of the 14th Ward carried the celebration to an even more surreal level: "The council can be proud of the fact that here in Chicago, the corporate authorities have led the way when other cities around the country were timid." He did not identify "the corporate authorities" who led the way. When pressed later, Burke said the city deserved some credit for banning distribution of free cigarette packs and limiting the availability of cigarette vending machines. "At least we didn't sit back and do nothing," he said. So misplaced were the comments from city hall regulars that two *Chicago Tribune* reporters, Patrick Reardon and Gary Washburn, were moved to assign credit where it was due. "It was strange praise to lavish on a governing body that sat on its collective hands for more than a decade," they wrote of Burke's comments. "For years, a lone South Side priest and his parishioners waged an ostensibly hopeless battle to get the council's attention—and action against such [alcohol and tobacco] signs." Opposing them were politically connected lobbyists and a vast amount of campaign funding, noted the reporters. "The battle was particularly lonely and solitary because Pfleger was challenging three industries with tight ties to the council."[8]

Meanwhile, Pfleger rejoiced with the overflow of Sabina members who packed the visitors' section of the council chambers on the big day. Then he went home to write a press statement. Considering the occasion, it was surprisingly low-key and humble: "Today, after waging a long uphill battle of protest, billboard red-washing, and lobbying, and encountering a city council delay in July, the community applauds the courageous action taken by the aldermen. By enacting one of the most sweeping anti-alcohol and anti-tobacco measures in the country, Chicago now takes center stage as one of the nation's first major cities to ban alcohol and tobacco advertising. Chicago has set a standard . . . and I expect this billboard ban to have a ripple effect across the nation."

The ripple has not been as sweeping as Pfleger hoped. Some large cities such as Oakland and San Diego, California, have been successful, and others have achieved partial success. But the same obstacles that blocked the anti-billboard movement in Chicago for ten years continue to frustrate efforts in many places. The record suggests only those cities committed to "the long haul" can expect results.

That was reinforced within weeks of the apparent victory. The new ordinance required that alcohol and tobacco billboard advertisements be removed within 180 days or when the current leases expired (usually six months at the most). But it was soon discovered that billboard owners were consorting with their alcohol and tobacco clients and quietly updating their leases to keep the billboards in place—some for up to twenty years! This would in effect nullify the new ordinance. Pfleger, Alderman Peterson, and other council and community supporters cried foul. Mayor Daley was irate. It was "never the intention that the ad firms grab all the billboards," he said. "They should have come clean. . . . The community doesn't want them. They have enough problems. They want them out!"[9] City attorneys got on the case, and on February 8, 1998, the city council unanimously passed an amendment that invalidated any new lease arrangements.

Four days later, a celebratory press conference was held on Halsted Street near 79th. It marked the unveiling of the first of a dozen new billboards in the community with the message, "Alcohol, Tobacco and Billboard Companies Obey the City Ordinance and Stop Targeting Us – Signed, Children of Chicago." They were cosponsored by St. Sabina and a minority health association. Pfleger provided a long narrative of the ten-year crusade, beginning with the neighborhood billboard survey and running through the painting campaign, his arrest and trial, the protests, the demonstrations and sit-ins, the sting operation, the pressure on the city, and at long last, the final achievement.

He was asked for his suggestions and secrets of success for anyone considering a grassroots campaign. His answer was inevitable: "I really believe the key to success in any campaign is to become committed for the long haul. On issues of importance success usually doesn't come quickly. To be successful, you need not only commitment but patience and endurance." He cited the example of his hero, Dr. King, "who taught that you had to be willing to go alone if necessary, to go when nobody else would go with you. When he stood up against the Vietnam War, everybody walked away from him. He stood by himself, but he said when you continue to do what you're doing, no matter how long it takes, good and truth and righteousness will always rise up and win. The important thing is you have to go the long term."

And he spoke of Nelson Mandela, who spent twenty-seven years in jail. "But he continued to be persistent in what he believed. This is the kind of commitment needed for success. No matter what happens, you've got to continue to speak it, continue to act right and not put it aside and let it fail. You've got to keep going out every week, keep passing out the flyers, keep painting the billboards, keep talking to groups, keep educating them. There will be times when nobody will believe it can be done, but you must believe it can happen, and eventually you will find that even those who may have gone adrift will return and say you must really believe this, that we can win, because you have stayed with us for so long."

†

WITH THE BILLBOARD war finally won, Pfleger immediately launched another campaign in 1998, one for which he had no difficulty arousing support from hundreds of minority religious leaders. He had heard of reports from parents about the *Jerry Springer Show* on NBC television, with its regular exploitation of poor and pathetic people, especially women, for the amusement of a rabid national audience. He watched segments and was appalled by the fist-fighting, hair-pulling, chair-throwing, profanity-spitting behavior encouraged by the genial host. He was concerned about its effect on children. He believed it was teaching them that violence was acceptable, even funny. Pfleger spoke with a producer of the show to no effect, so he hatched an action plan.

Within weeks a task force had been formed, including Reverend Jesse Jackson's Rainbow PUSH Coalition, the Southern Christian Leadership Conference, the Nation of Islam, and three hundred African American ministers (there were some white ministers too, including evangelist Billy Graham). Letters were sent to Springer's biggest advertisers and the stores that carried their products threatening an all-out boycott. A major demonstration was planned for Easter Sunday 1998 in front of the NBC Tower in downtown Chicago. Then the night before, NBC announced it was canceling the show, and that it would be instantly picked up by the FOX Broadcasting Company. Not to be undone, the demonstrators met at NBC, thanked the network for its good sense, then marched over to the nearby Fox affiliate waving placards that had been reprinted overnight to read, "We're in a Fox Hunt!" This demonstration was covered nationally by every network and sparked a public reaction. Springer's Nielsen ratings declined, and some important advertisers withdrew.

Fox and the *Springer Show* producers, Studios USA, agreed to curb the program's violence beginning in June and did so. But when the ratings did not revive, the producers quickly returned to their former outlandish style. Pfleger and other task force leaders flew to Los Angeles in August 1998 seeking a meeting. They were turned away without even getting into the building. Sporadic letter-writing efforts have continued, though the campaign resulted in a kind of standoff. Pfleger saw it as a partial victory since it served to undermine any legitimacy Jerry Springer might have had in the black community.

Richard Dominick, executive producer of the show, attempted to regain a foothold in the black community by offering to have Springer meet with children at a South Side auditorium to discuss the dangers of drugs and alcohol and to help conduct a food drive. Pfleger turned him down cold, prompting Dominick's retort: "If getting Jerry Springer off the air, if that is going to feed hungry children, I don't see how it will, but God bless him."[10]

Another campaign, one which achieved more publicity than success, involved paying the prostitutes who trolled the streets near St. Sabina for their time and using the opportunity to offer them an escape. The idea, as Pfleger explained it at a Sunday mass in 2000, was for teams of three men to approach prostitutes and ask how much they charged for half an hour (usually around twenty-five to forty-five dollars). If one agreed to be paid for her time, the team would take a three-tiered approach: first, assure her that God loves her and that the church loves her and wishes her well; second, inquire if St. Sabina could be of aid in any way through counseling, job training, substance abuse rehabilitation, or other resources for setting her on a new path; third, ask if she would like to pray for a few minutes with them. As he explained the idea, members of the congregation began to spontaneously approach the altar and put cash on it to fund the program.

News that St. Sabina was now paying prostitutes was unbelievable to some, scandalous to others. Said Pfleger, "You know what people always do when prostitutes are around. They call the police. That wasn't Jesus' approach. He didn't call the police. He reached out to them, talked and listened to them, offered them another way." The teams (sometimes with Pfleger along) worked for several years. The project ceased, says Pfleger, only when there were few prostitutes left on the street and several of the nearby motels that had catered to prostitutes and their customers went out of business. No statistics on the results were kept, but Pfleger cited several success stories, including that of Kathy Ellis, a forty-year-old drug addict with six children. The team told her the church would get her drug counseling and job training, clean her clothes, and pay for a haircut at a beauty salon. Sabina followed through on the promises, and Ellis, who attends Narcotics Anonymous meetings, got some order in her life. "Somebody cares," she told Pfleger. "When you're out there prostituting, you don't think anybody cares."

Working on two fronts, one negative (eliminating crime and exploitation) and the other positive (building up the resources of the community), St. Sabina by the late 1990s was making a visible impact.

7

CHALLENGES FROM ABOVE

PFLEGER IS JUST ABOUT THE COOLEST, HIPPEST, REALEST, MOST
SELF-CRITICAL, MOST JUST, MOST DOWN-TO-EARTH WHITE
MAN WE KNOW. HIS BONA FIDES ARE WELL ESTABLISHED IN
THE POOR AND BLACK COMMUNITIES THAT THE CATHOLIC
CHURCH NEEDS DESPERATELY TO REACH.
—MICHAEL ERIC DYSON

HE'S ALWAYS HAD a problem with authority. When that series of coincidences in 1981 served to make Pfleger the youngest priest to administer a parish in the archdiocese, clashes with Cardinal Cody were inevitable. The authoritarian-minded archbishop intended to leave him in that position only a short time, but Cody's death in 1982 left Pfleger in place after the arrival of Joseph Bernardin. Cardinal Bernardin made Pfleger pastor officially several years later, but the elevation was strictly pro forma—he had referred to himself as pastor all along, and church members universally regarded him as such.

However, relations between the two men soon grew chilly. Bernardin particularly objected to Pfleger's invitation to non-Catholic leaders like Cornel West, Al Sharpton, and Dr. Martin Luther King Sr., to speak

from the pulpit at St. Sabina, often during Sunday mass. According to
church regulations only priests or deacons are allowed to preach during
mass. Bernardin was especially concerned that these big-name civil rights
figures were always covered by the news media, and clips from their talks
invariably ran on the Sunday evening news programs. Pfleger countered
that other churches in the archdiocese occasionally invited non-Catholic
speakers, and Bernardin had not cracked down on them. "If you want
everybody to stop," Pfleger says he told the cardinal, "I'll stop. The law has
to be evenhanded."

More important, he argued, he had begun inviting civil rights activists
into the pulpit to further the education of St. Sabina parishioners, and
their presence drew overflow crowds. "Face it," Pfleger says, discussing his
position. "There's just not a lot of homegrown African American Catholic leadership in the archdiocese. The people need to be fed. We bring in
speakers who inspire, who have something to say."

The speaker dispute came to a head in November 1989 just as Pfleger
and the St. Sabina choir returned from Rome, where the choir, by special
invitation, had sung for Pope John Paul II. Urgent messages from the
chancery office were awaiting the jet-lagged pastor. Word had leaked out
that on the following Sunday the guest speaker at St. Sabina would be
none other than Louis Farrakhan, leader of the Nation of Islam. Bernardin considered this intolerable; the talk, he said, must be canceled. Pfleger
phoned Bernardin, saying that preparations and announcements had been
made, that Farrakhan had promised not to say anything incendiary, and
that a late cancellation would be embarrassing, insulting, and detrimental
to Catholic-Muslim relations. Bernardin remained adamant, insisting he
wanted the invitation terminated, period. Pfleger said he would have to
consult his parish council, and he did so immediately. He got back to the
cardinal and said the vote of the council was unanimous in favor of Farrakhan's visit. "I'm not going to cancel," Pfleger told Bernardin. "If you
want to stop him, you'll have to come and do it yourself!" The conversation
ended abruptly with both men breathing heavily. That Sunday Farrakhan spoke before a standing-room-only crowd and a phalanx of media
microphones and television cameras. Neither Bernardin nor anyone else

attempted to stop him, and the media reaction was that the firebrand leader proved uncharacteristically genial and conciliatory in his talk. Bernardin had no comment after Pfleger personally delivered a tape of the talk to the cardinal at his downtown office.

On several occasions Pfleger has explained his personal approach toward obedience to his bishop: "I've always been candid with my superiors. My primary allegiance is not to my country, flag, church, or cardinal. My allegiance is to God. I don't believe blind obedience to a pope, bishop, or pastor is healthy. Though I respect authority, when my moral beliefs contradict that authority, I will challenge an order." And if it comes down to an absolute confrontation, he said, "I respect the right of the one in authority to throw me out."

Two years later, in 1991, the tension between bishop and pastor lifted after Pfleger wrote a letter to Bernardin concerning the cardinal's failure to offer any support or advice as Pfleger faced a criminal trial over his defacing of billboards. Bernardin quietly attended a Sunday mass at St. Sabina. Weeks after, he drove to the rectory, where the two talked for some three hours. Pfleger said Bernardin told him that the mass had been one of the most spiritual experiences of his life and said, "Those people really love Jesus." He became thereafter more interested in the issues and activities at Sabina. He approved Pfleger's second and third terms as pastor of the parish and, Pfleger said, told him he could remain pastor indefinitely, as long as he wanted and was able to serve the needs of the people.

During one meeting of pastors from a section of the archdiocese, the cardinal asked the priests something Pfleger had never heard a bishop say before: "When people come to your church, do they find Jesus or not? And if not, what do they find, and why do they come?" Pfleger was so moved by the question that after the discussion he went up to Bernardin, grasped his hand, and said, "I am so proud to call you my shepherd." In 1996 when Bernardin was nearing death from cancer, Pfleger and several busloads of Sabina parishioners arrived at his residence on State Street and held a long prayer vigil outside, well into the night. The frail cardinal came out briefly, spoke to the crowd, and gave them his blessing.

The arrival of Archbishop Francis George in 1997 began a different era. George had the same objections that Bernardin had had with the ongoing series of guest speakers at St. Sabina. He also chided Pfleger regularly for violations of liturgical regulations and other breaches of Catholic Church protocol. In 1998, at the request of the parish, George came and celebrated a Sunday mass at the church. He appeared ill at ease as he began his homily, but he gained confidence when the congregation reacted with encouraging, supporting comments and frequent clapping. George said he was well aware of the continuing presence of racism in the United States. He told of his first encounter with segregation when, as a student in Nashville in the 1940s, he tried to sit in the back of a bus and was told that was reserved for Negroes. He noted that some forty years later, his own home parish in Chicago turned away Harold Washington when he was running for mayor.

He then said he loved St. Sabina because "I know where you stand. I've heard you're a great parish, a strong parish," one that "opens windows and brings a new spirit to Chicago" just as Pope John XXIII opened windows in the Vatican. Bolstered by the welcoming congregation, George may have gone further than he intended when he said a bit later in the talk, "I've read stories about Father Mike—that he said, 'This very conservative archdiocese isn't going to tell me what to do.' Well, I don't have to tell him what to do. If you give him enough rope, he'll hang himself!"

There was a second or two of stunned silence. Then George, recovering his composure, said, "But he always comes out right. There's more life than death here. The risen Lord is here." He was back in sync with the assembly, and at the conclusion of his talk they gave him hearty applause. It may well have been that Cardinal George's comment about Pfleger was not a momentary slip but a notification to the perceptive that he recognized the great divide between himself and this difficult pastor, and that he was aware of the difficulties they would both endure as they played out their irreconcilable roles in the years ahead.

†

FOR BOTH, THE month of February 2002 typified that tension on a grand scale. It was a period of unremitting stress, a roller coaster of ups and downs—and the rest of the year wasn't all that relaxing either. Cardinal George made it clear that he wanted to remove Pfleger from his position at St. Sabina. Pfleger had completed three six-year terms as pastor, and according to archdiocesan regulations a fourth term was out of the question. The term limits had two purposes: first, to give as many priests as possible the opportunity to serve as pastor, and second, to prevent pastors from becoming embedded tyrants in their own territories. Pfleger was relying on Bernardin's pledge that he would be an exception and could remain pastor at St. Sabina as long as he wanted. There was, however, nothing in writing. George, as Bernardin's successor, had the authority to rescind such a promise even if it existed in written form.

Toward the end of 2001, George had repeatedly pressured Pfleger to make plans for a new assignment. During a phone conversation on January 4, they discussed a variety of options. The cardinal was firm in his decision that Pfleger had to go now. Pfleger remained equally firm in his belief that now was not the time. For the next few weeks he mulled over the situation, prayed about it, discussed it with friends, staff, and other church leaders, and then sent George a three-page letter dated February 1, in which he passionately laid out his case for remaining pastor. One by one, he rejected the options that had been discussed:

> I really have no desire to go to Washington, D.C., [presumably for further theological studies or to take a post in some department of the bishops conference] and with my father being 90 years old and presently not in good health, a move out of the city would be impossible. I also do not think this is the time to write a book. I have had several people approach me about this over the years, but presently I have a lot of energy and passion and would rather do ministry now and write about it when I haven't got the same energy. I am also not interested in going to another Black Catholic Parish. As I mentioned in our meeting, I just do not feel there is a serious commitment from the Archdiocese to the African American

community and do not feel the calling or the desire to start over in a situation that has been let go and ignored without the support needed for it to be successful.

He stated that St. Sabina had become "a strong and effective African American Catholic Church that has not only trained its members to be leaders and proclaimers of the gospel, but I believe we have been able to make an impact on the community, city, and nation. I also believe Saint Sabina has gained respect within the Black church community of Chicago." Pfleger presented in detail the ministries of the parish, the outreach programs to the community, the successful elementary school, and the redevelopment efforts in the neighborhood. He continued:

Cardinal, I feel both called and committed to the present pastoring of Saint Sabina. I believe we have built a strong and vibrant model of church and would be happy to share that model with others in formal or informal ways but with Saint Sabina as a base and model. I believe we also have many new and exciting things before us. I want also to say that I do not feel worn, burnt out, or finished in my ministry to this faith community. I am therefore requesting an extension of my assignment as pastor of Saint Sabina for the next 4 to 6 years, with the desire to explore the possibility of someone who may desire to come in and study and learn about Saint Sabina to possibly consider becoming its future pastor. With the continued closing of churches and schools . . . and the seemingly consistent withdrawal and abandonment of ministry in the African American community by the Catholic church, I believe the continued presence of strong places such as Saint Sabina are crucial to our credibility. . . . Cardinal, I look forward to your response. If your desire is for me to be assigned here I will seek with the help of God to build a strong church for His glory. If your desire is for me to leave, I only ask that you give me a fair notice as to my termination so that I can seek other employment and ministry opportunities.

The polite tone belied the roiling emotions in Pfleger's soul. The only hint is at the end where he refers to the possibility of seeking "other employment and ministry opportunities." That reference would not be lost on Cardinal George. Talking about that letter years later, Pfleger stressed his habitual candor with his superiors. "I've made it clear to everyone that I like the Catholic Church; I believe in the Catholic Church, though there's much I disagree with. But if my only option to continue in ministry is to go to another church, then I'll go to another church."

After waiting for more than a week and hearing nothing from George, Pfleger virtually erupted when Cathleen Falsani, religion writer for the *Chicago Sun-Times*, called him on February 11 regarding another matter. He told her what was really on his mind—his fear that George was not going to renew his assignment at St. Sabina. He reiterated to the reporter many of the things he had written to George: that he would not accept another assignment in a black Chicago parish, that he resented the Catholic church's lack of commitment to the African American community, and especially the real possibility he would step away from the Catholic church. "My desire is to remain a priest," he told her. "My desire is to pastor at St. Sabina." But if this cannot happen, "I would have to look for other employment opportunities. I might have to look outside the Catholic Church."[1] The next morning, February 12, the *Sun-Times* front-page banner headline read, "CARDINAL OUSTING REBEL PRIEST." It ran with a color photo of Pfleger preaching in front of the painting of the black Jesus, taken at an angle by a *Sun-Times* photographer that made it appear that the halo in the painting was around Pfleger's head.

But events were outstripping the news. Later that same day Pfleger met with George and Auxiliary Bishop Joseph Perry for more than an hour at the cardinal's mansion. That evening at his weekly Bible study session in McMahon Hall, Pfleger announced a surprising breakthrough to some two hundred in attendance. The cardinal, he said, "is willing to extend my past term and, over the next few years, look into a new pastor for St. Sabina and other options for me in ministry." He expressed appreciation to George for the extension, adding, "I want to make it clear that I understand the policies of the archdiocese and that I respect them. But

I also believe there are unique situations, and unique parishes should be examined individually, and I've asked that it be done here."[2]

He did not explain exactly how this compromise had been worked out in such a short time. Quite possibly the prospect of losing Pfleger, as well as many of St. Sabina's parishioners, to another church had a sobering effect on the cardinal, and so he settled for time. Under the agreement, Pfleger could stay for a "few years"; he would not be getting a fourth term, however. As it turned out, of course, Pfleger did get a de facto fourth six-year term, which would have ended in 2008—and almost did end that year during the presidential primary. Yet when this was written in early 2010, Pfleger still remained in charge.

The morning after Pfleger's reprieve, February 13, a new *Sun-Times* banner headline reported: "REBEL PRIEST GETS A DEAL." On page three under the headline, "Priest promised to obey, but has long habit of rebellion," Falsani discussed Pfleger's penchant for challenging authority, civil and church, all the way back to his days as a seminarian. Meanwhile, Cardinal George celebrated an Ash Wednesday mass at the cathedral, marking the beginning of the penitential season of Lent. Afterward, reporters confronted him, asking why Pfleger didn't get a fourth term as pastor. George said the denial of another term was not a reprimand but an expression of church regulations that "do not allow pastors for life. . . . If every time a priest did an extraordinarily fine job we didn't move him, we wouldn't move a lot of priests." In the spirit of the season, he added, "The archdiocese of Chicago would not be irreparably damaged if I dropped dead right now, and that's true for most of us." He quickly denied any suggestions that he had backed down out of fear of losing Pfleger or his parishioners. "People don't stay in the church because of priests and ministers," he said. "They stay in the Catholic church because of Jesus Christ and because they have the faith."[3]

On February 14, Valentine's Day, George sent a short letter to Pfleger, putting the agreement they had settled on in writing. He wrote that due to Pfleger's extraordinary work in the St. Sabina community and his deep relationship with his parishioners, his term would be extended while they considered the future of St. Sabina, and Pfleger's place there. He sent a similar letter to Father Jack Wall, pastor of Old St. Patrick's Church in the upscale West Loop area. Like Pfleger, Wall had just completed his third term as pastor, and supporters were urging a fourth term for him. Like Pfleger, Wall got only an extension on his third term, said George, in order to complete building projects supporting the parish's liturgical, educational, and social service missions.

Had the storm passed? By no means. The next day, Joseph Perry, the auxiliary bishop who had met with Pfleger and George two days before, stopped by unannounced at the St. Sabina rectory to talk with Pfleger. He was not there, so Perry met with Kim Lymore, a Sabina pastoral associate and veteran church member. Afterward, she told the *Sun-Times'* Falsani that Perry had left a message for Pfleger. She was told to let Pfleger know he should "get out of the priesthood, start [his] own church." Lymore says she "was kind of shocked that that came out of his mouth. . . . He said that Father Mike had said . . . he would leave the priesthood and start his own church" if he couldn't continue at Sabina. "Then he said, 'I would [recommend he] do that immediately, so as not to be disruptive to the church.'"[4]

Pfleger was furious. "When a bishop comes and tells somebody who works for you that you should leave, and [she passes] the message along, it's hard for me to think this isn't personal. . . . To have a message passed on to me that I should leave the church by a bishop of the church, that's both painful and hurtful." He was still fuming a week later when he addressed a crowd of four hundred at a conference on slavery at a Chicago church. Referring to the Perry visit, he said, "I am not quitting. You are going to have to have the balls to fire me. If you want to fire me, fire me!" The real issue, he said, is the poor treatment black parishioners received from Catholic leaders. "We want African American culture to be embraced completely on equal grounds and not just tolerated. We want the Catholic church to understand what Nat Turner tried to make America understand—the slaves aren't happy being slaves. We are not just going to be satisfied being on the fringe."[5]

Perry wrote to Pfleger, saying he had been stunned by the *Sun-Times* article concerning his visit. He said he had actually come to discuss Archbishop Desmond Tutu's forthcoming visit to the parish, and in his conversation with Lymore she had told him of the pain the people were feeling because of recent events. Perry explained that he had been "wondering out loud" to Kim if perhaps the only solution was for Pfleger to go start his own church. He claimed to have said this with sympathy and concern, and that he did not ask her to deliver a message to Pfleger on his behalf. Lymore found Perry's take confusing. The article accurately reported what he had told her, she said. She heard no wondering-out-loud tone in his statement or in his advice that Pfleger get out immediately.

Meanwhile, twenty-one members of the St. Sabina leadership cabinet signed a letter to Cardinal George, asking for a meeting to "discuss the future of St. Sabina with you." George replied that he thought a meeting with so many would be cumbersome, and he would prefer to limit the group to the four members of the parish council and three others he named from the leadership cabinet. That prompted a terse reply letter from the cabinet saying, "Your request to meet with the handpicked aforementioned cannot be honored. If we meet, we will meet with the entire cabinet or we won't meet." George stood his ground, insisting that it was not possible to have a conversation with twenty people the same way that one can with fewer. He concluded icily that if the cabinet didn't agree and felt they should not talk, he would accept that, but thought it was a mistake and that they would regret it. He also remarked that it was strange to have Catholics say they would not speak with their bishop. By then the month of February was over.

Late in March, a small group from the cabinet did meet with George and reported the discussion was reasonably cordial. George said he would continue to seek input from St. Sabina members, wanted only what was best for the parish, and was in no hurry to replace Pfleger.

For much of the rest of the year, George was absorbed with his peers in the U.S. Conference of Catholic Bishops as they developed a national sex abuse policy in response to the crisis that racked the U.S. church. When George returned from Rome in November, he told reporters he had changed his mind about his earlier positions on many subjects. He seemed close to the view of Bishop Perry, declaring that perhaps Father Pfleger should leave the priesthood after all. "There are some men who probably shouldn't be in the priesthood. For me to say that is a big thing," said the cardinal. "A year ago I would have drawn back from that with horror and said no at all costs. Bishops are trained to protect priests, and so you protect vocations. . . . But in the last year I've reconsidered and said no, in some of these cases it would have been better for someone to say, 'Obviously you're in the wrong position.'" From the words he used, it seemed to some that George was comparing Pfleger with priests who abused young people. No, not at all, he said, and he backed off a little. "You have to respect Mike," he said. "He's done a lot of good things. But at some point he's got to sit down and say, 'Well, what do I do next?' That's a conversation I still have to have."

Pfleger simply restated his position. "My bottom line is I have to really follow where God has called me and be truthful to what God calls me to do. My desire has been to do that in the church. That's always been my first desire and commitment."

†

THE PUBLIC RESPONSE to the apparent stalemate indicated how divided people were on the issue. Pfleger-haters could scarcely contain their glee that he might go away. "Yes, get out now," said an anonymous letter writer. "You're a disgrace to the priesthood and a millstone around the neck of the Catholic Church!"

"He's been nothing but trouble since he was ordained," said another. "It's time for Cardinal George to say, 'Enough!'"

Others, including many traditional Catholics who had been support-ive of Pfleger and his work, were horrified and saddened by his threat to leave. "Reverend Father . . . why do you put your ministry above that which your bishop is asking of you?" wrote an earnest e-mailer. "I understand that you are saying that you are not being called to leave St. Sabina, yet [the bishop] is discussing with you spreading the light and the salt you have begun at St. Sabina's. You have just begun. I don't ever want to hear of your threat to leave the church that you love for any reason. That makes me personally fearful for you. I do not rejoice with your victories when you speak this way."

Many letter writers, e-mailers, and commentators appeared favorably disposed to Pfleger, some vehemently so. "[Your] eminence, have you visited St. Sabina community lately?" a writer asked the cardinal, sending a copy to Pfleger. "The church and the neighborhood have evolved as a pride of place; children and senior citizens feel safe. This was not the inner workings of an entrenched political figure, nor was it the result of a wealthy benefactor. This is a heightened form of ministry and stewardship. It is apparent from the comfort of the Gold Coast mansion, the sun rises and sets. Some of the pastors such as Fr. Pfleger are confronted with immense problems. They have thrived over difficult circumstances . . . with utter humility. What is deserving here is appreciation and affirmation—not hegemony."

"It is amazing to me that Fr. Pfleger has received so little support from within his own archdiocese for his life's work, yet rather has been the recipient of nonstop recrimination, persecution, and harassment," wrote a supporter to the *Daily Southtown* newspaper. "I do not believe history will be so kind to Cardinal George if he continues to listen to the petty mutterings of voices from within the archdiocese."[6]

"The suggestion that . . . Pfleger leave comes at a time when the Catholic Church has a multitude of critical issues that are eating away at the very core of the church's existence," stated a writer to the *Sun-Times*. Yet not once, said the writer, have we seen a headline that urged priest sex abusers to leave the priesthood. "It makes one think that perhaps the cardinal is using Pfleger to drown out some of the more serious issues in the church."[7] In his column in the *Sun-Times*, Michael Eric Dyson, a professor at DePaul University, spoke directly to Cardinal George: "You might not get this immediately, but Pfleger is just about the coolest, hippest, realest, most self-critical, most just, most down-to-earth white man we know. His bona fides are well established in the poor and black communities that the Catholic Church needs desperately to reach. If he's a rebel, he's a rebel like Jesus. So why not let him stay? After all, was man made for the Sabbath or the Sabbath for man?"[8]

And Judy Masterson, columnist for the Waukegan *News-Sun*, argued that Pfleger and others like him are called "to a higher obedience" that is not unlike that practiced by the early Christians who were regarded as "disturbers of the peace and outside agitators." She quoted Reverend Tom McQuaid, a Catholic priest who had worked with black parishioners in the Chicago archdiocese. "In the black community, there's a different understanding of pastoring," he told her. "Successful pastors are those who have been around for a while and established a relationship with a church. Culturally it makes much more sense for Mike to stay around. I'm not sure the Church understands there's a different reality there. . . . One size does not fit all in this case."[9]

In a long editorial, the *Chicago Tribune* tried to evenhandedly balance conflicting viewpoints. "George has always been known as a by-the-book prelate, so it is no surprise he would insist that the rules on tenure for pastors, while they can be stretched quite far, eventually must be forced and obeyed," declared the newspaper. "Pfleger has always been the prophet at the city gates. . . . It's no surprise he would fight to remain with his flock."

It would be a mistake to see George as a "heartless enforcer" of an arbitrary rule, said the writer, since succession planning is a necessary part of organizational life, and even Moses and Jesus had handpicked successors. That George backed off from ousting Pfleger immediately may not be due to timidity, said the editorial, but that "like a basketball coach, he looked down his bench for a substitute and found no one. One hopes it is also because he appreciates the special mix of skills and talents and personality *and spirituality* that Pfleger represents that enabled him to build St. Sabina into the vibrant community it is." When the time comes to replace Pfleger, said the editorial, the cardinal must realize "what a void will need to be filled."[10]

†

TO READERS OF Church history, there is something familiar in the bottom-line issue that marked the 2002 brouhaha and would emerge again in 2008. This conflict has been played out over and over again in Christianity almost from the time of Jesus Christ—the unavoidable tension between the institutional overseer and the charismatic leader.

The conflict between bishop-overseer Francis George and charismatic leader Michael Pfleger is classic because each embraces his role with such sincerity and sense of obligation. In requiring established time limits for pastors, George, as the *Tribune* editorial noted, was not enforcing some "fundamentally arbitrary rule." He was imposing order. That's what bishops do. In insisting that he be allowed to remain at St. Sabina indefinitely, Pfleger, as Judy Masterson noted, was appealing to "a higher obedience": serving the needs of a community that has been excluded or at best patronized by the institutions of U.S. society, including the Catholic Church. Exceptions to rules must be made in such cases. That's what charismatic leaders demand.

Complicating the matter is the fact that George has clearly stated his conviction that the Church must move in new directions to overcome the racism that stubbornly persists in society—and churches. In a strong pastoral letter published in 2001, less than a year before the succession controversy, he wrote,

> Striving to be a witness of Jesus Christ as a good neighbor to all is difficult. It seems easier to sit in our divisions and our hatreds. It seems easier to ignore the gap between rich and poor . . . to live tied up in the bonds of personal and institutional racism. But we cannot. . . . To embrace the vision proclaimed in Jesus' preaching of the reign of God, we need to see new patterns and possibilities. Too often, when decisions about the future of the Archdiocese are being made, the persons around the table do not adequately reflect the rich cultural diversity that shapes our Church, city, nation, and world.[11]

He ended the letter with a call for the Church to be all-embracing: "If she is faithful to her Lord . . . the Church will not only proclaim who He is but will herself act to become the womb, the matrix, in which a new world can gestate and be born. Listening and welcoming, the Church is a place of encounter, or racial dialogue and intercultural collaboration."

On the basis of George's stirring sentiments, it would appear he and Pfleger were on the same page. Certainly the argument could be made that St. Sabina had become under Pfleger's leadership a womb in which new realities were gestating, a place of encounter and racial dialogue. It may not have been precisely the kind of encounter and dialogue George and those who sat around his table, making decisions for the future of the archdiocese, would have liked. But there was not much gestating going on anywhere else. That could explain George's apparent ambivalence when he said on the same occasion that perhaps Pfleger should leave the Church, and then turned around and said, "You have to respect Mike. He's done a lot of good things."

It is the sort of dilemma that could keep a prelate such as he awake at night: should he abort what is gestating at St. Sabina or let it go to full term? The immediate crisis was over without a resolution. Pfleger continued his ministry as before. When questioned, he said, "The ball is in the cardinal's court."

Cardinal George declined to comment about his interchanges or relationship with Pfleger over the years in any way for this book. A spokesperson for George said Father Michael Pfleger is "a priest in good standing" in the Chicago archdiocese.

8

BASKETBALL AND RACIAL TENSION

I WAS UPSET BECAUSE I JUST WANTED TO PLAY BALL.
—ISAAC GLOVER, ST. SABINA SEVENTH GRADER

THE GREAT BASKETBALL crisis of 2001–2002 brought more national attention to St. Sabina than any of Pfleger's previous activities or campaigns. Ironically, it was a crisis Pfleger didn't want and attention he hoped to avoid. The man originally at the center of this controversy was Christopher Mallette, athletic director at the Ark and coach of the sports teams of the parish grammar school, St. Sabina Academy. A husky, articulate, high-energy leader, Mallette oversaw the academy students' participation in a myriad of leagues, including baseball, basketball, soccer, golf, and flag football. As a former linebacker on the Princeton University football team, he longed to introduce the kids to tackle football, but none of the leagues Sabina participated in featured the tackle version. However, a league called the Southwest Catholic Conference (SCC), made up of twenty-one virtually all-white schools farther west and southwest of the Sabina community did offer tackle football, so he began to explore the possibility of Sabina joining the league. He was also inspired by the idea of getting the kids into a large, white league, which could serve to break down interracial tensions before their arrival in racially integrated high schools. "I had this vision of unity in diversity," says Mallette, somewhat ruefully.

With a degree in American history from Princeton and a law degree from the University of Pennsylvania, Mallette moved to Chicago from Pennsylvania with his wife and children in the early 1990s to accept a position with the City of Chicago's corporation counsel office. When he first attended St. Sabina Church, he says, "I was really impressed with the message of justice and equality preached by Father Pfleger. It was almost nondenominational with genuinely authentic worship and a sense of the spirit of God in the place." He quickly became involved in the Sabina ministries, especially sports, and after a few years, he yielded to Pfleger's invitation to run the active community center and the school sports programs. He quit his job with the city, took a substantial pay cut, and waded into doing what he loved.

When he told the pastor of his interest in the Southwest Conference, Pfleger reacted with uncharacteristic hesitancy and caution. He was aware that the parishes of the SCC were the very ones to which many white families had fled from St. Sabina in the racial transition of the 1960s. And he knew from his own experience as a native South Sider (and from what Monsignor McMahon had shared with him in his early days at Sabina) about the hard feelings many of these "refugees" harbored toward black people, which had been passed on in many cases to their children and grandchildren.

Also fresh in his memory was the Grand Sabina Reunion in 1998 three years before, when all the graduates from the parish school from 1916 to 1966 were invited to a picnic, mass, and celebration of great memories. It was titled "Goin' to Sabina's one more time." But no one was going to Sabina's. A planning committee scheduled the event to be held on the grounds of St. Xavier University, some seven miles from the church, a convenient location for far South Siders and south suburbanites. Pfleger was not invited, nor were any graduates after 1966, a period of some thirty-two years, during which the school had continued to produce crops of grads every year. The cutoff, explained the promoters, was set at 1966 because that was "the year the music died"—that is, the year the mammoth Sabina Sunday night dances were cancelled. That made no sense to Pfleger, since the event was billed as a school reunion and had no connection with the dance. A more likely, and sinister, explanation was racial discrimination. The class of 1966 had 17 black students out of a total of 111, while by the next year (and every year after that) the graduating class was predominantly black.

Pfleger demanded to meet with the planning committee and did so at a South Side pancake house. When the tense conversation quieted, a leading member of the committee approached Pfleger and said bluntly, "We have nothing in common with them," referring to the post-1966 grads. Pfleger blew his stack, saying, "It's what I thought—pure racism! You cannot do this, and unless all are invited I will fight you!" The committee refused to reconsider the invitation list, so Pfleger called the president of Xavier and Cardinal Bernardin, expressing his anger. Xavier then cancelled the use of its facilities, and the cardinal revoked permission for an outdoor mass on the university grounds. Pfleger, in turn, shared his views on the matter far and wide but with little effect. The Grand Sabina Reunion was held at a suburban forest preserve on August 20, 1998, with an estimated four thousand guests and a mass celebrated by eleven priests.

With that experience still fresh in his mind, Pfleger had to ask himself if he really wanted to get the schoolkids involved in what might reopen Pandora's box. "I had a very uneasy feeling about our presence in that league," he says, "but I wanted to support Chris. I knew how competent he was. So I didn't object."

Mallette invited Hank Lenzen, the SCC executive director, to visit St. Sabina and get a sense of the whole operation. Lenzen was admittedly "blown away" by what he saw—the parquet floors in the gym, the quality bleachers, the weight room, the video games, the banners and lights. "We had music when the team comes on the floor like the Bulls have, and we even had a smoke machine," said Mallette. Lenzen thought Sabina would be a high-class addition to the league, and he shared his enthusiasm with the SCC executive committee. Meanwhile, the St. Sabina Academy school board and parents voiced support for the effort. Over a period of weeks,

Mallette met with the league committee, strictly followed the guidelines for admission, and formally presented Sabina as a candidate for membership. He believed acceptance would be a mere formality.

Then on May 24, 2001, he was told that Sabina had been turned down by an eleven-to-nine vote of the conference membership. Mallette was staggered, Lenzen was surprised, and Pfleger was outraged. The stated reason for rejection was fear by a majority of the member parishes that their children would be unsafe in the Auburn Gresham neighborhood, which admittedly had a higher rate of crime, drug, and gang problems than the neighborhoods of the SCC. According to the conference's treasurer, "Our concern is the safety issue of a young mother going over to St. Sabina's on a Thursday night for a fifth-grade girls basketball game by herself."[1] Reportedly, other conference members obtained statistics indicating that the Gresham police district (which includes St. Sabina) had thirty-two homicides in 2000, ranking it ninth highest among Chicago's twenty-five districts. Police data also reported eleven crimes, including robberies and batteries and four drug arrests, within two blocks of St. Sabina Church in the first three weeks of May.

Pfleger viewed the safety concerns as mostly disguised expressions of racism and said as much in a letter to all the pastors of the SCC: "To be denied admittance to the SCC based on the sole premise that certain coaches and parishes feared for the safety of their children is illegitimate, ridiculous, and insulting. . . . We are hurt and angry that our rejection was based upon a concern for the safety of the youth of other parishes. This is an insult to our staff, parents, parishioners, children, and community. We were deceived into believing that the SCC wanted to be inclusive, but the reality of the situation is that it does not. The most piercing part of the insult is that it comes from the church. We would never place our children in danger. It is very troubling that the board would insinuate that we would place our children in harm's way. . . . Our being denied entrance will be a tremendous loss to the SCC. Even more tragic in 2001, racism continues to be alive and well both in society and inside the Church."

Lenzen suggested a possible solution. He noted that some years before, Annunciata, a predominantly Latino parish, had been admitted to the league with the proviso that no home games be played at the Annunciata gym for five years, since SCC members were concerned about "travel and safety" in the area. The parish agreed, and the prohibition was removed after three years. Perhaps, Lenzen said, Sabina could abide by a similar policy.[2] "No way!" Pfleger replied immediately. "It's an insult."

A few days later, while talking to *Sun-Times* writer Cathleen Falsani on an unrelated matter, he spoke about the SCC rejection and his response. She, in turn, produced a front-page story on May 31, headlined "Black school can't join sports league," and the lid on Pandora's box creaked open. "The tragedy of all this is having to tell the kids that the reason we're not going to be in this league now is because they were afraid of their children coming into our neighborhood," Pfleger was quoted in the story. "This is how we pass on the hurt of racism to generations and generations."[3] A photo of the Sabina basketball team accompanied Falsani's article.

†

THE STORY OF these black children who were rejected by white parents was an immediate media hit. It was reported, re-reported, expanded, distorted, and commented on in newspapers and on radio and television, especially cable talk shows, not just in the Chicago area but across the country. The *New York Times* published a major piece on the rejection, linking it to racial tensions elsewhere. "The controversy comes at a time when the Catholic Church finds itself increasingly confronting issues of race," said reporter Pam Belluck. "As the traditional white-ethnic membership of urban parishes leaves the inner cities, churches like St. Sabina have opened their pews and especially their classrooms to African Americans."[4]

Frequently mentioned in the coverage was Cardinal George's pastoral letter on race released on the anniversary of Dr. King's assassination, just six weeks before the rejection of St. Sabina. In clear language he condemned all expressions of racism, whether overt or subtly concealed. He urged Catholics to welcome African Americans into their communities, and he rebuked any priests, sisters, or laypersons who would turn away "even Catholic African Americans from their parish or school." Now, here awaiting the cardinal's return from a tour of Poland was a case in point.

Immediately following the *Sun-Times* article, the Chicago archdiocese issued a statement, implying that racism was at the root of the SCC
decision: "If the reason reported—fear by certain coaches and parishes for
the safety of their children—is the sole reason for the decision, it is not an
acceptable reason. Such a reason presupposes that all black neighborhoods
are intrinsically less safe than all white neighborhoods and that white parents and children have more reasons to fear for their safety in the black
community than black parents and children do in the white community."

Auxiliary Bishop Joseph Perry, who is black, called the league decision "terribly embarrassing and disconcerting. It's embarrassing that it has
surfaced amongst our own rank and file, the same people to whom the
[cardinal's pastoral] letter was addressed." He added, "It's symptomatic of
something that's an undercurrent in our society and in our city that has
been there for a long, long time." The director of the archdiocese's Office
for Racial Justice, Sister Anita Baird, said concerns about safety could well
be a cover for covert racism. "We have to be honest and we have to name
it," said Baird, who is also black. "We have been taught this from generation
to generation, and unfortunately, now it is going to be passed on to another
generation, this fear that is based solely on the color of another person."[5]

Cardinal George, upon his return from Poland, attempted a middle
position, which immediately backfired. "The desire to protect a child is evidence of a parent's love," he told reporters after mass at the cathedral and then
added, "I hope we might find a way to take care of safety concerns so we can
have interracial leagues."[6] His neutrality offended St. Sabina parishioners
who viewed him as siding with the SCC obstructionists, and it aggravated
those SCC parents and others who had opposed Sabina's entry and wanted
nothing to do with "interracial leagues" under any circumstances.

The views of the latter could be discerned from some two hundred
e-mails, letters, and telephone messages sent to the Sabina rectory just
days after the controversy became public. Here are several excerpts from
anonymous messages recorded on Pfleger's voice mail:

I'm calling about forcing these children, our children, to play with the
children of St. Sabina. I think it's inappropriate. You live where you

Michael Pfleger about age 5
with his mother Marion.

Courtesy St. Sabina Church

St. Sabina marchers protest at a convenience store in 1989 allegedly selling drug paraphernalia to minors and loose cigarettes. Courtesy St. Sabina Church

Mayor Richard Daley with Pfleger at the dedication of the new Hawthorn Park skating and bowling center, 2004. Courtesy St. Sabina Church

(below) Pastoral Assistant Vince Clark with Father Pfleger during the Billboard Wars, 1991.

Chicago Sun-Times

Father Pfleger (from left) with Deacon Len Richardson, Cardinal Francis George, and church leader Isaac Glover during the cardinal's visit to St. Sabina, 1998. Courtesy St. Sabina Church

(below) Easter Sunday at St. Sabina. Courtesy St. Sabina Church

Pfleger's father Louis with the pastor's sons, Beronti (left) and Lamar, circa 1996.

Courtesy St. Sabina Church

(below) Father Pfleger with Dr. Cornel West, who draws overflow crowds when he speaks at the church. Courtesy St. Sabina Church

Father Pfleger in full voice during a sermon at the 11:15. Credit Tonka Maljevic

The pastor pauses for a moment at his heavily laden desk. Courtesy of Jennifer McClory

Three parish leaders (from left): State Sen. Jacqui Collins; April Dumas, director of The Beloved Community; and Helen Dumas, principal of the St. Sabina Academy. Courtesy of Jennifer McClory

Staff members (from left) Randall Blakey, director of ministries; Lisa Ramsey, director of the Sabina Employment Resource Center; Vince Clark, assistant to the pastor; and Kimberly Lymore, associate minister. Courtesy of Jennifer McClory

(left) Church member rejoices during Pfleger's return to the parish, 2008. Credit Tonka Maljevic

(below left) St. Sabina cabinet members (from right) Randall Blakey, Gerald Stewart, Helen Dumas, Cinque Cullar, and Len Richardson arrive at archdiocesan headquarters to meet with Cardinal George after Pfleger's suspension in 2008. Credit *Chicago Sun-Times*

(below right) Father Pfleger and protesters outside Chuck's Gun Shop, May, 2007. Courtesy St. Sabina Church

St. Sabina marchers carry 32 improvised caskets, representing Chicago school children slain in 1998. Credit Tonka Maljevic

(above left) Flanked by School Superintendent Arne Duncan (far left) and the parents of two slain school students, Pfleger calls for stronger anti-gun legislation in Springfield, 2008. Credit Tonka Maljevic

(right) Father Pfleger being handcuffed and arrested at Chuck's Gun Shop, June, 2007. Credit Tonka Maljevic

(below) The American flag flies upside down outside St. Sabina Academy as a sign of "distress" at the ongoing, wanton killing of children, 2009. Credit Tonka Maljevic

St. Sabina choir, dancers, congregation, and pastor in the midst of Sunday worship. Courtesy St. Sabina Church live, and you live because we pay taxes. And these children or their parents or the neighborhood is not a good influence on our children, and it might be good for you to be around us, but it's not good for us to be around you or have our children subjected to this stuff.

Your children are around because they're the product of prostitutes, they're the product of illegitimate births, they're the product of crack mothers and everything else. Not all of you are like that, but a lot of you in that neighborhood are.

You wonder why we don't want to play ball with you. Well, think about it. You aren't really Catholic anyway. We have seen some of your services and the way you wave your hands in the air like a Baptist or something. You got a little white man who talks like a black man because, God knows, we can't teach you to talk properly. We don't need to put up with that. . . . So you need to stay where you are. You know we're already supporting you anyway on welfare.

Though the tone of Pfleger's letter to the SCC priests suggested that he was ready to throw in the towel on this one, he really was not—nor were Mallette, the parents of St. Sabina, or the children from the school. The leadership of the SCC too felt an obligation to find a solution, lest its twenty-one parishes be forever tarred with the brush of blatant racist exclusion. Reverend Lawrence Dowling, the chaplain of the conference and pastor of St. Denis parish, says, "We just had to bring this thing back to a vote again. The bottom line was we had to make it right." When letters and talks began between Sabina and SCC, Dowling says he urged impartiality on both sides. "I've always been a big supporter of Mike [Pfleger]. I'm the one who nominated him for the Pope John XXIII award [that he later received] from the Association of Chicago Priests," he states. But he also feared that Pfleger's reputation and insistent accusations of racism would harm the deliberations.

At one point Dowling met with Pfleger and told him there were three distinct problems to be confronted. The first was the fact that racism was unfortunately "alive and well" among some coaches, parents, and others in the SCC. The second was that many parents' concerns about safety in the Sabina neighborhood were sincere and not to be lightly dismissed. The third complicating problem, said Dowling, was Pfleger himself! "I told him, your name is out there. You're a flashpoint because of the stands you've taken." As the discussions proceeded, it exposed the deep-seated roots of the controversy.

On June 3, during a racial healing prayer service at Sunday mass, Pfleger spoke of the issues, asked for support, and assured the congregation that the dignity of St. Sabina's children would not be compromised. He, Coach Mallette, and Randall Blakey, director of ministries, would serve as the negotiating team. Two days later, the SCC pastors met with archdiocesan officials and agreed to urge their parishes to admit St. Sabina to the conference. But the pastors noted that some coaches were threatening to forfeit games rather than play at Sabina.

The Sabina leadership declared on June 10 that before any follow-up vote was attempted, three critical issues must be discussed: first, the need for a policy to ban unwarranted forfeitures; second, the need for a policy to address racial taunts and insults; and third, a standard for ensuring safety at all the schools. The SCC parishes then unanimously voted to approve St. Sabina but failed to talk about any of the three issues proposed for discussion.

After meeting with St. Sabina parents in early July, Mallette sent a letter to SCC leaders insisting that the three critical issues were "not negotiable" and must be addressed. The league must guarantee "in writing that all coaches will show up with their teams," said the letter. "Anything less is unacceptable. . . . If the conference cannot say that every coach will show up, we cannot in good conscience participate in the SCC."

In a letter to Mallette dated July 6, SCC chairman Lenzen, on behalf of all twenty-one parish members, wrote that they would no longer be dragged into a confrontational discussion with people who only wanted to talk about race and not the safety of their own area. He said the race issue was a St. Sabina priority but not a priority of the SCC. "Is everything we do involved with race? Must it always be race when things don't go your way?" said Lenzen. He called the demand for a written guarantee against forfeiture unreasonable. He told the *Sun-Times* he couldn't get written commitment from everyone and couldn't force compliance.

In fact, several SCC parishes (Queen of Martyrs, St. Cajetan) had made it known that they had no intention of pledging to participate in games at Sabina, and a coach at St. Catherine said he wouldn't take his team to Sabina under any circumstances. All cited safety concerns as the reason. Dowling called all the conference pastors and begged them to keep quiet or to at least not say anything "racist or stupid."

In mid-July, St. Sabina leaders replied in writing that it would withdraw from the league if the issues were not discussed; the SCC again replied that this position was unreasonable. St. Sabina announced its intention to withdraw two days later. In a dramatic, game-saving move the next day, Cardinal George entered the fray, saying the SCC was not free to arbitrarily forfeit games, and St. Sabina was not free to withdraw from the conference. George called all the pastors, including Pfleger, to meet at a South Side church and urged them to act like "brother priests." In a follow-up statement, he praised those SCC pastors who were struggling to break the deadlock and insisted the three critical issues proposed by Sabina were legitimate and must be addressed. This is more than a squabble over race, he said, "because now the unity of the church is at stake. . . . And so there are no unilateral moves here. St. Sabina can't withdraw, the others can't say, 'I won't play.' I think it's very unfortunate. We should keep in mind the goal—that we want the kids to play together."[7]

Meanwhile, leaflets citing misleading statistics on black-on-white crime rates were placed on the windshields of those attending Sunday mass at SCC parishes by a white supremacist group, the National Alliance, based in West Virginia.

In early August the Sabina contingent entered into direct negotiations with the conference leadership under the direction of the archdiocesan chancellor, Jimmy Lago. At one point, George talked via speakerphone with Mallette, Blakey, Pfleger, Lenzen, SCC chairman Mike Phelan, and Lago, all huddled in the same room. He made it clear he would brook no more delays. When the principals emerged at the end of the day, they had arrived at a consensus acceptance of the three issues. Detailed draft documents were drawn up the next day. A dispute quickly arose over a proposed requirement that parents of players as well as coaches sign non-forfeiture agreements, but it did not get included in the final document despite Sabina protests.

The SCC parishes quickly voted to approve the three policy issues along with the admission of St. Sabina to the conference. By then it was too late for Mallette to organize Sabina students for tackle football, the reason he had sought entry into the SCC in the first place. Sabina's premier season with the newly integrated conference would start with boys basketball in December. There were some conversations about building on what had been achieved, perhaps through racial sensitivity programs in the affected parishes, but conference chairman Phelan said discussions about race were not on his "front burner."

He told the *Sun-Times*, "If some other people want to pick up the ball and say, 'This is where we want to go, and we've identified some results we think we can achieve,' yeah, OK. But if we're just going to sit down and say, 'Why do you feel this way? Why do I feel this way?' I don't see anything constructive coming out of it."[8]

The next month brought the terrorist attacks of September 11, and the destruction of the World Trade Center towers. Racial sensitivity discussions were swept off the table.

†

WHEN THE BASKETBALL season began, everything seemed to be going surprisingly well—at first. Security at the games was adequate to assuage fears; there were no forfeits at Sabina; and some parishes went out of their way to welcome the newcomers to the league. One even threw a pizza party for the team. But as the Sabina team (nicknamed "the Saints") dominated opponents in many games, the mood shifted. Cardinal George did not help when he attended a game and good-naturedly told the Sabina team, "Don't beat my boys too bad." If the white kids were the cardinal's boys, the team wondered, then who were they? By mid-December, complaints about refereeing became more common, as were charges of rough play, especially throwing of elbows. Mallette told the Saints, "Keep moving. They can't hurt you if they can't catch you." There was little chatting or fraternization between parents and supporters from the rival schools. Black parents clustered on one side of the gym cheering for their kids while white parents huddled on the other side rooting on theirs. An angry woman approached Pfleger during a game at St. Germaine and accused him of being an anti-white racist. Later a group of adults accosted him in the parking lot, asking why he was bringing trouble into their peaceful community.

With teams jockeying for play-off positions after the Christmas break, the tension increased. At St. Bede the Venerable, after a game which was called "especially dirty" by Mallette, a Sabina player was confronted by a member of the St. Bede team who reportedly said in a loud voice, "Time to leave, nigger!" Mallette regarded it as a clear-cut case of racial harassment and filed a grievance with the SCC. The executive committee acknowledged that the charge was valid but said Sabina failed to positively identify the offender. The incident, in fact, had been videotaped, and Mallette claimed the culprit could be positively identified. After considerable argument, the SCC finally agreed that the ideal remedy would be a mandatory mediation session at a neutral site with the two boys involved and their parents present. Failure by the accused to show up, said the executive committee, would result in St. Bede being barred from the play-offs. On the appointed evening, the Sabina youth and parents appeared; the St. Bede boy and his parents did not, sending instead a letter denying guilt. As a result, St. Bede was ruled ineligible for the play-offs. (The St. Sabina student later sued the SCC and the archdiocese, seeking more than one hundred thousand dollars for alleged racial taunts and for being compelled to dress for games in cafeterias and kitchens. The suit was resolved in 2007 with an unspecified amount paid to the youth.)

Meanwhile, matters only got worse. The Sabina Saints, who were compiling the best records in the league, had been using an especially talented seventh grader on both the seventh- and eighth-grade teams, as was considered acceptable in Chicago grammar and high school competition. The rules allowed for a youth at a lower level to compete also on an upper level team but not vice versa. Mallette was informed by the SCC that this procedure would not be permitted in the play-offs. The seventh grader could only play on the seventh-grade team. Mallette vigorously pursued an appeal, asking how and when this new rule had been hatched and where he could find a copy. As it turned out, there was no rule; it was "an unwritten rule." But it was going to be enforced anyway.

That decision soon became moot when Mallette was presented with a play-off schedule that had the two Sabina teams playing at the same time in two different gyms. In addition, Sabina was scheduled for no home play-off games at all despite having the top season records at both grade levels.

Then came the final blow: Mallette learned in March on the eve of the play-offs that the SCC, without informing him, had reversed the penalty on St. Bede, and they would indeed be participating. Phelan, the conference chairman, explained that the executive board had "changed its mind" and decided banning the team would be "too steep" a penalty.[9]

It was, Mallette said, "too much." On March 7, 2002, Pfleger, Mallette, and Blakey met with the team members' parents and leaders of the Sabina community. They reviewed the events of the season, discussed the endless controversies, and asked for the will of the people. "It was a difficult and painful decision," said Pfleger. "Do we win a trophy or teach a lesson in self-respect? Which is greater?" The gathering opted for self-respect. In a five-page letter to the SCC listing their grievances, including the failure to adequately address a racial insult, they wrote, "We have unanimously decided that due to this issue and a myriad of other issues, which demonstrate a lack of equity and integrity, effective immediately we will no longer participate in South Side Conference activities and events."

The next afternoon in the school lunchroom, Mallette shared the news with the students. "We didn't quit anything," he said. "We're standing up for something." Some students were shocked, some deeply disappointed, some angry, some in full agreement. "But in the end," said Mallette, "I think they all understood some things are more important than winning games. This was a teaching moment, and I was never prouder of our parents and kids than I was that day."

Mallette continued as Sabina athletic director and coach for another three years. There were no more dealings with the SCC during that time, nor have there been any overtures for reconciliation since his departure in 2005. He took a post as director of community safety initiatives in the mayor's office. Mallette and his family also left the parish, seeking, he says, "another level of spirituality, not one that's greater, just different." They are currently members of New Life Covenant Church on the South Side. Working at Sabina was "a ten-year boot camp for me," he says, "and St. Sabina is still a home to me. I have absolutely nothing critical to say about Father Pfleger. His spiritual DNA is all over me."

Still, some irksome questions remain. Should Sabina have remained in the league regardless of its grievances? Did the heavy hand of Pfleger, especially in the beginning, doom the effort? If he had said less, stayed out of the negotiations, and let Mallette handle everything, would the strident SCC voices concerning safety have been calmed? Or, given the level of rancor among some residents of the South Side and south suburbs, and given the long history of racial fear and flight in this densely populated area, was this perhaps the wrong place and the wrong time and the wrong people for such an ambitious venture in integration?

Reverend Dowling, the former SCC chaplain, would have preferred that Sabina remain in the league and blamed Pfleger in part for their pullout. "Sure racism was in the mix, no question," he said. "But how do you deal with the problem when race is being screamed all the time?" If Mallette had held on and been empowered to call the shots, said Dowling, "I suspect he could have made it work. He's a man of great integrity." Yet Dowling admitted that in recent years, since becoming pastor of St. Agatha parish, which has a heavily African American population, he has more sympathy for Pfleger's dogged determination to defend and stand with his people. He cited an occasion when he brought the St. Agatha school choir to McCormick Place to sing at a citywide rally for immigration reform. The affair was "so horribly mismanaged," he said, that his choir never had a chance to perform. "I got them together afterward," said Dowling, "and I said, 'I will never allow you to be disrespected like this again. Never again!'" He was feeling, he said, that sense of solidarity with a minority community that has marked Pfleger's entire career.

Mallette, who insisted the decision to leave the league was correct, said Pfleger's vocal presence in the controversy was important and necessary. "Look, I was getting hate mail myself, and, as a young father, I was afraid someone was going to put a bullet in a kid's back. Pfleger stepped in, put himself in harm's way, let the hatred be heaped on him. That's what he does."

In the local and national media blitz that followed Sabina's departure, ABC News interviewed a number of people about the league story. Auxiliary Bishop Joseph Perry and several priests who were pastors of SCC parishes expressed disappointment that Sabina chose to back away. "I would have preferred that he [Pfleger] hung in there," said Perry. So also did Lenzen, who said Sabina seemed to ignore the progress that occurred during the season. "Are there racial problems out there? Absolutely," he said. "I'd be a fool to think there weren't. But I know for a fact that a lot of good things have been happening." A handful of students from Sabina and SCC schools were also interviewed. Johnny Moore, a member of the Sabina team, said it was more important to stand on principle. "The championship didn't mean anything to us," he said. But William Adams, a player for St. Denis, an SCC school, insisted, "They would have made a bigger statement if they had won the championship." And Isaac Glover, a Sabina seventh grader, said, "I was upset because I just wanted to play ball."[10]

9

IT TAKES A VILLAGE

I'M SO CLEAR THAT I'M SUPPOSED TO BE A SOCIAL WORKER
HERE IN THIS PLACE AT THIS TIME.

—Sharon Tillmon

Michael Pfleger is sometimes accused of functioning as a lone
wolf, and though there is some truth to the claim, it is largely
a misperception. It ignores what is perhaps Pfleger's strongest skill:
his ability to recruit capable people who are willing to take on serious
responsibilities, often at personal sacrifice, to hurl themselves into St.
Sabina ventures or ministries, and to hold to their commitment for the
long haul. In their own right, these are people who are contributing to
the transformation of the community or the empowering of the congregation or both. Some, like Pfleger's principal aide, Vince Clark, have
been mentioned repeatedly in earlier chapters. There are many others
who have invested much of themselves in the Faith Community of St.
Sabina and comprise in many ways Pastor Pfleger's extended family.

Jacqueline (Jacqui) Collins is one such church member. A warm,
engaging woman who looks years younger than the calendar indicates,
she served, at Pfleger's request, as the parish volunteer minister of com-

munications from the late 1980s through the late 1990s. This was a critical time for St. Sabina. Pfleger was urging the congregation to get politically involved, and it was also the time when the parish was gearing up for the first big campaigns—against drug paraphernalia, billboards, and the sale of liquor to minors. Collins had the contacts and credentials for the work ahead. She had experience as an editor at Citizen Community Newspapers, a South Side Chicago chain published by Gus Savage, where she got to know and work with Jesse Jackson, Harold Washington, and other black leaders. She had served as an editor at the Columbia Broadcasting System's Chicago radio station (WBBM) before moving to the CBS television outlet (Channel 2) in Chicago. With her personal knowledge of Chicago media, Collins proved invaluable as communications minister, getting Sabina events covered and Sabina news on television and in print. Those who wondered how Pfleger and company were always getting coverage did not know the quiet role of Jacqui Collins behind the scenes.

In 1999 she left CBS and her communication post at Sabina for new challenges, though at the time she did not know what they would be. She attended Harvard University, earning a degree in public administration from the Kennedy School of Government, and continued on toward a master's degree in theology from the Harvard Divinity School. One summer she worked as an intern in Senator Hillary Clinton's office in Washington, D.C. On her return to Chicago in 2002, Pfleger phoned Collins with a suggestion. Thanks to the most recent U.S. census, he said, the state legislative district in which St. Sabina was located had gained an additional seat in the Illinois senate. Pfleger thought she should run. Collins was stunned. "I said no, no, I want to push for Hillary Clinton as a presidential candidate." Pfleger said she should think it over, pray about it, and remember that Christians have a responsibility to make an impact where they are.

She prayed and called back with a hesitant yes, though she had never run for office and was reluctant to take on a life of campaigning. Pfleger assured her she would have the support of Sabina members and the backing of Terry Peterson's 17th Ward organization. She called Senator

Obama, who encouraged her but warned she might encounter jealousy from some veteran legislators. Collins won the senate seat in 2002 and again in 2006, garnering 97 percent of the vote in the latter election.

Collins expresses amazement at the turns her life has taken. She had been raised as a Catholic, but the assassination of Dr. King in 1968 left her so disappointed and disillusioned that she left the Catholic Church. It did not seem to offer her anything constructive or hopeful. Then in 1986 she walked into St. Sabina Church one Sunday, not expecting much, and was surprised at the vitality of the liturgy, the friendliness of the congregation, and the bust of Dr. King in the sanctuary. "My twenty-year sojourn [outside Catholicism] was over," she says. "I decided to give the church one more opportunity." Collins began attending Bible study sessions, "and I could feel myself moving from just going through ritual to entering a relationship with Christ." She had heard Catholic social teaching described as "one of the church's most closely guarded secrets," and here she came to see it being practiced in a concrete way.

"As a state senator, I see my mission as being a lobbyist for those who have no representation," says Collins. And a sample of the bills she has introduced (bills which embody the sort of social justice that Sabina stands for) indicates she's been on mission: legislation extending the statute of limitations for prosecution of sex crimes against children, a law preventing public utility companies from disconnecting elderly and poor customers during winter months, a resolution creating a commission to document race and gender discrimination in contracts for state projects, a divestment act seeking to end atrocities against citizens of Sudan, legislation to halt subprime lending and mortgage fraud, and a law to halt confiscatory payday loan practices. She has received numerous awards for her work in these areas. For the opportunity to make a difference, Collins says she is grateful to God and to Pfleger, whom she calls "my inspiration."

†

IN THE MID-1980S Jacqui Collins recommended St. Sabina to Randall Blakey. As a cameraman for CBS television in Chicago, Blakey had covered some of Pfleger's early clashes with storekeepers who sold drug paraphernalia. Like Collins, he had been raised a Catholic and attended Catholic school but had "gotten away from the church because I wasn't getting anything out of it." Still, Blakey retained a sense of spirituality and felt something was missing from his life. His first encounter with the mural of a black Jesus moved him so profoundly he returned to the church for good.

He got involved in developing ministries at the parish, with a special emphasis on assessing the spiritual gifts of church members in order to direct them to where they could be most effective. He eventually earned a master's degree in theological studies from McCormick Theological Seminary in Chicago and was hired in 2001 as overall director of ministries for St. Sabina. In his thesis for the master's degree, Blakey noted that Pfleger removed "the large white crucifix affixed to the center of the sanctuary upon which hung a 'dead white Savior.' Father Pfleger replaced what he believed to be a culturally based icon with a more relevant symbol of God's presence in the black community, a strong, handsome black man depicting Christ who is alive with outstretched hands. Pastor Pfleger believed that if black people could see themselves within God's plan this change would work as a tool for them to embrace Christ in a greater way."

Blakey's job is to stimulate, nurture, and develop all who minister at St. Sabina to see themselves "within God's plan." He has to rein in the overly enthusiastic and generous members who sign up for everything, because he knows from experience that a burnout will inevitably follow. "I suggest just one ministry per person," he says, "and more only if it's clear they can handle both duties faithfully." He calls for most ministers to take a sabbatical in August so they can come back refreshed for the fall. Fostering the ministries at Sabina, from ushers and greeters to Sunday school teachers and tutors, and from Bible study presenters to Spirit of David dancers can be very rewarding acknowledged Blakey, but "it can also be a roller coaster" for the coordinator. "We all carry a treasure, but we carry it in earthen vessels," he says.

Blakey, who is now in his mid-forties and has a wife, Sonya, and two young daughters, says his job sometimes seems overwhelming. But "the sovereign hand of God keeps me here and sustains me." In his work he tries to implement an insight that came to him in his studies. He notes that in the first and fourth chapters of St. John's Gospel, two people (Nathaniel and the woman at the well) are moved to place their trust in Jesus because they realize they are known already by Jesus. Something transformative happens, Blakey says, when "belief is not based on signs but on knowing that you are *known*." For him personally, this means getting to know each person he deals with in a serious way, not taking anyone for granted. Ultimately, his goal is to assist these members to the kind of deep relationship with Jesus that transforms them into priestly leaders in the community.

†

ANOTHER WHO SIMILARLY chose to take on a daunting responsibility is Helen Dumas, the principal of the St. Sabina Academy for the past seventeen years. Dumas and her husband Martin had been active in the church for some years when Pfleger urged her to apply for the position in 1992. She had worked for twenty-five years in the Chicago public school system as a teacher and assistant principal, and though the idea of heading the St. Sabina school appealed to her it would entail a forty-thousand-dollar cut in her yearly salary. She hesitated at first, and Pfleger told her to pray over her decision. But since she had embraced "the vision that God set before Father Pfleger," she did apply for the job and was selected. Asked what that "vision" meant to her, Dumas says without hesitation, "It's leading people to a life that mirrors that of Christ, a life of compassion, service, and seeking social justice."

Under Dumas's direction, the academy is one of the largest and most distinctive black Catholic schools in Chicago. Enrollment reached almost six hundred in the mid-2000s but suffered a decline due to the 2008–2009 economic recession. Tuition and other fees amounted to $3,800 per student per year in 2009–2010. About 40 percent of the students get some kind of assistance through scholarships and grants, says Dumas, but the academy does not ask for or accept subsidies from the archdiocese. The student body comes from near and far—40 percent are from outside the Auburn Gresham area, from communities represented by thirty different zip codes. A major requirement is that school families belong to a Christian church (though two students recently accepted are Muslim); 35 percent of the students are Roman Catholic.

The academy has received consistently high ratings on student progress each year from the archdiocese and the Illinois Board of Education. That is a noteworthy achievement, Dumas notes, since virtually all the public schools in the region are under probation due to poor student progress. To maintain quality, the academy works with a cohort of four schools to bring in experts on leadership development four times a year to work with teachers and staff. Counseling and workshops are provided for parents who are having problems. Graduates of the academy are regularly on honor rolls in high school, become members of the National Honor Society, and go on to good colleges.

Before she became principal, Dumas and Martin had been strong advocates of the tithing system at St. Sabina. "We always believed if you give 10 percent to the church, God will find a way," she says. In 1989 when the parish was determined to end its debt to the archdiocese, the Dumases cashed in a ten-thousand-dollar life insurance policy and gave the whole amount to the debt campaign. They then took out a one-hundred-thousand-dollar policy and began paying premiums on that. Less than two years later, Martin, then forty-one, was hit with a sudden heart attack and died. "So here I was," says Dumas, "a single parent with a son in college and a daughter in grammar school." But thanks to the new policy's payoff, she was more than able to make her way. And with her commitment to tithing intact, she gave ten thousand dollars of the payoff to St. Sabina, where it went for the new baptistery in the center of the church dedicated to the memory of Martin Dumas. When Pfleger approached her about the principal job, Dumas thought, "Oh God, where are you leading me?" But the Holy Spirit had been with her before, she says, and she knew she would find a way.

†

ONE WHO CARRIES the spirit of St. Sabina beyond the walls of the church is Isadore (Izzy) Glover. As a longtime member of the Sabina Brotherhood, a support group for men founded by Pfleger, Glover formed a new organization called Men of Action to address community issues in the 18th Ward, west of Auburn Gresham, where he lives. He is also directly involved in the North Beverly Organization, south and west of the Sabina neighborhood. "One of our goals in the Brotherhood is to take activism into the larger community," he says. "We have a lot of members here who don't live right around Sabina, so we encourage one another to get involved where they are too." The Brotherhood currently numbers some thirty Sabina men who meet monthly for prayer, discussion, and often to hear speakers of note. "We've had some great ones at our meetings," notes Glover: "Archbishop Tutu, Maya Angelou, Harry Belafonte."

Glover, now in his sixties, was born in Canton, Mississippi. Though his family was Protestant he was sent to a local Catholic school, where he met Sister Thea Bowman, a young teacher. "It was mind-boggling for us to see a nun who was black," says Glover. After coming to Chicago, he graduated from Loyola University with a degree in education and began teaching in the Chicago public school system. He later worked in the private sphere before taking a position with the Chicago Board of Education in the human resources department eleven years ago. Glover and his wife, Sandra, have three children and have been married forty years.

His experience interacting with other men in the Brotherhood has had a beneficial effect on Glover. "We establish bonds with one another and we support one another," he says. "Men have a way of keeping things inside themselves, not letting anything out. That's disastrous. Here, we open up." He cites his own headstrong tendencies as an example of how the Brotherhood has helped him grow. "When I was wrong, I always had trouble admitting it. Then one day after my wife and I settled a difference of opinion, Sandra told a friend, 'You know that Brotherhood has done Isadore a lot of good.'"

Glover found the services at St. Sabina "very refreshing" when he first came in 1993. He was impressed with Pfleger and the quality of his sermons. "I noticed two things right away: first, Father Pfleger does not do short sermons; second, he does not just try to make you feel good. He challenges you to read, to think about what you're doing, the way you're living." Glover was impressed too with the quality of worship at the church. "The choir doesn't sing, the musicians don't play, and the dancers don't dance—not the way choirs, musicians, and dancers *perform* at a lot of churches. The people here aren't performing or entertaining. The Spirit is in them. Sometimes, when the musicians start, I begin to tear up. The Spirit is in them, and it's in me." He attributes the authenticity of worship to Pfleger, whom he calls a "perfectionist." "He will not settle for pretty good; he will not compromise. And that comes across every Sunday. It affects us all."

†

EVERY MONTH, SHARON Tilllmon provides food for twenty-five hundred people, hands out about twenty thousand dollars in cash or checks, spends six hundred dollars for people's clothing needs, and finds housing for about twenty families. She isn't a wealthy philanthropist; she is the director of the St. Sabina–Catholic Charities Social Service Center, housed in a storefront office under a burgundy awning on 79th Street. It is one of the busiest such centers in the city, providing the basics of food, shelter, and clothing to needy citizens regardless of age, race, sex, or religious affiliation. The funding for all this comes from state, city, and federal funds, from St. Sabina parishioners, and from other private donors. The parish social service center had for some twenty-five years tried to aid seniors, single mothers, the unemployed, the chronically homeless, those in emergency situations, and others who tend to fall between the cracks of society; but the cracks grew bigger, and many more were slipping through. Fortunately, through a collaboration with Catholic Charities in 1998, the center's operation has been upgraded and expanded.

Still, says Tillmon, "We are stretched. This year [2009] has been the most difficult we're ever had." Hard times, especially job layoffs and home foreclosures, have hit a whole demographic of families and individuals who never before needed a safety net. "It's not just the physical needs they have," she says. "It's the psychological blow of not being self-sufficient." Asked if the center is sometimes taken advantage of by people who don't really need help, she says frankly, "Nothing is foolproof, but we are professionals here. We do assessments; we're not jut applying Band-Aids. We're hopefully sowing seeds in good soil."

Tillmon radiates an air of confidence and efficiency as she explains the details of the center's operation, and she seems absolutely delighted with the heavy job she has. "I'm so clear that I'm supposed to be a social worker here in this place at this time," she says. "This is where I'm called to be." Tillmon, now in her fifties, had worshipped in Pentecostal churches most of her life. But when she took on the responsibility of raising her two nieces, she sent them to the St. Sabina Academy because of its reputation. She soon became impressed with the worship experience at the Sabina Sunday service, which was similar in some ways to the Pentecostal style. But she came to see a difference too. "At Sabina, worship is blended with justice and activism. Our leader [Pfleger] gets his ideas across in a way I'd never heard before. Our purpose is to give of ourselves. It is what we hear at church and at Bible study, so we take our religion outside the church walls."

As director of the social service center she is able to live the gospel precepts on a full-time basis—to feed the hungry, clothe the naked, find shelter for the homeless—and she gets paid for doing it. "I believe our mission is to revitalize this community, but you have to meet human needs first. We are stretched sometimes, but when you are where you're supposed to be, it's not so difficult." Besides, "there's the example of Pastor Pfleger who motivates us all," she says. "He is often at the center, sweeping the floor, unloading the trucks, doing what needs to be done."

†

MORE THAN SEVENTEEN years ago Bill Hynes went to an 11:15 Sunday mass at St. Sabina because his friend Peggy Moss said he should. He didn't really want to go. He had pretty much given up on the Catholic Church. He had heard that Sabina masses lasted an unreasonable three hours or more; and besides, it was a black church, and Bill Hynes is white. He was also an alcoholic and a drug addict. But he didn't want to disappoint Peggy, so he went and sat in the middle aisle, up toward the front. "All I can say," Hynes recalls, "is that the experience was powerful, unique, special. It spoke to my heart. The Holy Spirit was there. I took the only money I had, ten dollars, and put it in the collection and never looked back."

Hynes was in his mid-twenties then, with little thought of career, marriage, or the future, and his life was dominated by his addictions. "Addiction is in my family," he says, "every male, my uncles and cousins, my dad, everyone, and it's been ruinous. I'm the only one who ever got out." He went to Alcoholics Anonymous, he went to college, and he continued to attend the 11:15 service. After a while, he started to think about the future, even marriage. "But I thought, it's gotta be a girl who goes to the 11:15," he says, "because that's what I was addicted to."

In time he met Karen Moses, an 11:15 regular, and they were married and had three children. Hynes, who is now a registered nurse, approached Pfleger about starting a recovery program, similar to AA but melded with the spirituality at St. Sabina. "You know, at our church, people are used to coming up to the altar and making a personal commitment," he says. Hynes became creator and director of Sabina's "Jesus the Next Step," a program that uses music and Gospel readings in addition to standard AA techniques, and holds weekly meetings in the rectory basement. In addition, he has organized and led recovery revivals about once a year for the past ten years. Pfleger preaches at these gatherings, and up to seven hundred people who are in some stage of recovery attend. Hynes and his own family remain faithful to Sunday mass, always the 11:15.

†

JULIE WELBORN WAS raised a Catholic and attended Sunday mass all her life, so she was accustomed to the relatively low-energy worship style at black Catholic parishes. Then in 1993 Welborn attended a black Catholic revival at Holy Name Cathedral in Chicago; the Reverend Michael Pfleger was preaching. "All of a sudden," she says, "I found myself standing up at the altar with both arms up in the air praising God! I was totally surprised. That wasn't me!" But it was who she would become in the next few years.

Pfleger drew her into a relationship with God she did not have before, she says. "He connected me, so I didn't need a middle man." She became an active member at St. Sabina. "There are so many ways here to develop relationships with God—through Scripture study, worship, social justice action, political involvement," she says.

Welborn went to the University of Illinois at Chicago, earning a master's degree in communications. After volunteering for many ministries at Sabina, she added another degree, a master's in divinity, at the Chicago Theological Union in 2002, and became a full-time staff member at the parish as youth minister. Then in 2006, with Pfleger's encouragement, she and her friend Denise Nicholes established the Perfect Peace Café and Bakery on 79th Street, less than two blocks from the church. As a high-quality sandwich, soup, bakery, and catering operation—everything homemade—Perfect Peace stands in stark contrast to the raggedy businesses and boarded-up shops that formerly lined the street. Welborn admits this venture is a gamble, but feels its symbolic value to the community alone is worth the risk. And besides, she clearly loves what she's doing.

As one who takes St. Sabina very seriously, she expresses concerns about some aspects of church life. "There's such a focus on justice and being in the streets," she says, "that I'm afraid we don't fully touch the needs of a lot of people who come here—the singles, married couples, and families." She also worries that the Sunday mass service is so weighted in favor of worship and Biblical teaching that the eucharistic prayers and communion can seem like an afterthought. "It's not that Pfleger neglects the Eucharist," says Welborn. "He talks about it in instruction classes and Bible study, and he does the eucharistic part of the service with care. But a lot of the folks who come here are drawn by the Bible preaching and teaching and may need a deeper understanding of the Eucharist."

Even for lifelong black Catholics like herself, St. Sabina demands some adjustment, in Welborn's opinion. "Father Pfleger is a type A personality with his hand on everything, and he's always on fire. So it's hard for parishioners and staff to match that level of energy and commitment." Nevertheless, she adds, "St. Sabina sets a table and creates an atmosphere that is accepting of everyone and makes it possible for people to fall in love with Christ."

†

LISA RAMSEY IS another high-energy achiever whom Pfleger has tapped for a demanding job. In 2005 Pfleger called and asked her to head the Employment Resource Center the church had organized with funding from city, state, and private sources. She agreed, becoming manager of the new facility two blocks from the church. With a staff of thirteen providing counseling, motivation, and recommendations, the center is especially busy during these times of economic recession, assisting more than three hundred job-seekers a month. Ramsey credits Sabina and God with setting her in a place where she's able to use one of her greatest gifts, "helping people see their God-given potential."

As an ambitious, energetic, single woman with management degrees from the Massachusetts Institute of Technology and Columbia University, Ramsey had pursued a marketing career with several large corporations and quickly climbed the ladder. While working in Boston, she left the Catholic Church for ten years, turning to a nondenominational church, which she found didn't meet her needs either. "I was restless, tired of being threatened with hellfire and brimstone," she says. "I wanted a home, a church that taught the Bible authentically." After she moved to Chicago, a coworker recommended St. Sabina to Ramsey. "I went one Sunday and sat in the front pew. And when the service started, I knew I was home." She reveled in Pfleger's "humble teaching and his application of the Bible to everyday life." She became an active Sabina volunteer.

At the same time, Ramsey was troubled about her career. Her job as a senior marketing manager entailed meeting with owners of smaller food companies and persuading them to sell their businesses to her larger firm. Since coming to Sabina she wondered if she was really offering value to the lives of these owners or manipulating them into entering contract agreements far more beneficial to her company than to the sellers. In 2003 Lisa Ramsey was summoned by top officials and told she was being laid off from her $140,000-a-year position. She recalls with a laugh that she threw her arms up in the air and shouted, "Thank you, Jesus!" Her reaction was certainly not what they expected. For her, it was the answer to a prayer that had been growing in her heart for some six years, "Lord, show me what to do!"

"I still wanted a six-figure salary," she says, but in the light of the gospel preached at Sabina, other things seemed more important. She saw her firing as an answer to that prayer. Then out of the blue came Pfleger's phone call. For Pfleger, the creation of the center has also been the answer to a prayer. "You can't expect a community to make any kind of a comeback if lots of folks are unemployed," he says. "It just won't work."

†

LEONARD LANGSTON NEVER expected to be running one of the most active Catholic community centers in Chicago when he graduated from Morehouse College in 2004 with a master's degree in public policy and administration. He had drifted from Catholicism in his teens and become a member of Trinity United Church of Christ. Then one Sunday he attended a mass at St. Sabina and left the church three hours later with one clear conviction: "I've got to get involved." He looked around and found the Ark, Sabina's busy youth center, to be a natural fit for a young adult volunteer like himself. He impressed those in charge, and to his surprise was offered the director's job at the Ark in 2007 at the age of twenty-four.

Langston's mild manner and teenage looks belie his role and responsibilities at one of St. Sabina's most important points of intersection with the Auburn Gresham community. Pfleger is determined to keep the center as a safe haven for young people from the storms of the outer world. On an average day during the school year, the Ark's programs, including mentoring, homework assistance, arts and crafts, karate training, and even flight simulation instruction serve over one hundred young people, while another one hundred will take part in basketball leagues, basketball tournaments, and open gym nights for self-directed games. The Ark also provides gym time and instruction for the St. Sabina Academy students. In the summer the Ark is especially busy, offering a summer camp and a Friday Night Live menu of dance instruction, arts and crafts, video games, and other activities, all designed to get youth six to eighteen off the streets on Friday evenings, which can be especially perilous.

Langston's laid-back approach suggests that this is no big deal. "It's an awesome job," he says. "I like it because I'm working with the future, and I have a chance to shape it positively." He was married in 2009, and his wife, Jennifer, is a doctor specializing in childhood kidney ailments. Besides serving as Ark director, Langston is one of the Sabina armor bearers.

†

KIMBERLY LYMORE CAUGHT the spirit of St. Sabina fairly early in the Pfleger era, and she has become a major figure in the congregation and a full-time associate minister at the church. She has been studying theology and ministry since her arrival, with a special interest in the relationship between worship and action for justice. Lymore is a trim, quiet-spoken, fashionably dressed woman. She drifted away from her Catholic roots in her earlier life, earned degrees in business and computer science, and worked for many years as a systems analyst for major Chicago firms like Baxter Labs and Amoco.

When she came to St. Sabina in 1983, "the gospel singing, the hymns, the contagious friendliness of the place" stirred her spirit, and she got involved in a big way. The congregation wasn't as large as it is now, she says, maybe three hundred at the main service. In those days, she recalls, Pfleger was still experimenting with the liturgy. "Some services had so much drama and activity," Lymore says, "that church members were calling him 'Cecil B. De Pfleger,' but he's somewhat toned down the dramatics since." During the next seventeen years, Lymore became a visible volunteer leader in the parish. She was a lector on Sunday, a member of the worship committee, technology expert and computer troubleshooter, bulletin editor, retreat organizer, and Bible study leader. Meanwhile, her interest in ministry and spirituality grew. She went on to get a master's degree in ministry from the Catholic Theological Union and later a doctorate in ministry from McCormick Theological Seminary. In 2003, Lymore accepted an offer to serve St. Sabina as associate minister, taking a thirty-thousand-dollar-a-year pay cut in the process.

As part of her work for the doctoral degree, she wrote a thesis about St. Sabina, using the typology of sociologists Carl Dudley and Sally Johnson, who described five different kinds of Christian churches: survivor, prophet, pillar, pilgrim, and servant. Clearly, wrote Lymore, St. Sabina qualifies as a "prophetic church," one that is "proactive," that has "a vision of God's coming reign," is "ready to risk whatever is necessary to follow God's will," and has "vigorous leaders who articulate the vision and are ready to withstand the inevitable abuse that comes with suggesting changes." For such a church to succeed, noted Lymore, church members must be mobilized for action by meaningful worship experiences, and that is precisely why Pfleger insists on emphasizing praise and worship for such long stretches of time during the Sunday service.

However, Lymore sees a problem. "With a congregation of roughly two thousand members," she wrote, "only about two to three hundred people participate in the social justice type events or corporate witness. . . . It is clear not all congregants make the connection between the worship experience and the Christian's social justice–oriented mission." Many parishes would be overjoyed if 10 to 15 percent of their members were regular participants in social justice action, but Lymore suggests that is not good enough for a prophetic place like St. Sabina. She proposed a number of reasons why more parishioners do not make the connection, despite the structure of the Sabina service and Pfleger's consistent addressing of justice issues. In her thesis, she addressed just one of the possible reasons, "a lack of understanding of how worship should move us to social justice."

She formed a focus group of church members and designed a three-week program in which they discussed why they came to St. Sabina and why they stay, and they reflected on their own life experiences. The meetings climaxed with attendance at a rally in downtown Chicago for parents and relatives of schoolchildren slain by gunfire in 2008. She hoped through the group participation, the members would come to better understand the worship-justice connection, but she had to conclude that the goal remains elusive. "The connection is not easily made by people. Even with the intense level of worship at St. Sabina . . . and the explicit attention to social justice issues . . . there are people who do not make the connection. . . . There are also people that do . . . participate in social justice activities but do not have a clear understanding of the connection."

But she saw definite benefits from the discussion and interaction within the focus group, and Lymore believes Sabina leaders need to provide more opportunities "for our congregants to engage in critical reflection on a topic, event, speaker, or the Sunday sermon and Bible study." At present, she wrote, "all of the adult formation venues entail someone standing in front of them delivering a 'message' in order to inform their thinking. . . . The African American community is rich in oral tradition. Adults need opportunities that allow them to share their stories, which can be very empowering." She sees critical reflection as an important next step in St. Sabina's ongoing education and empowerment of its people.

10

ADVISERS: FRIENDLY AND OTHERWISE

Father Pfleger is more like Jesus than the church—
not that the Catholic Church does not do good
things—but Father Pfleger goes into the highways
and byways.

—Louis Farrakhan

That Michael Pfleger's closest adviser and longtime mentor is Louis Farrakhan comes as a shock, often a turnoff, for many people. His unapologetic association with the outspoken leader of the Nation of Islam is one reason why Pfleger is routinely labeled a bigot or an America-hater by conservative commentators and hordes of bloggers. It's distressing to many to learn that Pfleger's number two adviser is Reverend Jeremiah Wright, the retired pastor of Trinity United Church of Christ and the minister whose fiery rhetoric stirred endless turmoil in the 2008 presidential campaign that led to Barack Obama's departure from that church. Pfleger, who has had both men speak at St. Sabina, does not hesitate to give his unqualified support to both.

"Louis Farrakhan is the most brilliant man I know. I've never been with him when he didn't make me think," Pfleger says. He lists Farrakhan's "integrity, his unwillingness to compromise, his consistency and honesty" among the qualities he most admires. Pfleger says he calls Farrakhan at least once a month, more often when he's wrestling with a tough decision, every day when a crisis is brewing. They have dinner at each other's homes, and Pfleger drives frequently to Farrakhan's farm in Michigan for more extended discussions. Their subjects are wide-ranging—the Bible, the Koran, war, race, politics, religion—"and I've gotten a full education on Islam," says Pfleger.

He denies that Farrakhan is a racist or bigot. "I've known him from the 1980s, and I've never heard a racist or offensive word. I've listened to his tapes and lectures, and I believe the man speaks the truth." When Farrakhan has spoken about Caucasians as "blue-eyed devils," says Pfleger, he's talking about those whites "who choose to be participants in the oppression of others" and are therefore "representatives of the devil, the source of all evil." Similarly, he contends, Farrakhan is not anti-Jewish but is justly critical of Israel's politics vis-à-vis the Palestinians in the same sense that former President Jimmy Carter has been critical. Besides, he adds, Farrakhan has greatly "toned down his rhetoric" and word choice in the past six years so that his views will not be taken so easily out of context.

Pfleger first met Farrakhan in the mid-1980s when he was invited to Farrakhan's residence for dinner along with other ministers in the black community, including Father Clements. Says Farrakhan, "I couldn't help but notice that Father Pfleger's spirit was so genuine. The beauty of that spirit, his commitment to justice and equity, was greater than that of many other pastors. I grew to love him and refer to him as my brother."

That Pfleger is white is of no consequence to Farrakhan, who chooses his words carefully. "His skin color is not an instrument of negativity," he says. "He is a fellow struggler for justice. In a way, Father Pfleger is more like Jesus than the Church—not that the Catholic Church does not do good things—but Father Pfleger goes into the highways and byways. He is more like the Master, an activist trying to heal the conditions that oppress people. I honor him as a disciple of Jesus Christ."

In their frequent visits, "we have shared many beautiful things," he says. "We discuss Scripture. We try to analyze the condition of blacks and whites in this world. We do not argue. We dwell on the nature of the Spirit of God as revealed by wise men all over the world." Farrakhan implies some change has occurred in his own approach and attitude, saying that there has been "a growth in our spirits, a lifting of the religious message from a nationalistic to a universal level." He quotes St. Paul's words in the New Testament, "Let that mind be in you that was in Jesus Christ where there is neither Jew nor Greek, slave nor free, male nor female," and he insists that "this spirit can transform racial division." When Pfleger was ordered to take a leave from St. Sabina in 2008, Farrakhan offered him a place to stay at his Chicago home or Michigan farm but emphasizes, "I have never encouraged any division between Father Pfleger and Cardinal George."

In 1993 when Farrakhan toured the country in an effort to soften his reputation as a hidebound bigot, Pfleger tried to assist him. In an op-ed piece in the *Chicago Sun-Times*, he castigated the media for its insensitivity. "As long as the editorial writers, reporters, and newscasters can continue to focus everything on Minister Farrakhan's relationship with the Jewish community, they can ignore and obscure every aspect of his gifts, talents, solutions, and ministry to the country. . . . I only pray that America will one day become free enough to listen to them."

Like Farrakhan, Pfleger's other first-line adviser, Jeremiah Wright, is a militant speaker who challenges African Americans to combat inequality and prejudice and whose fierce rhetoric can easily be misconstrued. He came to Trinity United Church of Christ in 1972 when it had fewer than one hundred members and built up the congregation to more than eight thousand by the time he retired in 2009. He and Pfleger met by chance in the early 1980s at Delores' Barber Shop on Ashland Avenue when Pfleger and his son Lamar stopped in while Wright was getting a haircut. "When I heard he was a Catholic priest and had a son, I thought, 'How can that be?'" says Wright.

Intrigued by this unorthodox Catholic clergyman, Wright decided to attend a Sunday mass at St. Sabina and was amazed at what he beheld; "The service was more revolutionary than mine was." He says he heard African drums leading in the entrance procession, saw a troupe of well-trained dancers, listened to an impressive choir singing a variety of traditional gospel hymns along with African music, and marveled at the congregation "up on their feet, shouting, clapping," praising the Lord. "It was wonderful," says Wright. "I thought if I tried some of those things at my church, they'd run me out of town on a rail." He began to "sneak over to Sabina" when he wasn't otherwise occupied, and he became "convinced of the authenticity of this white man's speech and style. I realized it wasn't fake. A black congregation can tell." Wright especially admires Pfleger's penchant for applying the gospel message to current events like war and politics. "He's willing to pull off the mask, pull off the scab. He deals with uncomfortable truths."

Pfleger had been intrigued by Wright's approach ever since he drove by his Trinity United Church of Christ and saw the sign on the lawn demanding "Stop Apartheid." It reminded him of Jerry Maloney's gutsy sign outside Precious Blood Church in the 1960s: "Stop the God Damned Bombing."

"Jeremiah is a true patriot who loves this country enough to criticize and challenge it," he says. "He's served the country [in the U.S. Navy]. He has been a guide and mentor to me." Pfleger says he particularly appreciates how Wright educates his congregation on global issues, including the situation in the Middle East and in countries in Africa and Latin America. Pfleger sees Wright as a prophetic voice and an accomplished practitioner of black liberation theology.

Wright says Pfleger has counseled him and his wife regarding problems in their marriage and has helped other members of his family. He considers Pfleger his pastor. Wright's youngest granddaughter is a student at St. Sabina Academy. The friendship between the two men became even more solidified after both were roundly castigated in the 2008 presidential race for the politically charged sermons they had delivered.

†

A THIRD PERSON Pfleger regards as an important adviser, Father Ed McLaughlin, has little in common with Farrakhan or Wright. He is a quiet-spoken, thoughtful Catholic priest, sixteen years older than Pfleger, who pastored a large suburban parish until his retirement. He has kept in touch with Pfleger since 1974, when Pfleger was a deacon at a parish in Glenview at which McLaughlin, then a seminary professor, occasionally said mass. Through telephone calls and occasional lunches, says Pfleger, "Ed tries to keep me in touch with reality." He means not only developments and rumors in the greater institutional Catholic Church but also maintaining a sense of balance in his zeal for justice.

"I've always admired Mike's leadership ability, his spectacular ideas, and the thoughtful way he operates," says McLaughlin. "His spirituality is effective in the parish. People feed off his vision and prayer life. I listen to him, support him, give him my slant on things, though he's not really an ecclesial guy, just barely Roman Catholic." McLaughlin is concerned that his friend, despite his gifts, is vulnerable to disappointment and anxious about the future, especially since he views Cardinal George as eager to remove him. "It's a tense situation," he says. "Mike needs Sabina and Sabina needs him. Face it, nobody is going to measure up to him. You can't clone Mike Pfleger."

In an effort at peacemaking, McLaughlin met with George in 2009 and presented the cardinal with a parable. When God was preparing to destroy all living things, he began, Noah simply obeyed God's command. Except for Noah, his relatives, and the creatures on the ark, the world was destroyed. When later God was about to destroy the cities of Sodom and Gomorrah, Abraham tried to negotiate with God but failed, and the cities were destroyed. But when God decided to destroy the Israelites, Moses said, "What are people going to think of you if you destroy your own chosen people?" This time God relented and Moses won. "So if you oust Pfleger," said McLaughlin, making his less-than-subtle point, "it will be taken as if you don't care about the black community!" George heard the message, says McLaughlin, then insisted he's not out to get Pfleger, just hoping to have a smooth transition when the time comes.

Another priest who has actively supported Pfleger, Father Bill Kenneally, is a retired pastor in the archdiocese, well known for his innovative tendencies and wry wit. He doesn't feel Pfleger gets anywhere near the support he deserves from his fellow priests. "I think there's a sort of resentment because he's not a team player, and he gets away with things.

It's the kind of jealousy toward anyone who stands out. I think Mike needs affirmation. He gets it in heavy doses from his parishioners. An artist may be selling his paintings very successfully, but it's not satisfying unless you're getting affirmation too from your peers, your fellow artists." Also, he notes, there once existed a sense of camaraderie among Chicago priests involved in what was known as "black work." They encouraged and mentored one another, he says, but that's just not operating as it once did.

And this lack of support extends to his own family. His two sons are at the far ends of the country, Lamar in Seattle, Washington, Beronti in Sarasota, Florida. Of his many cousins in the Chicago area, only two attended his father's funeral in 2008. The rest are basically estranged from him over the stands he has taken in the church and community. Shortly after he adopted Lamar, one cousin said to him, "I'm glad you did this, but why did you have to adopt a nigger?" For Pfleger, his family—indeed, his life—is St. Sabina.

Father Don Nevins, a Chicago pastor and seminary classmate of Pfleger, agrees that there exists a painful kind of estrangement between Pfleger and many priests. But he thinks it's partly Pfleger's fault since "he does his own thing and almost never comes to class meetings and anniversaries. So he sort of becomes his own worst enemy." Nevins was in charge of a 2009 evaluation of Pfleger's performance as pastor, a procedure that's done in all Chicago parishes every five or six years. Questionnaires were sent at random to some forty Sabina parishioners, to all staff members (including Pfleger), and to ten designated parish leaders. The results are not made public, but Nevins says on a scale of one to seven (with seven indicating extreme satisfaction), Pfleger consistently got upper sixes and sevens. In fact, says Nevins, he was rated higher by the people than he rated himself. "A main concern of church members was that he wasn't taking enough care of himself," Nevins says. "I recommended that he get another term. I can see no reason to take him out."

†

CATHLEEN FALSANI, WHO covered Pfleger for the *Chicago Sun-Times* for ten years and who probably knows him better than any other newsperson, calls him "as complicated and maddening, wonderfully faithful, loyal, and generous of spirit as anyone I have ever known." She acknowledges that she has had her differences with Pfleger yet sees him as "a man of God who most of the time makes the right choices." She disputes critics who accuse him of being a publicity seeker reveling in the spotlight. "Yes, he's in the spotlight," she says, "but it's always to put attention on an issue, not to build his own ego." Nor has Pfleger, as a prophetic leader, sought to build a fiefdom, says Falsani; rather, he has supported his church members, especially women, in developing their talents and assuming responsibilities as far as is possible within current Catholic regulations. In being at times "abrasive, shrill, hot-headed, and egotistical," Pfleger displays the characteristics of a dynamic leader, in Falsani's view. In some ways, she says, he is in the mold of the African American pastor—exercising a kind of "paternalistic headship," and it is something his congregation has come to respect.

Falsani, who now lives in California with her husband and ten-year-old son Vasco, whom they adopted from Malawi, recalled two instances when Pfleger reached out to her. Six years ago when she was notified in the middle of the night that her aunt was dying, she called him, and he prayed with her on the phone for an extended time. Then in 2009 when Vasco was in the hospital about to undergo heart surgery, Pfleger arrived unexpectedly, comforted her and her husband, and counseled them about the importance of letting the child make the ultimate decision about adoption. His advice, she says, was for them "transformational."

†

CERTAINLY, ST. SABINA under Pastor Pfleger is not without its critics and its dropouts. Some who were initially caught up in the spirit and activity, who attended mass and Bible study, who labored in various ministries, who marched and marched, eventually burned out. Others have found the length or the dramatics or the decibel level of the Sunday service overwhelming and depart to churches where the service is quieter and shorter. And there are some too who find fault with basic elements in the Pfleger approach or in Pfleger himself and finally go their own way.

One who was candid enough to talk about his experience is Virgil Jones, a man now in his late forties who for a time was about as close to Pfleger as anyone has been. Jones came to St. Sabina in 1986 after deciding to leave the major seminary just two years before his ordination as a priest. He quickly became a committed volunteer in the myriad activities in and around the church. "My allegiance to Mike Pfleger's vision was total," he says. "I gave it my all." He became an active participant in the sting operation that used high school students to ferret out storekeepers selling liquor to underage teens. He was involved in religious education in the school, assisted in sacramental preparation for children and adults, attended Bible study, marched against gangs and drugs, worked with young people, and helped win the eventual battle over billboards. In 1993 when Pfleger hired him as full-time associate pastor, his dedication to Sabina only increased. For practical purposes, Virgil Jones was second in command under Pfleger.

Then about 1988, Jones says, "my work began to feel not like ministry; it began to feel like work. It wasn't as rewarding anymore." Questions and doubts undermined his dedication. "Are we overusing the media?" he wondered. "Why do we have to let them know every time we do something? Why can't we just do it?" He also became concerned about the quality of education at Sabina Academy, fearing that the school, as its enrollment soared, would descend from superior "to mediocre at best." Pfleger, he thought, was determined to admit as many children as possible without at the same time increasing the quality and number of teachers and staff. Jones says he saw too a shift in ministry. "We were fighting against things I didn't agree with," he says. He had reservations, for example, about the pastor's decision to fly to California to attend a press conference regarding the Jerry Springer show. He thought some of Pfleger's sermons were "overly repetitive and sometimes more about politics than the word of God. My allegiance to his vision waned."

Personally, Jones says, he didn't feel he was being ministered to. "I had potential, but I wasn't being developed as a leader." The reason for that, it seemed to him, was Pfleger's "way of doing things alone, his patriarchal style," not letting his closest associates in on decision making. "My circle of influence was small. . . . I was just spinning my wheels. I felt he needed people to hold him accountable."

Jones got a call from a search firm and realized there might be more opportunity for him beyond St. Sabina. When he spoke to Pfleger about leaving, he says, "our relationship changed. I think he felt I was betraying him, and I didn't want that." He left in 2000 to become director of LINK Unlimited, an organization that helps minority youth get into good colleges. Jones, like Chris Mallette and others who have departed from St. Sabina, denies that his differences with Pfleger negate the things Pfleger has accomplished and the tremendous good he has done over the years. "We really love this man," he says. "I'm a better person for the influence he's had in my life."

Bob McCoy, a church member for more than forty years, has disagreed with Pfleger on a number of issues, including worship style, and he even considered leaving the parish several times. "I prayed over it, and every time something would happen that made me stay," he says. "So here I am." He knows others who have left for a variety of reasons, some seeking a quiet church, some seeking even more ebullient worship. "We're not tied down to one institutional style here," he says. "Worship should be a free experience assisting your relationship with Christ." McCoy himself attends the more subdued and somewhat shorter Sunday service at 8:30 A.M.

Pfleger admits a parting of the ways occurs with some regularity at Sabina, and he regards that as understandable. "Don't come to church for me," he has said more than once in a sermon, "because I will let you down. But he [Jesus] will never let you down." He likens different churches, even different denominations, to automobiles. "The make or model of the car is unimportant. The question is, will it take you where you need to go, to Jesus? My concern is that people are being fed. If it's not happening here for someone, then they need to go where it will happen, with my blessing."

†

BEYOND THE BORDERS of St. Sabina, there are literally thousands who detest, resent, loathe, abhor, despise, execrate, and hate Reverend Michael

L. Pfleger. Their commentaries and pronouncements on him are easily found all over the Internet, which, like the universe, seems to go on
without end forever. His media visibility as a white Catholic priest in a
black church, one who seems to welcome conflict, who bypasses civil laws
and the regulations of his own church, who sides with dangerous and
unworthy people, and who tries to justify his stands on the basis of our
own American Christian faith, makes him a prime target for critique and
condemnation.

He is a heretic, say the bloggers. He hates white people—his own
white people. He hates America—his own country. He supports baby-
killers. He hangs around with dangerous persons. He lures simple folks
into his lair and mesmerizes them with unintelligible shouting, planting
thoughts of antiwhite revenge in their minds. He is a renegade, a rebel,
and a recalcitrant. He must be excommunicated, silenced, driven out of
the village; Michael Pfleger is not like the rest of us.

It is possible to go through these critiques for hours without finding
a single qualification, a single mitigating factor, or even a suggestion that
the writer could be wrong. And in the search it is almost impossible to
encounter anyone who claims to have met him, heard him speak in person, visited his church, or read anything he has written. The information
all comes from the other Web sites, televised video clips (mostly on Fox),
or, more recently, YouTube.

But there are a few whose knowledge of the man goes deeper. One
of these is Tom Roeser, a retired executive who remains a tireless writer,
blogger, radio host, television commentator, and chairman of the board
of a Chicago Internet daily newspaper. His interests are politics, about
which he is unreservedly Republican and conservative in his views, and
the Catholic Church, about which he is stridently orthodox (calling himself an "authenticist"). It would be a mistake to lump him in with the
know-nothings who clog the Internet highway with their ravings. He
does his homework, he means what he says, and his views are widely circulated. And that is why the Roeser take on Sabina is alarming. No one
has dogged Pfleger during his career with more indignation and complaint than he. Asked to sum up his impressions of the situation at St.

Sabina over the past twenty years, he declined. But since Pfleger's name gets into his blog almost as regularly as it appears in the Chicago (and national) media, it is possible to garner his views.

Roeser has long held that the Archdiocese of Chicago should have removed Pfleger from his parish years ago because he "has been a main cog in the exceptionally viable black wing of the Cook County Democratic machine, a figure whose personal endorsements of candidates has been adjudged worth many hundred thousands of black votes." In fact, he declares, St. Sabina is "a wholly owned subsidiary" of the Chicago Democratic organization. "Only when Pfleger becomes a 'persona non grata' with the Democratic Party that pulls the ecclesial strings will the archdiocese be forced to do what it has not had the courage to do heretofore—subdue him."[1]

There is no question Pfleger has used his relationship with elected local and state Democratic politicians, including Terry Peterson when he was alderman in the 17th Ward, Barack Obama when he was state senator for the district that covered Auburn Gresham, and Mayor Daley to get the senior high-rise buildings, the employment resource center, the social service center, and the other facilities that have literally turned around the immediate Sabina neighborhood. Pfleger admits he lobbied for these changes, using the same arguments and rationale that are available to any pastor, minister, or community leader in any governmental entity in the country. It is the historic, unseemly tight connection between the Catholic Church and the City of Chicago political machine that enrages Roeser. Corruption through bribes and paybacks has bedeviled city business for generations, but there is no evidence that the Sabina-backed projects involved any illegality or behind-the-scenes deals.

It was Roeser's firm hope that when Pfleger went over the top in his 2008 put-down of Hillary Clinton at Trinity he would be "stripped of his pastorate and do what he has threatened to do in the past—start his own church [where] he would attract no more attention than the usual down-and-out leather-lunged Elmer Gantry storefront preacher he resembles." Within ten days of Pfleger's mishap, Roeser put out two lengthy columns arguing for the pastor's dismissal. Pfleger, he said, "should be unhorsed, decommissioned, defrocked, laicized, and sent out to pasture." But he had doubts that "the flaccid, equivocating archdiocese . . . [would] muster the will to exert the discipline . . . just as it failed to halt latent pedophilia and active homosexuality in the seminaries." His hope proved in vain—Pfleger returned to his pastoral duties after two weeks.

Roeser's bigger and longer-standing beef is Pfleger's "serious theological impropriety and flagrant disobedience." He has actually attended a mass or two at St. Sabina and informs his readers that the masses are "liturgical nightmares and bear little resemblance to what was intended as a divinely ordained means of applying the merits of Calvary" to the faithful. "It is a good question whether the 'masses' at Sabina's are valid. More likely they are not and the Catholic congregants are being misled as to their efficacy."

Then, revealing his extreme cultural bias and gross insensitivity as he often does, Roeser writes, "For the mass that is polluted with railing and shouting anent race hatred and partisan Democratic politics . . . sets its heavily non-observant, secular attendees huzza'ing and bouncing off the walls in orgies of primitive emotion against whitey that is a sacrilege."[2]

In a final salvo, Roeser gives his recommendations on what must happen when Pfleger, whom he likened to "a Frankenstein monster," does finally depart: "A new pastor of any race should come and be prepared to see wholesale defections from St. Sabina, but these defections would be either largely non-Catholic interlopers who savor stentorian shouting rallies instead of mass or nominal Catholics who don't understand the significance of the mass." Returning the parish to its original status of church rather than "raucous meeting hall" is essential, he says.[3]

Jim Bowman, a former newspaper religion reporter who attended a mass at St. Sabina in 2003 when Al Sharpton was present, proved less disparaging than Roeser in his own blog but could find nothing of substance in the service itself. "The people embrace a virtually nonsensical worship service," he writes, "full of loud music and emotive display. Joy reigns, though a dance and choral presentation at the end featured maybe twenty black-clad young people and a white-clad dancer in a 'slave song' performance whose whole purpose was to raise for loving embrace the memory of being a slave or of holding up under the dreadful experience. It was a daunting, depressing show that apparently met deep yearnings of the congregation, which apparently wants to be reminded of and dwell upon the horrors of old. . . . The preaching was by slogan, often shouted. No argument need apply here, just repetition of things already well digested by the audience, which was overjoyed to hear them for the umpteenth time and responded regularly with single right hand raised in air, two hands clapping, swinging, swaying and/or shouting assent."

On the other hand, Bowman was impressed by the externals that he could understand, from the "excellent shape" of the church, "down to the cushioned pews and center-of-nave glorious baptismal font." He also took note of outside externals like the senior citizens residence and parish-sponsored Catholic Charities office. Despite Pfleger's "flouting of church law and regulations" and "his brazen embrace of his community's prejudices," he gave Pfleger credit for running a "going operation that packs them in on Sunday and pays its own way."[4]

Pfleger usually takes about as much notice of bloggers as he does of the letter writers who attempt to skewer him by mail. He was, however, surprised by an elaborate and lengthy analysis of the Sabina service by a British-based Internet organization called Ship of Fools, which sends unidentified "mystery worshippers" to Christian congregations around the world to assess the quality of weekend worship. Their lengthy reviews are often critical, even sarcastic. The mystery worshipper who was present at St. Sabina October 19, 2008, was literally overwhelmed by what he beheld. "To describe the worship as high energy is an understatement," the worshipper writes. "It was like I've never experienced before: liturgical Catholic meets black Pentecostal—on steroids: heartfelt and extempore prayers without any waffle . . . people appeared happy the whole time . . . quite simply the best sermon I have heard for a few years . . . people serious about their faith and its impact on the world around them. . . . The whole three-hour experience was as near to heaven as I could imagine. The music was spine-tingling, the sermon was rousing and totally applicable to the daily struggles of the hearers."[5]

In this case, Pfleger took notice. Copies of the mystery blogger's analysis were made available for interested church members.

II

THE THEOLOGY OF ST. SABINA

<hr>

THE BIBLE IS THE MOST SOCIAL ACTION BOOK EVER WRITTEN.
—MICHAEL PFLEGER

XCEPT FOR A two-week vacation in Hawaii every year, Pastor Pfleger does not take a day off and never has since he came to St. Sabina. He gets up every morning between 5:30 and 6:00 and begins with an hour of reflection and study after greeting God as "Abba" or "Daddy." "I try to have an intimate relationship with God," he says. "He knows me, he knows me by name, he knew me in my mother's womb." If there's something weighing on his heart, and there often is, he will talk to his Father about it, hoping for some advice or consolation. Other times he will read Scripture, especially the psalms in the Old Testament, or some of the writings of Martin Luther King.

Early in the week he will begin mulling over sermon ideas for the following Sunday. He may listen to some tapes of Dr. King or Jeremiah Wright or Louis Farrakhan, trying to capture the energy and passion of their preaching. It's the same passion he was first touched by at the Hopewell storefront church on the West Side when he was a seminarian. He has always found white preaching too cerebral and distant from the rousing, action-oriented, sometimes in-your-face preaching of the black church. Pfleger often reads material from *How Shall They Preach* by Dr. Gardner Taylor, considered the dean of black teaching, or he will reread a chapter from *Black Preaching: The Recovery of a Powerful Art* by Henry Mitchell, another acclaimed teacher. Other sources he may use are the writings of John McKenzie, a Jesuit priest and biblical scholar who opened the minds of many Catholics to the riches of the Bible in the 1960s and 1970s; James Cone, the chief architect of black liberation theology; or Sister Thea Bowman, a poet unafraid to condemn racism in the Catholic Church. He studies the Scripture readings for the coming Sunday, considers the major news events of the day, and begins jotting down notes.

By Thursday he's ready to sit down for two hours and write out the sermon by hand. He says he aims for a thirty-five-minute talk but it usually comes closer to fifty. And when you consider the amount of spontaneous material he throws in, the clapping and commenting of the congregation, and the number of orders he gives to the people in the pews: "Turn to your neighbor and say, 'Neighbor, God is love!'" a Pfleger sermon can run as long as ninety minutes.

If Pfleger has not mastered the art of black preaching, he has come close to it, as veteran preachers visiting St. Sabina often acknowledge. Black preaching relies on a wide variety of techniques, including repetition, parallel word structures, vivid and earthy imagery, metaphors related to life experiences, an abundance of slang expressions, and paragraphs that end with a kind of climax. It can soar, becoming lyrical, even poetic, and it can arouse in a congregation emotions ranging from intense sadness to near ecstatic jubilation.

Here is Pfleger speaking to a church full of teenagers, their parents, and relatives at an eighth-grade graduation mass:

Let me tell you something. You can't live casual; you have to live determined! You can't just go with the flow 'cuz the flow can take you out and drown you in the ocean. You can't just ride with the current 'cuz the current is going in the path of destruction. We can't afford to just hang because if we hang, the devil will hang us. You're

gonna follow some plan—either God's or the devil's. There ain't no
in between!

And a little later in the talk:

Don't help an unjust society by giving them cause to reject you. Don't
help an unjust society by getting poor grades or dropping out of
school. The devil will try to dress you in wrong thinking, that it's not
cool to get good grades. The world will try to dress you in the clothing
of wrong behavior, tell you something's wrong with you if you aren't
sexually active. Sex doesn't prove you're a man; sex doesn't make you a
man. The dogs, the birds, the squirrels, the cats, they all have wild sex.
Sex will prove you're some poor fool who can't control his own body!

The sermons reveal not only technique, they open up aspects of
four foundation stones that are firmly embedded in St. Sabina teaching.
Though none is expressly Catholic, they all have a degree of compatibility
with Catholic teaching, and all have characteristics that tend to overlap
with those of the other stones.

†

THE FIRST IS his deep belief in activism grounded in faith and supported
by robust praise and worship of God. Nothing, absolutely nothing, is
more important to Pastor Pfleger than social activism. It is at the heart
of his ministry, and it's what he prays and preaches about. He took the
opportunity at a talk to a gathering of Protestant seminarians to tear into
"comfortable" Christianity. "A major purpose of the Church is to create
leaders," he said, "the kind of people who will lean on the Lord like the
apostle John leaned his head on Jesus' breast at the Last Supper. And he
heard the heart of Jesus, the heart of God, who looks for the lost and
abandoned. The Church needs prophetic leaders who care about what
God cares about." He spoke about pastors who "are the biggest failures
in the world" because "they pimp their community, preaching a prosperity gospel, while outside a great crowd is waiting for justice." He cited the

comment of the singer Bono, who said of his worldwide relief efforts, "I'm doing what the Church doesn't do anymore."

"The Church is either a moral voice to the world or it's an immoral voice," said Pfleger. "We're called to change the world. We have to see this in a world plagued by starvation, murder, genocide. Our responsibility at St. Sabina is right here in this [geographical] area. If the Church is for us just huddle time, then we are a mockery."

Later, Pfleger expanded on his frustration over churches that dismiss activism. "People like to separate justice issues from church issues. They say, 'Why all this social action stuff?' I say, no, no, what I do isn't just social action stuff. I do biblical stuff. The Bible is the most social action book ever written. If I preach the Bible, I preach a God who is a God of justice. People want to cut away from justice, cut away from politics. So the Church becomes a business." Pfleger argues that the Church in some sense is a business but with a big difference from normal business where the customer is always right. "Our aim is not to please the customer but to please the owner, God!" he says. "If we don't realize that, the Church becomes an idol, and we're all idol worshippers!"

The connection between religion and activism is a major reason people are attracted to St. Sabina and a major reason why many stay. Terrence Marshall Haley, who heard newsman Harry Porterfield talking about the church on television one day in 1986, attended a Sunday service at St. Sabina and clearly remembers his first Sabina action: participating in a protest march outside a Borg-Warner plant, urging their divestment from the racist regime in South Africa. "I thought these Sabina people were really into something," he says. "I'd never understood before how this was related to religion, how the love of God is best manifested in doing what Jesus did. St. Sabina is my home because it's here that I committed to the Lord." Haley, an administrative clerk for Blue Cross–Blue Shield, has been marching ever since, and his thirst for activism has made him an infectiously enthusiastic volunteer in other venues as well: Sunday school teacher, armor bearer, election judge, poll watcher, church greeter. Haley says he is not an exception. "Oh yeah, I've seen how getting active changes people," he says.

Pfleger's direct, take-no-prisoners dedication to social and political action has its roots in a mélange of sources, beginning with Dr. King's life and writings. It comes too from his own Church, which has been beating the drum of Catholic social teaching for well over a century through a series of papal encyclicals. The most recent, by Pope Benedict XVI, urges Christians to engage directly in political and social issues, adding, "Awareness of God's undying love sustains us in our laborious and stimulating work for justice . . . amid successes and failures, in the ceaseless pursuit of a just ordering of human affairs."[1]

Between 1950 and 1970, the Chicago Church became a generator of social action theory and practice, largely through the charismatic vision of Monsignor Reynold Hillenbrand, rector of the major seminary at Mundelein. A generation of activist priests, including Jack Egan, Dan Cantwell, and Martin Farrell, and activist laity, including Pat and Patty Crowley, brought the Church into engagement with major urban issues like poverty, segregation, and racism. Egan, who openly supported Pfleger's work, died in 2001, but that period clearly had an effect on Pfleger and other Catholic activists.

In a noteworthy speech he gave at the Union League Club in Chicago in 2006, Pfleger defended his (and the Church's) participation in political matters:

> There are those who think religion and politics should not even be in the same building, let alone the same room. There are certainly those who think they should be in the same bed—lovers that mutually seduce each other when it is for their personal convenience or ideology. Then there are some who think they can be at the same restaurant but should be seated at separate tables. But I believe that politics and religion should not only be in the same restaurant, but they should be seated at the same table—each being true to self; each holding its individual integrity and each authentic to its very different purpose and calling. . . .
>
> Yes, I believe religion must always be at the table even if that means pulling up a chair and sitting down when we are not invited.

But it also means not apologizing for our presence—not sitting as a silent partner—or not compromising our religious principles, and like the Apostle Paul says, whether convenient or inconvenient.

He discussed how religion had been misused by governmental entities to justify the Holocaust and slavery and the apartheid system in South Africa, and how it had been used to endorse and crown candidates as though they were anointed by God himself. "But there have been many times," he said, "when the exchange between politics and religion has created healthy conversations and transformative action. Chicago has presented a model for this." He spoke of cooperating with Mayor Daley in halting the sale of liquor to minors and working with members of the city council in finally obtaining a ban on billboards advertising cigarettes and liquor. "On Wednesday I stood with [Daley] at a press conference, committed to lobby with him in Springfield for a higher minimum wage," he said. "When I speak of the rebirth of Auburn Gresham, I always say it could not have happened without the commitment of the mayor. But we, as religious leaders, must remain both free and independent. I believe Dr. King gave us a good blueprint for the relationship between religion and politics. Sometimes it meant going to jail for protesting unjust political laws and sometimes it was sitting in the offices of presidents, governors, and mayors, negotiating just laws." It seemed like sound advice, but Pfleger would learn two years later how precarious maintaining a balance can be.

†

THE SECOND FOUNDATION stone at St. Sabina is liberation theology, a school of thought within Christianity that emphasizes the obligation of the Church to relieve the oppression of the poor, especially through political action. Beginning in the 1960s, it laid deep roots in Latin America, spreading through small faith communities whose members studied the Bible as the story of God working to free his people from bondage. Jesus is viewed as the ultimate liberator, not only from sin and death but from the social or governmental oppression of the vulnerable. The Church must exercise "a preferential option for the poor," insisted theologians like Jon Sobrino in El Salvador and Ernesto Cardenal in Nicaragua.

But since a major theme of liberation theology is conflict, Catholic officials in Rome have attempted to stifle it, charging that it overdoes themes of victimization, arouses antagonism rather than cooperation, and is infected with Marxist influences. The ban, however, has not been completely successful.

A variation on the school, called black liberation theology, was developed in the United States by James Cone in the 1960s using the same basic themes but focusing on the liberation of African Americans from oppression by white persons and institutions. It too has become controversial for the same reasons that were proposed against the Latin American model.

Pfleger, however, believes black liberation theology is making a valuable contribution to the Church because "it challenges believers to change their lives right now." Too much of the time, he says, the Church is talking about heaven while people are saying they're hungry here on earth. Dr. King was surely an early liberation theologian, he insists, and so was Dorothy Day, founder of the Catholic Worker Movement. And so was Bishop Oscar Romero, who was assassinated in El Salvador while saying mass because he supported the peasants against the country's wealthy landowners. That Church leaders have not encouraged a commitment to liberation theology Pfleger regards as "pathetic and cowardly." Nevertheless, black liberation theology is alive and well at St. Sabina.

James Henry Harris, a Baptist pastor in Norfolk, Virginia, and author of *Pastoral Theology*, has set out some basic ingredients of the practice of liberation in a black parish.

"Black folk," he writes, "expect the preacher to reassure them of God's power, not to question or doubt it. They expect the pastor to help them cope with joblessness, poverty and discrimination by transforming their despair into hope." These members of the Church must be encouraged to "actively participate in human liberation," including their own. The Church must "begin the process of nurturing our neglected communities back to health. In order for the black community to become a viable place for external investment, blacks will first have to invest in themselves."

The black churchgoers will in part invest in themselves by understanding "that tithing . . . significantly affects the liberation of black folk. A tithing church will be able to influence public policy issues such as housing for the poor and equal employment opportunities."

Black churches should employ "gospel music, youth choirs, innovative worship settings, and the use of other musical instruments in worship" rather than just "piano and organ." In this way, "Black theology should remind Christians of the reality of their heritage and help them become proud of the struggles that their parents and forebears endured. . . . All should acknowledge this aspect of the black experience in America."[2]

Harris was not writing about St. Sabina, but it might as well have been his model, since it incorporates these components in an extraordinary way. However, the tendency of the liberation approach to repeatedly recall the history of past oppression and to identify the victims and victimizers of the modern world leaves it open to criticism and distortion. Often, strong words can be taken out of context and repeated over and over on television shows or made instantly available to millions via Web sites like YouTube.

Pfleger acknowledged that snippets from his Sunday sermons at St. Sabina could lend themselves to misuse in this way. For example, on the Sunday before the presidential inauguration on January 20, 2009, he said in the midst of his talk, "Do not remove the ancient landmarks. We must not forget the history that tilled the ground, that paved the road for 1/20 [inauguration day]. . . . You gotta know the history that leads to 1/20, a history stained with the blood of the known and unknown. A history of strange fruit that hangs on trees in Birmingham, a history of people who were hanged and shot, people who walked in Montgomery . . . the history of the known and unknown beaten, jailed, bit by dogs, and knocked down by fire hoses. Stand up! Call out the names before heaven of uncles and grandparents! Do not forget and remove the ancient landmarks."

If that short segment had appeared on YouTube, Pfleger could have been taken to task for dwelling in the past when many felt the real point of the Obama inauguration was to point to the future. In fact, the over-arching theme of the sermon was a call for church members to pledge themselves to the cause of Christ, to become the voice of the voiceless and the Good Samaritan to the needy stranger: "When Barack Obama raises his hand and promises to protect the Constitution, we will raise our hands and say we are committed to Jesus Christ in season and out of season." The point about "ancient landmarks" was a momentary nod to liberation theology and was altogether appropriate in the context. Outside context, it becomes ready material for mischief or malice.

Or consider these words from a well-known civil rights advocate: "The Negro is still not free. One hundred years later, the life of the Negro is still crippled by the manacles of segregation and the chains of discrimination. One hundred years later, the Negro lives on a lonely island of poverty in the midst of a vast ocean of prosperity.... There will be neither rest nor tranquility in America until the Negro is granted his citizenship rights. The whirlwind of revolt will continue to shake the foundations of our nation until the bright day of justice emerges."

Out of context, the words convey hopeless complaint and a menacing threat. Within their full context, the "I Have a Dream" speech of Martin Luther King, they are part of what is considered one of the most elevating and inspiring orations in American history.

The issue of context took on special importance in the 2008 presidential campaign when a portion of a sermon by Reverend Jeremiah Wright delivered six years earlier, at his Trinity United Church of Christ was aired on national television and quickly found its way to YouTube. It was given in the aftermath of 9/11, when many Americans wanted revenge for the slaughter and destruction at the World Trade towers. Ironically, Wright said he was trying to put a spotlight on "the insanity of the cycle of violence and the cycle of hatred" that has bedeviled the human family for too many years. To those overwhelmed by "the unthinkable act" of the foreign terrorists, he spoke of "the bloody assaults" America has waged on other peoples—on the slaves brought over from Africa, on Native Americans, on U.S. citizens of Japanese descent interred during World War II, on "the innocent citizens" America has killed in Iraq, Sudan, Panama, Libya, and the wholesale annihilation of the people of Hiroshima and Nagasaki.

Coming to a climax, Wright declared, "Now we are indignant because the stuff we have done overseas is brought back into our own front yard.

America, the chickens are coming home to roost! America builds bigger prisons and passes a three-strike law and then wants us to sing 'God Bless America.' No, no, no! Not God bless America but God damn America! It's in the Bible for killing innocent people. God damn America for treating its citizens as less than human. God damn America as long as she acts like she is God and she is supreme!"

What we have failed to learn, insisted Wright, is that "violence breeds violence, hate breeds hate, and terrorism breeds terrorism." It is time, he said, for serious "self-examination" of our relation with God and our relations with others.

For months, those three words, "God damn America," dominated the electronic media. Out of context, they *proved* that Wright was anti-American and antiwhite. Within context, they reflected one man's rage against the violence that characterized much of American history and which, soon after Wright's harangue, would engulf the Middle East in yet another war, one seemingly without end.

In a series of public appearances and radio and television interviews, Pfleger defended his friend and mentor. "Jeremiah is one of the most loyal, loving people I know," he said. "He is a true patriot who loves his country enough to criticize and challenge it. . . . For people to take a sound bite and loop it over and over is ridiculous and irrational. If you took a sound-bite of Jesus saying, 'You got to hate your brother and mother, sister and father in order to love me,' they'd say Jesus was a madman. The people at Trinity know Jeremiah; they know the man." If he says something that seems harsh, he added, they'll look at the context, and they will understand because they understand black preaching and the basics of liberation theology. Pfleger's own brush with context and harsh words would come just six weeks later during his guest sermon at Trinity.

†

THERE IS AN undeniable current of evangelicalism running through the Sabina religious identity, and it constitutes a third foundation stone. Its characteristics are an emphasis on a personal commitment to Christ or being "born again," a determination to share one's belief with others, a central focus on the crucifixion of Christ as the sole means of salvation, and an acceptance of the Bible as the one and only source of religious authority.

Pfleger himself underwent a born-again experience as a seminarian, and a common event at the conclusion of his Sunday sermon is an altar call, an invitation for people to come up around the altar and renew their own commitment in some way. At times Pfleger balances this with a call for repentance or a call to come forth and give up something specific that may be compromising their dedication to Christ. One Sunday in a mood of hyper-enthusiasm, he stood on (not at) the altar and asked smokers to come forward and throw their packs of cigarettes at him as they declared their break with the old habit. And they did, dozens pelting him and the altar with packs while renouncing their addiction. This stress on personal affirmation doesn't mean Pfleger has abandoned the idea of baptism as one's entrance to the church; it is an important sacrament at St. Sabina. But Catholic teaching has always maintained that baptized persons must personally accept and live by their commitment to Christ as they mature, and it is this that he focuses on.

In a typical aside in the midst of a sermon, this one on patriotism, Pfleger said, "I honor the flag, but I don't worship it. The flag won't save me. The flag ain't comin' back for me. But he [Jesus] said, 'I'm coming back, I will be with you always, I will never desert you.' The flag has let me down at times, but he will never let me down."

The evangelical requirement of sharing one's faith with others has become almost an obsession at St. Sabina, and a Sunday hardly passes without Pfleger urging his people toward missionary activity. In one memorable sermon, he used the story in the Gospel of Mark about four men who carried a paralyzed man, then opened a hole in the roof of a house to get to Jesus, as an illustration of what evangelism is all about. First, he said, these men realized that, though the paralyzed person was not dying, he was "not reaching his potential," and they wanted that for him. "Is it important for us that every human being reach their potential?" he asked. "Do we have compassion?" Pfleger interjected that at a pastors' meeting he attended, someone commented that 8 to 10 percent of young people today are "lost." "Since when do we have the audacity to decide who's lost and who's saved?" he said. "How dare you give up on anybody? There are no throwaways in God's kingdom!"

Also, Pfleger said, the men understood that all four of them were needed to carry the paralytic. "To reach his potential, all four carried the mat, all four had to do their part." At a Sabina service, everyone has to do their part—the greeters, ushers, lectors, Eucharist ministers, sound technicians, choir members, and so on. If somebody isn't doing their job, "then something fails," he said.

Besides, he noted, the four had "the expectation" that they would succeed, that Jesus would see the man and he would walk again. "We don't receive the things of God if we don't expect to get them," he said. "Many of us suffer expectation bankruptcy, and we file for Chapter 11. It's not enough to believe in Christ. We have to believe that everything in the book is for you and me. It's yours, or God is a liar! Stop surrendering your dreams; blow the dust off the dreams on your shelf. You gotta have the crazy faith I have."

And finally, the men were willing to go the distance despite uncertainty about the outcome. Pfleger was yelling now. "Give me what you got! Some people sit at worship every Sunday and don't do nothin'. If you can't [do something], get your sad butts up and go get in shape! They're not members; they're long-term visitors!" The four men were taking a real risk in what they did, he said. "What if the paralyzed man said, 'Leave me alone'? What if they picked him up and he was heavier than they thought? What if that man had an attitude? What if they tore the roof off and Jesus said, 'Don't interrupt my preaching'?" In the story, the man was lowered through the roof, and Jesus healed him. The man picked up his mat and walked. He reached his potential, said Pfleger, thanks to four nameless individuals "who believed God is able to do what he said he would do." He ended by urging the congregation to pick up their own mats, their excuses, and give their all. "This life is no one-hundred-yard dash," he said. "It's a marathon."

There is practically nothing that occurs at St. Sabina without an evangelical wrinkle. The cross is a familiar topic in sermons and Bible study. In opening his sermon at the beginning of Holy Week 2009, he dwelled for a long time on the words, "I'll never know what it cost to see my sins up on the cross. What a cost, what a cost! Whatever I go through cannot be compared to what he did for me." There is, insisted Pfleger, "no salvation, no glory, no resurrection without the cross."

The Bible, another essential ingredient of evangelicalism, is at the center of St. Sabina life, from the extensive time given to praise and worship that opens every Sunday service, to every sermon Pastor Pfleger delivers, to every weekly Bible study session, to every wedding and funeral at the church. And it's embedded in the prayers quietly said in a kind of huddle before every mass or march or civil action. St. Sabina could be called (and has been called by some) an evangelical church—except for the fact that it is officially Roman Catholic. Pfleger sees no contradiction in this. Since the Second Vatican Council in the 1960s, the Catholic Church has promoted the study, preaching, and knowledge of Scripture as essential. In its document on divine revelation, the council said, "The force and power in the word of God is so great that it remains the support and energy of the Church, the strength of faith for her sons [and daughters], the food of the soul, and the pure and perennial source of spiritual life." Father Tom Walsh, who was an associate pastor at St. Sabina from 1986 to 1992, says these were the years when Pfleger began to put extreme emphasis on the Bible in sermons and in his encouragement of Bible study. These were also the years when Sunday attendance mounted. "In 1986 the church was a little more than half full," says Walsh. "By 1992 it was full every Sunday."

Pfleger attributed his enthusiasm for regular, weekly Bible study to a dream he had one night when half asleep. "There were all these people sitting around a banquet table piled high with food, but they just sat there because their mouths were muffled and their hands tied. Was it a dream or a vision, I don't know. I took it as a sign we had to get serious about studying and understanding Scripture." When asked why he does not have regularly scheduled weekday masses, Pfleger says he did schedule them for a while but decided it was preferable to concentrate on the two hundred or more who attend Tuesday night Bible study than the five or six who attended the weekday mass.

One problem with this heavy emphasis on the Bible as the pillar of the church at St. Sabina is that it leaves Catholicism's other pillar, the Eucharist (the presence of Jesus in consecrated bread and wine), without equal billing. To be sure, every mass at the church has the eucharistic prayer, including the words of consecration, and the reception of communion by the congregation. But coming several hours after Scripture has been so vigorously celebrated and preached, this quiet, latter part of the service can seem like an afterthought.

Another problem for evangelical Bible enthusiasts is the Catholic Church's belief that "tradition" (the teaching of the church down through the centuries) is also a source of doctrine so that the Bible is not "the sole and final source" of authority for the believer, as orthodox evangelicals maintain. Pfleger says he regards the eucharistic prayer, including the consecration of bread and wine, as a transition from the prayer and worship that precedes it to the reception of communion that follows it. "Jesus' body and blood becomes our food," he says, "so that we can go out and become feeders to the world." At times, he notes, the reception of communion does not mark the end of the Sunday service, as it does at many Catholic masses, but leads directly to an after-service action outside, such as march or rally. "It's all about being the body of Christ in real life," he says.

†

PERHAPS ST. SABINA'S most visible and visual feature is what is known as inculturation—a strong commitment to blend the Christian faith with the particular cultures and histories of the people it serves. A determination to make St. Sabina a distinctively African American church has marked Pfleger's tenure since, as one of his first moves on arrival, he painted the parish's donated bus green, black, and red. Anyone who enters the church knows instantly that this is an African American house of worship, starting with the dominant black Jesus mural, the African-styled Holy Family figures, the block-like altar that resembles a drum, and the other furniture in the sanctuary. Some visitors have been offended by this pronounced display of race, arguing that Catholicism should present itself as a universal faith, transcending race, nation, and culture. The truth is a certain amount of inculturation has been inevitable and acceptable from the beginning of Christianity and is openly visible in the distinctive cultural expressions found in the church architecture, art, and devotional practices of all ethnic groups like the Irish, Poles, Germans, and Latinos in Chicago and other large cities. Pfleger believes African American culture should not be the exception.

For more than one hundred years, Catholic leaders have encouraged inculturation. In 1944, Pope Pius XII said ministers of the gospel should not try to "transplant European civilization and culture, and no other, to foreign soil." The task, he said, is to integrate "the principles of Christian life and morality" into existing cultures. And Pope John Paul II added that this process is not just for the benefit of a given social, ethnic, racial group but also for the benefit of the Church itself, which gains from the wisdom and insights of distinct cultures. It is this celebration of black culture that moved an elderly Elbert Johnson to tell Pfleger it was what he had been looking for in Catholicism all his life. And it was the same thing that struck a youthful Randall Blakey when he first entered the church, forcing him to reevaluate his previous assumptions and look at the Catholic Church with new eyes.

†

DESPITE A HEALTHY measure of Catholic presence in these four components, Pfleger's critics insist he spends too much time trying to change the world while giving little notice to the basic teachings of the faith as found in the *Catechism of the Catholic Church* and refusing to promote eucharistic adoration, holy hours, the rosary, pilgrimages, indulgences, or other old staples of the Church. Pfleger's reply is that he is a Catholic, and St. Sabina is an official institution of the Archdiocese of Chicago with all the benefits and limitations pertaining thereunto, though he sometimes prefers to think of his parish as catholic with a small *c*, in the sense of "universal" and open to everyone. He fully accepts the pope as head of the Church but sees the papal role as primarily one of spiritual and moral leadership rather than preoccupation with ritual correctness. "He has to be a voice of conscience to the whole world," Pfleger says, "keeping us focused on important things like the children in Uganda, the genocide in Darfur, the injustice in the Middle East."

He believes the devotional needs and preferences of black Catholics are very different from those of whites, Latinos, and others. Nevertheless, in doctrinal matters he is quite traditional, almost fundamentalist, in some areas. He firmly adheres to the articles of the creed: Father, Son, and Holy Spirit, heaven and hell, the resurrection of the body, and life everlasting. In his Bible study classes, he presents the words of Scripture as literally true and has little interest in the more liberal approach of modern biblical research. In some cases, however, he will make exceptions.

"I don't think of heaven so much as a place," he says, "but as just being in the presence of God. If a child comes to a strange house, he will hesitate to enter it, but if he hears his father's voice inside, he'll want to get in to be with his father. That's heaven, the eternal presence and worship of God." Hell, on the other hand, is simply the absence of that glorified presence, says Pfleger, admitting he has little interest in the image of hell as a place of eternal fire.

He believes strongly in the existence of angels and the devil, especially the devil, who slips into his sermon almost every Sunday. "I believe in both kinds of devils," he says, "the two-legged kind and the spiritual kind who rebelled against God. Look, you can't live long in this world without believing in Satan. Life will teach you about God and the devil; it's the greatest textbook. Anyone who denies the existence of either is delusional." This grim emphasis on the dark side, obviously influenced by the many tragedies he's had to deal with in the Auburn Gresham community, makes him highly critical of what he calls "cotton candy theology" that sees God as continually smoothing the way for believers. "I believe Satan roams freely seeking whom he may devour. When I go to a funeral and someone says that God wanted that person more than we did, I get pissed off," he says. "No, when I see murders and rapes of children, I know there's an enemy out there who's trying to trip us up. We have to stop blaming God and just help people get through it."

He has absolute confidence in Christ's physical resurrection from the dead and the bodily resurrection of everyone who has ever lived when

Christ returns. "That is my hope," he says, "because otherwise we've been bamboozled!" Ultimately, he is relying on the coming with Christ of a new heaven and a new Earth where, Scripture says, every tear will be wiped away and there will be no more death or mourning. Meanwhile, too much of his time is taken up just helping people "get through it."

Dealing with day-to-day parish decisions, Pfleger can be quite strict. He will not marry any couples who have been living together unless they agree to move into separate quarters and attend church for six months. He will preside at funeral masses only for church members, although he will hold a service at a funeral home for a nonmember. Often he is sought out for this by grieving parents, many non-Catholic, who know of his concern for young people. On sexual matters, Pfleger tries to be pastoral. If a couple wants to avoid pregnancy, "the first choice is abstinence," he says, "but you have to look at the circumstances and help people make informed decisions." He is strongly opposed to abortion. "I think God wants life for all his children and is against anything that prevents them from reaching their potential, including racism, sexism, ageism, and death before birth." But he is very concerned about pro-lifers who get hysterical about saving life in the womb and are then indifferent to the quality of life outside the womb.

When counseling a woman considering abortion, Pfleger says he urges carrying the pregnancy to full term, and he offers prenatal care paid for by the parish or puts her in touch with a psychologist or an adoption agency, if any of these choices will be helpful. Regarding homosexuality, he also takes a pastoral position. He doesn't promote it, but if he is dealing with a committed gay couple, he does not feel he should turn them away or condemn their relationship. "Real commitment is not something we have enough of in this world," he says.

Given the four foundation stones and the Catholic character discussed here, St. Sabina is not a typical Catholic parish. It represents one man's and one community's attempt to blend a set of characteristics borrowed from a variety of sources and put together for the enrichment of the people who live in it.

12

PREELECTION MELTDOWN

[FATHER PFLEGER'S REMARKS] ARE BOTH PARTISAN AND AMOUNT TO A PERSONAL ATTACK.

—CARDINAL FRANCIS GEORGE

ON MAY 25, 2008, Michael Pfleger took the pulpit at Trinity United Church of Christ to give the sermon of the day. He was introduced by Reverend Otis Moss, the new pastor, as "a brother beloved, a preacher par excellence, and a prophetic, powerful pulpiteer." Pfleger's talk lasted forty-seven minutes. It was largely about the need to achieve human unity by overcoming racism, and it went fairly smoothly—except for two spots. The first was an apparent slip of the tongue when he said, "I also believe America is the greatest sin against God." But he caught himself immediately, saying, "Whoa, whoa, whoa!" He backed up a bit and then made his intended point: "So then the greatest sin against God [is] racism. It's as natural as the air we breathe." Most people have never heard of that slip. What they have heard and seen—hundreds, thousands of times on YouTube and television—is the second spot, the ninety-second screed toward the end of the talk when he mocked presidential candidate Hillary Clinton.

Leading up to it, Pfleger said that preelection "conversation must be honest enough to deal and demand that we acknowledge first the sin [of racism]. You can't turn to something you ain't identified. . . . It must be honest enough to expose white entitlement and supremacy wherever it raises its head." Then he turned toward the Trinity pastor and stated, "But Reverend Moss, when Hillary was crying, people said that was put on. I really don't believe that it was put on. I really believe she just always thought, 'This is mine.'" There was applause and laughter as he went on, imitating her voice: "'I'm Bill's wife. I'm white, and this is mine. I just gotta get up and step into the plate.' And then from out of nowhere came, 'Hey, I'm Barack Obama.' And she said, [voice rising] 'Oh, damn! Where did you come from? I'm white! I'm entitled! There's a black man stealing my show!'" He pulled out a handkerchief, dabbed at his eyes, and began to sob.

Then, as if realizing he had gone over the top, Pfleger said, "I'm sorry. I don't want to get you in trouble. The live-streaming just went out." People were now standing up and cheering. "I'm sorry. I'm sorry," he said in a joking way. "The following message does not represent our church and does not represent this station. It is purely on the host of the show. Oh God, I gotta get outta here. Y'all are way past your hour of power."

As the congregation quieted down, Pfleger went back on message for another seven minutes, calling for a nationwide conversation about white entitlement. He ended with a challenge: "Trinity, do you have the faith to demand the conversation that America has ignored all its history? This day and this time you will ignore it no more—because the church is beginning to speak up!"

He returned to his own church that evening without the slightest suspicion that this short, satirical interjection would ignite a firestorm that even after two years is still smoldering. It isn't so much what he said as when and where he said it that explains the brouhaha that followed.

Hillary Clinton's moment of near tears occurred before the New Hampshire Democratic primary, in early January, almost five months before Pfleger took the pulpit. And though she had been expected to lose New Hampshire by a wide margin, she won the state handily. The pundits speculated that her momentary show of vulnerability turned out to be a major factor in her surprise victory. She continued thereafter to win other states, cutting into the heavy lead Obama had built. By late May, with the Democratic convention just three months away, the race between the two looked closer than expected. Obama's opponents, both Democratic and Republican, viewed Pfleger's performance like manna from heaven, an unexpected opportunity to trash the vote leader through guilt by association with his ally and "spiritual adviser," Reverend Pfleger. At the same time it provided an opportunity to rekindle the earlier firestorm over Obama's relationship with his longtime pastor, Reverend Jeremiah Wright, producing together perhaps an anti-Obama conflagration of apocalyptic proportions.

Syndicated columnist David Limbaugh, brother of Rush, was fanning the flames within two days of Pfleger's appearance on YouTube: "It strained credibility that Obama would have been unaware of the toxic environment of his Trinity United Church of Christ and its pastor, Jeremiah Wright. . . . But now we have the Rev. Michael Pfleger bursting on the scene . . . and spewing the most offensive, racially charged remarks imaginable. . . . Please explain, in view of the ongoing revelations about his associations, how Obama hasn't lost credibility to present himself as one who could unify this nation."[1] During the following weeks, the ninety-second riff took on a life of its own. For a time it embarrassed, angered, and slowed down the best efforts of the Obama election machine.

†

PFLEGER HAD MET Obama in the mid-1980s when the young community organizer in the southeastern part of Chicago visited St. Sabina after hearing about the people-centered projects and actions developed at the church. Pfleger saw in Obama great leadership potential and kept in occasional touch with him thereafter. Between 1995 and 2004 he donated $1,500 of his own money to Obama campaigns. He heartily endorsed Obama in 1996 when he became a senator in the Illinois legislature, and Obama was sponsor of the $250,000 state grant that created the Auburn Gresham Employment Resource Center. He also endorsed Obama in 2000 when he ran for a seat in the U.S. House of Representatives and lost. Obama was soundly beaten in that race by incumbent Bobby Rush, a former Black Panther who had become a competent legislator and was well respected in his South Side congressional district. "I got dumped on [for opposing Rush]," says Pfleger, "but I saw in Obama the kind of vision, intelligence, and passion we needed." Pfleger was a visible supporter of Obama in his successful campaign for the U.S. Senate in 2004.

In 2006, when Obama was contemplating a run for the U.S. presidency, Pfleger issued a press release, stating his concern that harm might come to Obama from those "who are not ready or willing to see an African American gain such attention or power, let alone seize the White House. Personally, I hope and have encouraged Senator Obama to run. He is the best and brightest hope for American's future." He concluded with a plea: "We must send a loud and clear message to one and all. 'Do not touch this man, for if you do you will answer to us all.'" During the campaign, Pfleger shared his positive views about the candidate during Sunday mass, served on a Faith Advisory Group of clergy supporters of Obama, and was a prominent member of the organization Catholics for Obama. Before the critical Iowa Democratic Caucus, he personally traveled to Iowa to campaign for the candidate. Then just two weeks before Pfleger's sermon at Reverend Wright's church, Cardinal George sent a letter ordering Pfleger to sever his relations with pro-Obama political groups and to cease supporting the candidate from the pulpit.

He complied insofar as campaigning from the pulpit—but reluctantly. "I felt I have a right as a U.S. citizen to support candidates," he said later. "In the past I've invited some to the church to state their positions and answer questions. I've worn buttons and lapel pins and had bumper stickers on my car when Jesse Jackson and Harold Washington and Richard Daley and others were running for office. And nobody complained before." The cardinal's ban was especially irritating, he added, because more than a few bishops and priests were openly criticizing Obama's pro-choice positions and, in effect, telling Catholics they must, in conscience, support John McCain for president.

So it was with some frustration that he stepped into the pulpit on May 25. He mentioned Obama only once, noting that some voters had already publicly stated they could not vote for him because of his color, and then talked about race, white entitlement, and Hillary Clinton. It apparently did not occur to him that his words could boomerang back at him and strike Obama too, just as Wright's words had.

Four days later, television news, radio talk shows, and YouTube made his performance the first order of business, some commentators wondering breathlessly if Obama could possibly survive this assault on Hillary Clinton by his friend. Pfleger was unprepared for the immediacy, intensity, and immensity of the reaction. He quickly issued a terse, unsatisfying press statement, saying, "I regret the words I chose Sunday. These words are inconsistent with Senator Obama's life and message, and I am deeply sorry if they offended Senator Clinton or anyone else who saw them."

Obama's reaction was more to the point: "As I have traveled this country, I've been impressed by not what divides us, but by all that unites us. That is why I am deeply disappointed in Father Pfleger's divisive, backward-looking rhetoric, which doesn't reflect the country I see or the desire of people across America to come together in common cause." In the aftermath of the Wright controversy, the Pfleger misstep was just too much, and Obama announced that he and his family were withdrawing their membership at Trinity United Church of Christ. "Our relations with Trinity have been strained by the divisive statements of Reverend Wright, which sharply conflict with our own views," he said.

Cardinal George was irate when he called Pfleger, but his public comments were relatively mild. "The Catholic Church does not endorse political candidates," he declared. "Consequently, when a priest must speak to political issues that are also moral, he may not endorse candidates nor engage in partisan campaigning." Father Pfleger's remarks "are both partisan and amount to a personal attack," he added. "I regret them deeply. . . . To avoid months of turmoil in the church, Father Pfleger has promised me that he will not enter into campaigning, will not publicly mention any candidate by name, and will abide by the discipline common to all Catholic priests." Meanwhile, the St. Sabina rectory was awash with messages of hate and threats. "They want to kill me," Pfleger told parish members. "It's been very ugly." There was little subtlety in the letters and e-mails that came pouring in by the hundreds on a daily basis:

> *What are you trying to prove? How big an ignorant, arrogant, caustic, antagonistic, and racist bigot you really are?*

> *I for one am not going back to church until Archbishop George acquires a backbone and makes you pay a serious price for your behavior.*

> *I am trying to get an airline ticket . . . to come and see you personally! You will not like my response. As a matter of fact you might not remain on your feet long. See you soon.*

> *You people don't have a parish priest. What you have is a white nigger.*

> *As a Catholic you disgust me. . . . May you burn in hell where God will place you.*

> *Obama is done, done, done. No electability whatsoever, and this should clinch it.*

In this mass of communication, there was a scattering of thoughtful and sympathetic pieces, as well as some that thoroughly agreed with Pfleger's message. One woman even offered him a "lovely guestroom" in Reno, Nevada, should he feel "now or in the future" the need to "get away."

†

IN HIS SUNDAY sermon June 1, 2008, one week after his Trinity appearance, Pfleger tried to calm the storm, offering a rationale for his words.

> For whatever damage that was caused to any human being and for any offense felt, especially to any of the candidates or their families, I am deeply sorry, and I pray that my apology will be accepted even by those who say they won't accept it. The last few days have been the

most painful of my life, even more so than the murder of Jarvis, my foster son. When the world is meeting you for the first time from a dramatization in a sermon that I felt was in the sacredness of a sanctuary, among people who know me, and then find a YouTube that in no way defines the sermon or the message that I preached, nor the person or pastor that I am, it is painful. It is also grieving to me when a 1.5-minute YouTube video becomes the headlines across the world . . . while the tragedy and death of earthquakes, cyclones, and tornadoes that have taken the lives of people around the world, while the killing of children across the country and here in Chicago . . . have become stories on page eighteen and nineteen.

Elsewhere in this talk, he said, "I apologize for the words I chose . . . for my dramatization. . . . For anyone who was offended and who thought it to be mockery, that was neither my intent nor my heart. . . . Hate me if you will. Hate my imperfect dramatization. Hate my imperfect articulation. I have never presumed to be anything but imperfect. I pray I can still beat the drum of justice, even if sometimes I am off beat." He did not acknowledge (either then or later) that he had gone well beyond the boundaries of propriety and had acted in an obviously partisan manner.

Sun-Times reporter Falsani challenged him in an interview about his statement that his remarks at Trinity were in the "sacredness of a sanctuary" and only for those present who knew and understood him. He replied that Trinity staff told him the live-streaming had been down all day, "and they didn't know whether it was back up. I regret that I was naïve enough to believe [the dramatization] was just going to be kept among the church."

Falsani also wanted to know how he could claim the Trinity debacle was more painful to him than the death of his own son. Pfleger said he knew the death of his son was not his fault; he had not shot Jarvis, whereas in this situation he had shot both himself and his church. "I've spent my life trying to serve God and build up this faith community. I felt all of that was at risk. . . . I've done everything to make this church strong. I don't want to hurt this church. I don't want to hurt these people who are at their jobs or workplaces having to defend their pastor. That shouldn't be what they have to do. I did not want to hurt this church's reputation."

Falsani was not impressed, telling him his defense "sounded like the worst kind of narcissism."[2]

Then, matters took a more ominous turn. Cardinal George called Pfleger and said he wanted him to step back and take a leave for some weeks, at least until the clamor calmed down, and he wanted him to leave the rectory. He suggested an apartment on the North Side he could move into. All this threw Pfleger into a state of near panic. He knew full well that the cardinal had long been eager to get this troublesome pastor out of his hair. "I saw this as an open door to oust me from St. Sabina," he says. "I feared everything I loved and believed in was over." He called George the next day and said, "I don't think I can do this." But George was adamant: he had to go and he had to go now; there would be no compromising. That night ABC television news reported that Pfleger had been "suspended indefinitely" from his duties. However, George's press statement was less blunt:

> To put recent events in some perspective, I have asked Father Michael Pfleger . . . to step back from his obligations and take leave for a couple of weeks . . . effective today. Fr. Pfleger does not believe this to be the right step at this time. While respecting his disagreement, I have nevertheless asked him to use this opportunity to reflect on his recent statements and actions in the light of the Church's regulations for all Catholic priests. I hope this period will also be a time away from the spotlight and for rest and attention to family concerns.

George also announced he was appointing Father William Van-ecko, pastor of nearby St. Kilian's parish, as temporary administrator at St. Sabina, a move which strongly hinted that Pfleger's absence might be longer than "a couple of weeks."

After conferring with his staff and parish cabinet, Pfleger left the rectory, declining George's housing offer and moving instead into an empty apartment across the street from St. Sabina. Mayor Daley phoned and arranged to meet him and former Alderman Terry Peterson for dinner. The mayor was supportive, Pfleger says, but could offer no assurances about the future. For the next two weeks, he went back "to where I started," rereading Dr. King's writings, praying, and bolstering his faith. He talked with Ed McLaughlin about his situation and spent a day with Louis Farrakhan at his farm in Michigan. They drove around the blooming June countryside for hours talking, says Pfleger, reminiscing and eventually getting lost.

In Pfleger's absence from the parish, St. Sabina members rallied at the church (with a warmly welcomed Reverend Wright among those in attendance), calling for the return of their pastor. "We wholeheartedly disagree with the cardinal's decision," declared Gerald Stewart, president of the parish council. "We respectfully request the cardinal immediately reinstate Father Pfleger as full pastor . . . and request an immediate meeting with Cardinal George to discuss the future of the entire faith community of St. Sabina."

The request for a meeting was honored two days later when nine members of the Sabina cabinet, including Stewart and Randall Blakey, director of ministries, met with Cardinal George at the downtown chancery office. As Blakey recounted it, the meeting went extremely well: George explained that he ordered Pfleger out of the rectory because of his concern about the "overwhelming pressure" the man was under; he put in a temporary administrator since that is required by Church law; and he saw no reason why Pfleger could not resume his duties after his two-week sabbatical. "We were quite relieved at that point," says Blakey, "so we saw no reason to even bring up our fears." At Sunday mass on June 8, a spontaneous celebration of jubilation lasted for more than five minutes after Kim Lymore, associate minister, announced the good news that the pastor would soon return.

†

PFLEGER LOOKED MORE triumphant than penitential when he stepped up the middle aisle in his mass apparel on Sunday, June 22. "The Bible says the righteous man falls seven times," he said in his sermon, "but the

Scripture doesn't end there. It says, 'You get back up!"—and he shouted for emphasis, "You get back up! You get back up!" Later he thanked "those who chose to balance what I have sought to do in my ministry and in my life over a 1.5-minute YouTube that showed around the world. I have chosen to be an activist, as were my mentors, Martin Luther King and Jack Egan. . . . We must all become activists who level the playing field" because "there are haters out there who will distort the truth and wait for their opportunity. . . . We still have an unequal justice system. We still have more people of color in poverty, in jail, in poor education systems, a lack of health care. All the statistics will tell us we have not come as far as we've liked to come."

"I return to the pulpit," he said, "committed to Jesus Christ." In a voice choked with emotion at the end of the service, he began to sing the refrain of the traditional hymn, "Blessed Assurance": "This my story, this is my song. Praising my savior all the day long." Softly at first, then with fuller voice, others joined in until the whole congregation was on its feet, singing, waving their hands, sending the music up to the ceiling of the old church. It was over at last. He had faced another crisis and survived.

Since that day, Pfleger has been asked many times to explain what he was thinking of when he mocked Hillary Clinton at Trinity. His answer has always been the same. "I apologize for any way I got in the way of the message. I do not apologize for talking about race. I do not apologize for talking about entitlement. I apologize when the person gets in the way of the message. I apologize when my flesh and my personality get in the way because then the people don't get the message." In other words, he acknowledged that his dramatization, which so delighted his audience, actually distorted beyond recognition what he was trying to convey. Clearly, he hadn't thought through the media implications of a sermon gone bad.

As a matter of fact, the subject of entitlement was at the time a legitimate issue in the public arena. Columnists, editorial writers, and television commentators had been suggesting that Hillary Clinton did indeed feel entitled to the White House, her former home for eight years. She practically said so herself during the primary campaign. She was Bill's wife, she was a respected member of Congress, and she had an impressive list of other accomplishments. It would only be natural that she feel a tinge of resentment toward this newcomer who was getting so much attention and adulation.

But did Senator Clinton feel entitled because of her race? White entitlement had also become a subject of discussion in 2008, as it often does when a white candidate is running against someone of another race. As described by Peggy McIntosh, associate director of the Wellesley Center for Research on Women, white privilege "is like an invisible, weightless knapsack of special provisions, maps, passports, code books, visas, clothes, tools, and bank checks," which aid white Americans in every aspect of life from grocery shopping to getting into good colleges and earning promotions at work. White people don't think about these privileges ordinarily, she says, but they're just there nevertheless.[3] That was undoubtedly an idea Pfleger wanted to introduce to the Trinity congregation, but he put it so baldly in his skit, ridiculing Hillary and intimating she was consciously banking on her superiority over this "black man" and deeply disturbed that her racial entitlement was not working as it was supposed to. If a similar skit had been done by Jon Stewart on *The Daily Show* or Dave Letterman or a cast member on *Saturday Night Live*, it would probably have provoked little indignant reaction because these are venues where satire and cynicism are celebrated. But performed by Obama's "friend" in the church of Obama's former pastor? That was beyond the pale.

Nothing Pfleger has said publicly has satisfactorily explained his conduct in the Trinity pulpit. He has rarely acted so erratically. Even when he's shocked supporters and critics alike with his conduct (defacing hundreds of billboards, for example), there was method in his madness, and he's often emerged vindicated. Here, there was no really satisfying mitigating circumstance—except one, which he chose not to mention. His father Louis was seriously sick at the time, and it was feared he would not survive. Pfleger had been spending a lot of time with his father at the hospital, and it could well be that worry and concern blurred the younger man's vision, leading to the ill-conceived pantomime. Louis Pfleger died six weeks after the Trinity sermon.

Speaking on the subject even before the media frenzy, several black academics discussed the inability of most whites to grasp the nature of black preaching, which is often drenched in deliberate exaggeration; uses wild, inventive metaphors; is rarely spoken from staid, white pulpits; and may become rowdy and extremely funny at times. Linda Thomas, a professor at the Lutheran School of Theology in Chicago, said black preaching "can be a loud, passionate, physical affair," which has as its goal a call to challenge those in power and raise questions for society to grapple with. "If white people are surprised by the rhetoric," she says, "it's because most have never visited a black church."[4]

The final word belongs to a Chicago priest who sent Pfleger a copy of the homily he delivered one Sunday in the midst of the controversy. In its conclusion, he said, "A long time ago, Jesus approached Mike Pfleger and said, 'Follow me,' and Mike Pfleger has done that, followed Jesus down a path, which, I dare say, most of us could not have gone down. Last week, Mike Pfleger messed up big-time, but how would we feel, how should we feel, if Jesus had gone out to dinner with Mike Pfleger that very night? How would we feel if Jesus says to us, 'It is my desire to say to Father Pfleger, as I once said to a woman caught in a situation where she messed up, Mike, I don't condemn you. Go your way; continue your great ministry. But don't do this kind of thing anymore.'"

13

GUNS AND CHILDREN

═══════════

THERE'S A WAR RIGHT HERE IN CHICAGO.
—MICHAEL PFLEGER

PFLEGER HAD JUST finished presiding at a wedding on May 30, 1998, when someone rushed into the church and told him that his seventeen-year-old son Jarvis had been shot on 79th near Carpenter Street. He ran out of the rectory to find Jarvis lying on the sidewalk outside a convenience store two blocks away, a crowd of people gathering around. He had been struck in the neck by a single bullet as he and several friends emerged from the store. Witnesses said it appeared to be a random shot from a passing bicyclist who pulled a gun and fired into the group and then sped away. An ambulance carried Jarvis to Christ Hospital, and Pfleger followed in his own car. He felt relief when told Jarvis's condition was considered critical but not grave. The next day Pfleger found Jarvis conscious and able to move his head, but he could not talk because of the injury. He seemed to be paralyzed on the left side. Pfleger stayed with him a long time, telling Jarvis, "You're going to make it; you're going to achieve!"

Early the following morning, Jarvis's sister came to the rectory, sobbing with the news that Jarvis had died unexpectedly during the night.

181

Pfleger was struck numb. The rest of that day was taken up with funeral arrangements and calls from the media, church members, and other supporters. When he finally returned to his room in the evening, he sat in a chair without moving, all night, for the next eight hours. "It was like I was totally paralyzed," he says. "I was mad at God. How could he allow such an ending for this kid, how could he extinguish his dreams for the future, this kid who was finally putting his life together, this lively, mischievous kid who had so much possibility?"

For the first time, Pfleger seriously questioned his decision to go into ministry. "I decided I could not get through this. Only God could get me through." And he vowed if he did get through it, he would be more aggressive in battling guns and violence. He said the funeral mass five days later in a church packed with young people, and he told them, as he told himself, to curb their grief for the moment and to commit themselves to fight the insanity in the streets. For him the struggle was now personal. And it would continue to be so in the years ahead.

†

THE PROLIFERATION OF guns had been on his radar long before this tragic hour. Since coming to Sabina, he had offered sympathy and prayers as he wept with the many parents and relatives gathered around the caskets of young gun victims. It had gotten to the point that South Side people he didn't even know would call and ask if he would come and help them survive the horror. And he went as often as he could. He knew well the fearful, fatal role guns were playing in aggravating the tensions that arose in the midst of social instability, so when the Sabina marchers were out fighting tobacco advertising or gang activity, guns were on the agenda too.

Pfleger had tried to develop creative strategies. In 1993, for example, he helped coordinate a city-wide gun turn-in, which confiscated several hundred weapons from the public. When one of the students in the Sabina Academy later asked him what he could do, Pfleger got the idea of a toy gun turn-in. "It occurred to me the great educational benefits that could result from children turning in their toy guns," he says. "It would give parents an opportunity to talk about violence and guns . . . and the children an opportunity to address something that is always at the back of their minds."

A week or two later, the nearly five hundred children in the school were assembled in church for a pastor-led, antigun revival. Hanging in front was a sign that read, "Those who teach touch the future," and beneath it a quilt with the names of the forty-nine public school children who had been cut down by gunfire already that school year. "You have a divine destiny and purpose, and nothing or no one will take you from what God has planned for you," Pfleger said. Then as the assembly chanted, "Guns kill people, I want to live!" and "No more guns in my house!" The kids hauled box after box of plastic, metal, and rubber toy weaponry and dumped them in two thirty-gallon drums for disposal. The turned-in items included everything from a realistic-looking .38-caliber revolver to a canary-colored high-range plastic water cannon. Then Gloria Randolph, whose son, twenty-one, had been shot and killed four years before, spoke softly to the schoolchildren. "What you surround your lives with, what you play with, these are the things you will use as adults," she said. She pointed to the forty-nine names on the quilt and added, "because play can lead to this."[1]

In 1993, there were indications that the public might be fed up with the toll of gun slaughter—about sixteen thousand deaths a year. And some states were taking action. Connecticut had passed an assault-gun ban; Massachusetts was considering the same, while Virginia had limited gun buyers to one purchase a month. That same year, Congress finally passed the Brady Bill requiring a five-day wait and a background check for any gun purchase. Meanwhile, the National Rifle Association, the unquestioned champion of the right to bear arms, had been hit by sagging membership for a third straight year and had a more than twenty-million-dollar deficit. *Boston Globe* columnist Ellen Goodman rejoiced that the gun lobby for the first time was on the defensive, and Attorney General Janet Reno prayed, "If only this nation will rise up and tell the NRA to get lost."[2]

But appearances proved deceiving. The heralded Brady Bill contained loopholes, one of which exempted those purchasing firearms at flea markets or gun shows. In early 1994, when Pfleger and members of the Illinois Coalition protested one Sunday outside an expo center in Harvey, Illinois, that sponsored monthly gun shows, they found that weapons were flying off the shelves. "It's ironic," Pfleger observed, "that when people are in church praying for peace and an end to violence, this was a packed convention center with people walking out with shopping bags filled with guns." It was doubly ironic since Illinois had its own state law requiring a seventy-two-hour waiting period for all gun purchases.

The NRA was forging a comeback with its successful Eddie Eagle GunSafe Program. Billed as an alternative to existing gun safety educational programs, it used an eagle cartoon character to teach children from kindergarten through third grade to obey a four-step procedure whenever they came upon a gun: "stop; don't touch; leave the area; tell an adult." The NRA claimed the program, widely implemented in schools by the mid-1990s, had resulted in an 80 percent reduction in gun death among young children. Critics, however, including the Violence Prevention Center in Washington, D.C., disputed the claim and declared that Eddie Eagle was nothing more than "Joe Camel with feathers." The aim, said the center, was to put a friendly face on a hazardous product, just as the tobacco industry had been doing with its own popular character. The center also found that the NRA's tax-exempt sister organization, the NRA Foundation, operated as an educational arm to prepare the next generation of shooters and was receiving money from the gun manufacturers as well as the tobacco industry.

Smelling the smoke, Pfleger fired off a stinging press release that declared, "The NRA through the Eddie Eagle program seeks to sell the same lie that the tobacco industry said for years, 'We do not want children to use our products.'" Now with the Liggett Group's admission that smoking does cause cancer and that some tobacco advertising had been aimed at hooking young people, he wrote, the public can see "the blood line" between tobacco and gun manufacturers and sellers. "As sick as this romance is, we should not be surprised," Pfleger charged, "for both these industries have spent their corporate lives deceiving, lying, and killing. And both believe that future financial success depends on making tobacco and guns children-friendly and attractive. Both of these industries have one goal in mind—making money. And one target in mind—our children."

That statement was released in November 1997. Six months later, in May 1998, Jarvis lay crumpled on the sidewalk bleeding from the neck.

†

TWO DAYS AFTER the burial, Pfleger was railing against the NRA's newly elected president, Charlton Heston. He was outraged that the man "would allow himself as a quality actor to be used to create an image for an industry that is a pusher of guns . . . to our children. Heston was much better playing Moses than Judas." And he railed at the NRA itself. "They're vultures," he said. "I don't understand how anybody can look at the violence we're suffering from . . . and line themselves up with the thugs of the NRA."

An NRA spokeswoman accused the media of "allowing us to be portrayed as if we're a bunch of criminals" and denied the NRA should be blamed for school shootings. "These are behavioral problems," she said, "not firearm problems." Pfleger retorted, "Our kids have a right to be in the neighborhoods. The shooters are in the wrong place, not our kids."[3]

He desperately wanted more action, more attention, more light on the problems—not just on guns but also on all the other realities plaguing the community. In August, he organized the most ambitious and largest Sabina march to date. A crowd estimated at more than three hundred took part. Up in front with Pfleger were Paul Vallas, then chief executive officer of the Chicago public school system; Jim Ryan, Illinois attorney general; and Terry Hilliard, Chicago police superintendent. They made a point of stopping at houses where known gang leaders lived. Pfleger introduced the people who answered the door to the high-ranking officials standing there, and he assured them that whatever the problem of anyone in that house, whether with drugs, guns, gangs, school, police, or law, they could go directly to these men in charge and get results. The marchers also stopped at a liquor store, which reportedly did not have a license, and Hilliard had the local police commander shut it down immediately when the owner could not produce one.

Afterward, Vallas called Pfleger and community leaders like him "living saints who are selfless and who serve as catalysts in the communities." He says, "We've taken the Pfleger model and promoted this system [in the public schools]." The Vallas school initiative involved antiviolence forums, conflict resolution training for parents, a video aimed at deterring teens from joining gangs, and a job readiness program, as well as community marches and rallies. Pfleger said the August event was "an awesome display of government, church, law enforcement, and education all on the same page to end violence." He then delivered an impassioned plea for unity. "To combat all the problems . . . we must grow to spiritual maturity where Democrats and Republicans, Rainbow PUSH and the Nation of Islam, the government and law enforcement stay connected to confront the issues that are destroying us. The police can't do it alone, the Church can't do it alone, the neighbors can't do it alone, the schools can't do it alone. The Bible teaches that God cannot work where there is disunity, and one of the most powerful lessons [from the prophet Ezekiel] is that God did not breathe the power of the Spirit until the bones connected to each other."[4]

Concern about guns accelerated in April 1999 in the wake of the Columbine High School massacre in Colorado, in which twelve students, one teacher, and the two assailants died. Pfleger began to emphasize that unity at the community level, whatever its value, could not solve the problem alone. "The gun people have declared war on our kids," he said. "We've got to come after them . . . in lawsuits. We've got to create a groundswell from legislatures to community involvement and create a momentum against this gun industry that's trying to kill our children and get rich on it."

A month later at the National Press Club in Washington he joined Sarah Brady, whose husband was shot in the assassination attempt on President Ronald Reagan. Both spoke out against a Missouri referendum that, if approved, would allow widespread carrying of concealed weapons. "It would allow people not only to have concealed guns but to take them into schools, bars, buses, stadiums, just about everywhere," Pfleger warned. He was especially upset too that Anheuser-Busch, the beer giant, was supporting the proposition. "Now it's selling beer and guns," he said. "This takes it to a new level."

By the early 2000s, when the level of street violence continued unabated, Pfleger connected it with the war in the Middle East, just as Dr. King, thirty-five years before, linked racial oppression in the United States with the war in Vietnam. During a press conference at the Cook County morgue in 2003, where the bodies of six slain employees of a Chicago warehouse had recently been stored, he accused the Bush administration of fostering the notion that "violence is acceptable." Americans could not consistently watch the violence that their country was manifesting in Afghanistan and Iraq and hear the talk of "we're gonna get them dead or alive," and not have it become part of American culture, he said. "Violence has become acceptable behavior . . . and that trickles down to our cities, our streets, and our families."

Also in 2003, the Community of St. Sabina renewed its old interest in billboards, this time by renting ten of them in or near the Auburn Gresham neighborhood with the message, "Stop the killing—Pressure Congress and the White House for stronger gun laws; Remove all guns from our homes; Children and adults, please report any guns you see." Listed was a Chicago police phone number people could call anonymously. And in 2004, the community marked Dr. King's seventy-fifth birthday with a huge billboard at one of the busiest downtown ramps off the Kennedy Expressway with the message, "Honor Dr. King. Let's remove guns from our homes and communities."

In 2004, Pfleger helped form a citywide Clergy for Safer Streets alliance, which celebrated Valentine's Day by calling for citizens to turn in guns at five churches and a synagogue. "You can't buy flowers or candy for someone who's dead," he said. "Gun violence is in every neighborhood, every community." The campaign attracted a few weapons the first day and more trickled in during the following weeks, but it was far from a mass surrender of weaponry.

Also in 2004, the Illinois Supreme Court dismissed a major lawsuit filed by Mayor Daley against twenty-two gun manufacturers and twelve gun shops in the Chicago suburbs. The suit sought $433 million in penalties, claiming firearm manufacturers and marketers constituted a "public nuisance" by easing the illegal entry of weapons into the city. In Chicago ownership or possession of handguns had been illegal since 1982. Yet guns had been responsible for 570 deaths in the city in 2003 alone. The deadly weapons had come from somewhere, and an investigation prior to the suit revealed that Chicago police posing as criminals were able to purchase 171 guns from suburban shops without complying with existing laws. The suit, which aroused the wrath of the NRA, managed to survive for years until thrown out by the state supreme court.

†

In 2007 Pfleger and Jesse Jackson joined forces to put pressure on one of the biggest gun sellers in the area, Chuck's Gun Shop and Target Range in suburban Riverdale, just beyond Chicago's city limits. Antigun experts claimed this was the handy location where South Side gangbangers went to procure weaponry. In fact, Chuck's had been identified as the place where many guns were allegedly purchased legally yet somehow ended up in the hands of killers, including the one who killed Michael Ceriale, a Chicago policeman in 1998.

Jackson and Pfleger, accompanied by members of St. Sabina and Operation PUSH, began a series of demonstrations outside Chuck's demanding a meeting with the owner, John Riggio. Despite minor publicity, nothing noteworthy occurred until May 26, 2007. On that day some two hundred demonstrators were present, many with placards saying, "Vote Riverdale Gun-Free." Pfleger and Jackson were accompanied by Arne Duncan, then superintendent of Chicago Public Schools and a longtime opponent of guns himself. When Riggio locked the door and refused to appear, Pfleger shouted into a bullhorn, "We're gonna find you and snuff you out. You can't keep hiding because you're afraid. Obviously, you've been doin' something wrong. Like a rat you're gonna hide, but like a rat we're gonna pull you out. We're gonna snuff out John Riggio." He added, "We're gonna snuff out legislators that are voting against gun laws. We're coming for you because we're not going to sit idly."

Most of the television and newspaper reporters who were present paid scant attention to the event. Fox News, however, was quick to point out that "snuff" as a slang word means to kill or murder in some dictionaries (while in others it has a first meaning of "to blow out" as a candle), and Fox broadcast Pfleger's words to a national audience. Pfleger responded immediately that he had no idea snuff was slang for killing. "Police were there," he said. "Reporters were there. No one understood me as calling for murder. I was talking about exposing the gun shop owners and legislators who support them." What he really wanted was Riggio to come out and tell the people what community he lived in and whether there were any gun shops in his own neighborhood. Pfleger's supposition (later proved correct) was that Riggio lived in a community where shops like his were prohibited.

Three days after the demonstration the Illinois State Rifle Association issued a press release headlined, "Priest Calls for Murder of Gun Shop Owner." This set off a battery of follow-up stories on cable news and the Internet and a salvo of hate mail aimed at Pfleger himself. John Michael Snyder, a prominent pro-gun advocate, called Pfleger's words "an absolute outrage" and declared that "ecclesiastical penalties should be invoked" against him. "Hopefully Chicago-area Catholics will demand that authorities initiate canonical proceedings against this loose cannon."[5] In his own response to the incident, Cardinal George seemed to side with the interpretation of the rifle association. "Publicly delivering a threat against anyone's life betrays the civil order and is morally outrageous, especially if the threat came from a priest," he said in a public statement, adding, "It is up to civil authorities to determine if a threat was made." George did not call Pfleger or seek a personal explanation from him. This storm died down almost as quickly as it began, but the snuff incident, like other accusations against Pfleger, entered the lexicon of his critics, to be brought up whenever his name should arise on any subject.

Undeterred, Jackson, Pfleger, and a phalanx of supporters returned to Chuck's a month later. This time Riggio came out and invited the two clerics to come into the shop—alone. They refused, claiming the shop was full of "hostile" Riggio comrades. Riggio than allegedly pushed Jackson, and he pushed back. Police quickly intervened and arrested both Jackson and Pfleger, charging that their demonstrators were blocking entrance to the shop. The charges were promptly dropped.

†

PFLEGER COULD NOT let the subject of guns alone. Funerals of young victims occurred with too much regularity on the South Side, and more and
more often relatives were pleading for him to be there. It was as if he
had become the God-appointed ambassador whose presence could offer a
kind of comfort in the midst of horror. "I cry every time one of these terrible things happen," he says. So he swore to come at the problem from
yet another direction. A bill under consideration in the Illinois House of
Representatives, HB48, would put some restrictions on the availability of
handguns by requiring virtually all private sales to be handled through a
licensed gun dealer. State law already required buyers to have a firearm
ownership card, which indicated they had passed a background check, and
sellers were supposed to keep records on all sales. But there was no real
enforcement of this latter provision, making it hard to trace sold or stolen
weapons. To fill that sizeable loophole, HB48 insisted private sales also
involve dealers, who are required by law to file their records with the state.

In the view of Pfleger, who frequently notes that there are more safety
restrictions on the sale of teddy bears, this would close some gaps and
maybe save some lives. So he hurled himself and St. Sabina into a twelve-
month campaign to make HB48 a reality. For the year of 2008, busloads
of Sabina members headed by their pastor went to the Thompson Center
in downtown Chicago and held a rally and vigil whenever a public school
child was murdered. They carried signs ("Stop the Killing of Our Children") and handed out leaflets about the bill, urging passersby to call their
state representatives and urge support. No one kept a tally on how many
trips downtown were made, but by mid-December, seventeen children
had lost their lives. Between attending wakes and vigils and conducting
services at churches and funeral parlors, Pfleger was near exhaustion.

In mid-October, for example, a packed St. Sabina Church was the
scene of the funeral of seventeen-year-old Kiyanna Salter, whose nick-
name was "Gorgeous." She had been a passenger on a Chicago Transit
Authority bus along 71st Street when two men got into an argument.
One pulled out a pistol and fired, missing his intended target and kill-

ing Kiyanna instead. She had been a top student at Julian High School, was studying Japanese, and was interested in a medical career. Speaking softly, her mother told the gathering in the church, "It's going to happen again." She begged parents to guard their children: "You have to love them, talk to them, hug these children."[6] The week before, Pfleger had buried a thirteen-year-old girl, and two more teens the week before that. "There's a war right here in Chicago," he said.

On December 17, St. Sabina sponsored a rally in the auditorium of the Thompson Center for family and friends of those slain. More than six hundred attended to hear the names and see photos of the victims. Mayor Daley and Arne Duncan were among the scheduled speakers, but neither came. Duncan had just been nominated by President Obama to be the new U.S. Secretary of Education, so the featured speaker was Louis Farrakhan, whom Pfleger introduced as "my friend and brother." In his talk, Farrakhan wondered whether, as a nation, we regard oil and status symbols like designer clothes and jewelry as our real wealth rather than our children. "If our treasure is in our people, why not spend our billions to make giants out of these young people we have been given?" Farrakhan received a standing ovation.

As the time approached for a decision on HB48 in early 2009, Pfleger kept in close touch with house members who told him the vote would be close. He urged his congregation to contact their representatives in the capital and express their support for the bill, and he took several busloads to Springfield so people might have the opportunity to make their case face-to-face with members of the house. There were five members who had been straddling the fence on the bill, but it appeared they were leaning now in favor of HB48. Pfleger dared to feel a bit optimistic, though he knew the NRA had been lobbying heavily for the bill's defeat.

The results on voting day, March 25, 2009, left him stunned and angry. HB48 was defeated by a vote of sixty to fifty-five, the five straddlers having all sided with the NRA. All the effort had not been enough.

In his sermon at the 11:15 mass the following Sunday, he shared the news about the bill. "I'm disappointed," he said, "not discouraged. Believe me, it's not over. It's only over when God says it's over." His subject for the day was based on Psalm 63, which speaks of a time when King David was "in a dry place," thirsting for God. Pfleger said, "There's a tendency to let a dry place define you. But you have to mature, to get beyond that. You gotta come to a place where you say, 'I gotta see the kingdom of God at work in me. I need heaven to come to my earth. You can't get your thirst quenched by people. So you let the dry place become an opportunity to get closer to God." He was getting louder now. "In a dry place you want something that will take you through hell. I need the living one, like the woman at the well needed living water. Open your mouth, give me your word! All things work together for those who love the Lord."

Then in an unusual shift toward the end of his talk, he turned away from the congregation and looked up to the mural of Jesus standing in the hands of his Father, and he was literally screaming, "Show me your power! Let me see your power! Show me your power! Let me see your power!" Over and over, he said the words until his voice began to falter. Here was a vulnerable Michael Pfleger—in pain, in agony, in hell, letting out his pent-up disappointment in public, mourning the failed curb on guns, mourning all those lost children, and his own lost Jarvis.

Finally, he turned back toward the congregation. "The devil wants us to think he's in control," he said, "but he has limited, restricted, territorial power. God's authority takes over and supercedes. I want a divine intervention like David, like Mary at the tomb of her brother Lazarus." The band began playing softly, and choir members were singing. "Come up," Pfleger said, "come up and worship in the sanctuary." They came quietly out of the pews, dozens and dozens came and gathered around their pastor. "Renew your vows to the Lord," he said. "Promise to honor him all days, all days, in sickness and in health." They stood there silent for some minutes, and then the service continued.

†

WITHIN A FEW days he had written a letter to the members of the Illinois house: "To all the legislators who voted no to HB48, I ask the question, why? I watched and listened to your hollow arguments and your statements wondering whether HB48 would make things any better or not, whether there was a better bill that could do more . . . but why weren't you willing to see, to give it a chance? If you do nothing, nothing will change. If you do something, you are putting yourself in position to make a difference. . . . Yes, I watched and listened to your arguments loud and clear, but I also hear the blood of my foster son who was killed by gun violence and the countless other sons and daughters . . . crying out from the grave. Perhaps, like Cain in the book of Genesis, you ask, 'Am I my brother's keeper?' The answer then and the answer now is yes! I wonder when another is gunned down, if you will feel anything. I continue to pray for the safety of your children and our children."

After that, he obtained the signatures of some fifty ministers and rabbis from across the country on a letter to Obama, urging the federal government to intervene in the gun violence problem. It was yet a new tack that he felt held promise, and he continued to find ways to bring attention to this scourge he could not cure. In early May, with summer coming, bringing a likely increase in violence, he was inspired to hang the American flag outside the Sabina academy upside down. Doing so is an internationally recognized signal of distress, and Pfleger told the reporters who came to see what he had done that everyone in Chicago should be "distressed" by the slaughter that never seems to slacken. When veterans' groups and others protested that he was misusing the symbol, he agreed to return it to its standard position for Armistice Day, then hung it upside down again afterward.

In October, he met in Chicago with U.S. Education Secretary Arne Duncan, U.S. Attorney General Eric Holder, Mayor Daley, and other leaders to welcome a five-hundred-thousand-dollar federal grant to help quell violence in the South Side area around Fenger High School, where a recent gang beating had occurred. Encouraged and hopeful, Pfleger decided to put the flag back in its rightful position. But six weeks later, as several more children were murdered, he returned one more time to his old staple, billboards, announcing that St. Sabina was renting twenty of them with an offer of five thousand dollars for information leading to the arrest and conviction of any person who shot or killed a child. The first one was placed in the Englewood neighborhood, adjacent to Auburn

Gresham, near where twelve-year-old Jahmeshia Conner boarded a bus in mid-November on her way to school. Her strangled body was found several days later a few blocks away. Pfleger met with the girl's father and afterward told reporters, "We're saying we refuse to become immune, to just shake our heads and put up a few teddy bears and balloons each time a child is killed."

Asked later if he is not totally depressed by frustration and failure, Father Pfleger said, "Frustrated? Yes. You'd think the lives of kids are valuable enough to protect. But I don't see the situation as hopeless because God is bigger than evil and he overcomes evil. If I didn't believe that, I'd have given up a long time ago. I'm like the kid in the Gospel who comes to Jesus with five loaves and two fish. When Jesus touches them, they multiply and feed five thousand people. So my job is to keep coming to God with something for him to touch, to keep coming with something. And when he touches it, it won't be my doing. It will be God's."

EPILOGUE

W HEN IT WAS announced in March 2010 that Cardinal George
would preside at an event honoring Father Michael Pfleger with
a "lifetime achievement" award for his service in "dismantling racism,
injustice and inequality," some speculated that the cardinal might use
the occasion to thank this priest for his "lifetime" contributions and
remove him at last from St. Sabina. Others, most notably a stridently
pro-life, anti-Pfleger Web site, bristled that George, head of the U.S.
Bishops Conference, would even consider honoring Pfleger given his
indiscretions and his friendship with unworthy figures like Louis Farrakhan and Jeremiah Wright. As it happened, the presentation on April
7 at the brand-new Christ the King Jesuit Preparatory High School on
Chicago's West Side left the Pfleger future up in the air where it had
been ever since the 2008 Hillary Clinton uproar. The awardees, selected
by the archdiocese's Office for Racial Justice, included not only Pfleger
but Joseph Perry, the Chicago auxiliary bishop who "wondered" in
2002 if Pfleger might best be advised to start his own church. In a brief
talk, George noted that work for justice accomplishes little unless it is
informed by love and then spoke of Pfleger, partly in rebuke but mostly
in affirmation:

Father Pfleger has been a controversialist, and controversy is easier to report on than is love. Father Pfleger has spoken in anger, sometimes unjustly or uncharitably, and anger is easier to capture on camera than is love. But Father Pfleger is a Catholic priest and a pastor, and in that capacity, like all good priests, he acts out of love. Ask his people. Ask the sick he has visited and the dying he has attended. Ask the troubled he has consoled. Ask the young people he has counseled and the school children he has supported.

The overflow crowd in the school chapel (including three busloads of St. Sabina members) cheered and applauded.

Pfleger tells me he intends to proceed as if every day at Sabina could be his last, but meanwhile he's pursuing several goals. "First, I want to continue making this an extremely strong church, a self-sufficient church, a model of spirit-filled, justice-determined action. I want to see the day when St. Sabina is not an exception in the archdiocese but the norm. I want to infect believers with the knowledge that social justice is the basis of our mission. I think church leaders have really outsourced our mission, leaving it up to government and private business to solve our problems. We've forgotten our real mission is freeing the captives, feeding the poor, reaching out to the outcasts.

"Second, I'm concerned about our school. We've got to find a way to build a Catholic school system that makes education available to everyone who wants it and our enrollment grows so that we don't have enough seats for all the students. What we have now is an elitist system that only the wealthy can afford."

Is there any thought of retiring? "No, no, not yet," he says. "Someone asked me, now that I've turned sixty, am I ready to ease back a little? And I said no! If anything, I'm becoming more and more radical with age. Pfleger will always be Pfleger."

But, I remind him, he will not always be at St. Sabina. "We already have great leadership here," he says. "My dream is to find a successor as pastor, someone I could train, who believes and embraces what St. Sabina is all about, who could work with me and others here for several years and then take over to bring St. Sabina to the next level." He is aware that will be a difficult task. "The Catholic Church today is under a mandate to bring back a conservative, cautious tradition," he says. "There's a conscious turn in that direction. More and more this is what's being taught in the seminaries, and more traditional guys [priests] are coming out all the time. The days of the Berrigans and Egans are gone."

So the backward move is inevitable, I say, and when you leave, Sabina will be brought into line and become another traditional Catholic parish? He shakes his head. "No, not necessarily. God's got a plan, and it can supercede even the plans of an archdiocese." He does not want to elaborate.

I ask him what he will do when he has to leave, finally moved out by the archdiocese after all these years. Would he consider accepting a pastorate at a small parish, maybe a long way from this church, where he would have a relatively free rein to operate as he has at Sabina?

"What have you been smoking?" he asks. "It ain't gonna happen—not unless there's a change in the philosophy of the Chicago archdiocese."

Well, maybe in another diocese? I ask. "You're still smoking," he says. "Look, I will always be in ministry. I'm never gonna retire. I'll consider my options when the time comes."

He said in 2002 that he would think about "other employment opportunities," even outside the Catholic Church, if forced to leave St. Sabina, so I ask if that's still an option. That is not what he's saying now. He's not even thinking about personal decisions. He's much more preoccupied with the future of his parish. "If we could only get to the point where places like St. Sabina were really validated," he says, "not just tolerated. That's what I really want."

St. Sabina's future is on other minds as well. Kim Lymore says, "It will depend more on how Pfleger leaves than when he leaves." If he is ordered out bluntly, against his will, without the opportunity to prepare a successor, the church could experience a substantial depletion, she says. If, however, his departure is amicable and he is able to endorse his successor, there is no reason to think Sabina could not continue to flourish. "There is a solid foundation of leadership here."

Randall Blakey predicts some will leave when Pastor Pfleger goes, as is always the case in such transitions, but he thinks the bulk of this faith community is stable enough to carry on. Like Lymore, he believes much will depend on the attitude of the new pastor. "If he is not strong and committed," he says, "there could be a mass exodus."

Julie Welborn also has confidence in the community, whose members have been molded over the years by extraordinary liturgy, preaching, Bible study, and the unfailing call to the building of the kingdom of God. "We'll be all right," she says, if when the time comes "Pastor Pfleger is able to leave gracefully and on top!"

NOTES

PROLOGUE

1. Cited in Eileen McMahon, *What Parish Are You From?: A Chicago Irish Community and Race Relations* (Lexington: University Press of Kentucky, 2009), 67.

CHAPTER 2: DEEP ROOTS

1. A few of the quotes attributed to Pfleger and others in chapters 2, 3, and 4 came from interviews I conducted in 1989 and appeared originally in the *Chicago Reader*, "The Holy Terror of Saint Sabina's," November 17, 1989.

CHAPTER 4: THE PARAPHERNALIA WARS

1. Editorial, "Change tactics in war," *Southtown Economist*, July 20, 1989.

CHAPTER 5: PAINTING THE TOWN RED

1. Scott Hume, "Regulate Outdoor Advertising…" *Advertising Age*, August 13, 1990.
2. Tom Seibel and Andrew Herrmann, "Priest charged in paint 'war' over smoke, drink billboards," *Chicago Sun-Times*, July 11, 1990.
3. Laurie Abraham "Lost revenues: City balks as billboards overrun poor areas," *Chicago Reporter*, November, 1990.
4. Robert McClory, "Jury acquits priest on 'necessity' defense," *National Catholic Reporter*, July 19, 1991.
5. Colman McCarthy, "Priest sees red over billboard pushers," *Washington Post*, July 12, 1991.

CHAPTER 6: VICTORY AND BEYOND

1. Chinta Strausberg, "Billboards to be removed," *Chicago Defender*, August 15, 1991.
2. Fran Spielman, "Drinking crackdown," *Chicago Sun-Times*, July 23, 1993.
3. Chinta Strausberg, "Pfleger, Shaw keep up heat," *Chicago Defender*, July 17, 1993.
4. Nancy Ryan, "Tobacco, alcohol billboards face near-total city ban," *Chicago Tribune*, July 26, 1997.
5. Chinta Strausberg, "Billboard clients, firms fight back," *Chicago Defender*, July 10, 1997.
6. R. Bruce Dold, "Even the 'wrong' billboard deserves protection," *Chicago Tribune*, July 4, 1997.
7. Chinta Strausberg, "Tillman hits billboard ban," *Chicago Defender*, September 11, 1997.
8. Patrick T. Reardon and Gary Washburn, "Billboard foes beat system," *Chicago Tribune*, September 11, 1997.
9. Chinta Strausberg, "Council votes to bring down alcohol, tobacco billboards," *Chicago Defender*, February 7, 1998.
10. "Activist Arm Twisting," *Hollywood Reporter*, April 24, 1998.

CHAPTER 7: CHALLENGES FROM ABOVE

1. Cathleen Falsani, "Cardinal ousting rebel priest," *Chicago Sun-Times*, February 12, 2002.
2. Cathleen Falsani, "Cardinal lets Pfleger stay at St. Sabina, for now," *Chicago Sun-Times*, February 13, 2002.
3. Cathleen Falsani, "Rebel priest gets a deal," *Chicago Sun-Times*, February 13, 2002.
4. Julia Lieblich and James Janega, "George: 'No pastors for life,'" *Chicago Tribune*, February 14, 2002.
5. Cathleen Falsani, "Bishop to Pfleger: Just get out," *Chicago Sun-Times*, February 22, 2002.
6. Cathleen Falsani, "Cardinal: Maybe Pfleger should go," *Chicago Sun-Times*, November 18, 2002.
7. Editorial, "Cardinal should reconsider," *Daily Southtown*, February 21, 2002.
8. Michael Eric Dyson, "Cardinal is misdirected," *Chicago Sun-Times*, November 27, 2002.
9. Judy Masterson, "Church should learn lessons from Pfleger's situation," *Lake County News-Sun*, February 14, 2002.
10. Editorial, "Of a priest, a prelate, a parish," *Chicago Tribune*, February 17, 2002.
11. Cardinal Francis George, "Dwell in My Love," pastoral letter, April 2001.

CHAPTER 8: BASKETBALL AND RACIAL TENSION

1. Cathleen Falsani, "'Safety' issue isn't valid: archdiocese," *Chicago Sun-Times*, June 1, 2001.
2. Pam Belluck, "Race Issues Surface in School's Bid for Church League," *New York Times*, June 6, 2001.
3. Cathleen Falsani, "Black school can't join sports league," *Chicago Sun-Times*, May 31, 2001.
4. Pam Belluck, "Race Issues Surface in School's Bid for Church League," *New York Times*, June 6, 2001.

NOTES FOR PAGES 112–180

5. Cathleen Falsani, "Safety issue isn't valid: Archdiocese," *Chicago Sun-Times*, June 1, 2001.

6. Cathleen Falsani, "St. Sabina deal falling apart?" *Chicago Sun-Times*, July 15, 2001.

7. Maureen O'Donnell, "George finds St. Sabina issue 'vexing,'" *Chicago Sun-Times*, July 30, 2001.

8. Cathleen Falsani, "St. Sabina ready to play first conference game," *Chicago Sun-Times*, November 28, 2001.

9. John W. Fountain, "Team Leaves White League In Silence Instead of Cheers," *New York Times*, March 11, 2002.

10. Chris Bury, "No Easy Layup for Catholic B-Ball League," *Nightline Report, ABC News*, May 6, 2002.

CHAPTER 10: ADVISERS: FRIENDLY AND OTHERWISE

1. Tom Roeser, "Pfleger Sermon Jeopardized Obama's Chances," On the Other Hand blog, June 11, 2008, http://blog.tomroeser.com.

2. Tom Roeser, "What must happen until Pfleger is justly dealt with," On the Other Hand blog, June 2, 2008, http://blog.tomroeser.com.

3. Tom Roeser, "Pfleger Sermon Jeopardized Obama's Chances," On the Other Hand blog, June 11, 2008, http://blog.tomroeser.com.

4. Jim Bowman, "Mass Appeal," Blithe Spirit blog, February 10, 2003, http://blithespirit.wordpress.com.

5. Five Pints [pseud.], "St. Sabina's, Auburn Gresham, Chicago," The Mystery Worshipper blog, October 19, 2008, http://www.ship-of-fools.com/mystery/2008/1639.html.

CHAPTER 11: THE THEOLOGY OF ST. SABINA

1. Section 78, "Caritas in Veritate" (Charity in Truth), 2009.

2. James Henry Harris, *Pastoral Theology: A Black-Church Perspective* (Minneapolis, MN: Fortress Press, 1991) 64–70.

CHAPTER 12: PREELECTION MELTDOWN

1. David Limbaugh, "Obama's Unity Charade," DavidLimbaugh.com blog, June 2, 2008, http://www.davidlimbaugh.com/mt/archives/2008/06/new_column_obam_4.html.

2. Cathleen Falsani, "'This is a dangerous time in America . . . you have to whisper your thoughts,'" *Chicago Sun-Times*, June 3, 2008.

3. Peggy McIntosh, "White Privilege: Unpacking the Invisible Knapsack," English Forum blog, September 29, 2009, http://usapetal.net/wpmu/eh226/2009/09/29/white-privilege-unpacking-the-invisible-backpack.

4. Barbara Bradley Hagerty, "A Closer Look at Black Liberation Theology," *All Things Considered*, National Public Radio, March 18, 2008.

CHAPTER 13: GUNS AND CHILDREN

1. Lucille W. Younger, "Guns kill, I want to live!" *Chicago Defender*, October 28, 1993.
2. Ellen Goodman, "Fear, violence finally have broken NRA's spell," *Boston Globe*, October 18, 1993.
3. Chinta Strausberg, "Pfleger calls new prez of NRA a 'Judas,'" *Chicago Defender*, June 9, 1998.
4. Chinta Strausberg, "Violence Busters," *Chicago Defender*, August 10, 1998.
5. "Outrage over Father Pfleger's 'snuff' threat spreads," Illinois Review blog, May 31, 2007, http://illinoisreview.typepad.com/illinoisreview/2007/05/outrage_over_fa.html.
6. Angela Rozas, "It'll 'happen again,' mom tells funeral," *Chicago Tribune*, October 14, 2008.

INDEX